Pedagogy,
Symbolic Control
and Identity

Critical Perspectives Series

Series Editor: Donaldo Macedo

A book series dedicated to Paulo Freire

Debatable Diversity: Critical Dialogues on Change in American Universities
by Raymond V. Padilla and Miguel Montiel
Pedagogy of Freedom
by Paulo Freire
Latinos Unidos: Ethnic Solidarity in Linguistic, Cultural, and Social Diversity
by Enrique Trueba
Pedagogy, Symbolic Control and Identity: Theory, Research, Critique
by Basil Bernstein

Forthcoming:

Ideology Matters
by Paulo Freire and Donaldo Macedo
Cuba's Economic Crisis
by Elisa Facio

Pedagogy, Symbolic Control and Identity

Theory, Research, Critique

REVISED EDITION

Basil Bernstein

ROWMAN & LITTLEFIELD PUBLISHERS, INC.
Lanham • Boulder • New York • Oxford

ROWMAN & LITTLEFIELD PUBLISHERS, INC.

Published in the United States of America
by Rowman & Littlefield Publishers, Inc.
4720 Boston Way, Lanham, Maryland 20706
http://www.rowmanlittlefield.com

12 Hid's Copse Road
Cumnor Hill, Oxford OX2 9JJ, England

Copyright © 1996, 2000 by Basil Bernstein

Originally published in 1996 by Taylor & Francis, Ltd. Revised edition first published by Rowman
& Littlefield in 2000. Reprinted by permission.

British Library Cataloguing in Publication Information Available

Library of Congress Cataloging-in-Publication Data

Bernstein, Basil B.
    Pedagogy, symbolic control, and identity : theory, research, critique / Basil Bernstein.
        p.   cm.
    Originally published : London ; Washington : Taylor & Francis. c 1996, in series:
    Critical perspectives on literacy and education.
    Includes bibliographical references (p.) and index.
    ISBN 0-8476-9575-1 (cloth : alk. paper) — ISBN 0-8476-9576-X (pbk. : alk. paper)
    1. Educational sociology.   2. Sociolinguistics.   3. Knowledge, Theory of.   4. Identity.
LC191.B456 2000
306.43—dc21   99-087951

Printed in the United States of America

For Marion

Contents

Postscript

Acknowledgements

Acknowledgements are rarely easy to write, not because of narcissism and absence of gratitude, but because so many inevitably do not appear: never more so than in the case of this book. From Parlo Singh, without whose intervention this book may not have appeared, to so many who in different ways and from different perspectives have contributed. Part II is witness to my debt to research students. I have been particularly fortunate here at the Institute of Education to have worked with Andrew Brown, Paul Dowling, Harry Daniels, Janet Holland and John Mace. I am also indebted to Paul Atkinson, Brian Davies, Sarah Delamont, Alan Sadovnik and Joseph Solomon, who in their different books have created a major source of discussion and criticism. I have strayed far from my original concerns but I am immensely grateful to Ruqaiya Hasan and her colleagues for rekindling this concern and showing me how it can be generalised and integrated into the larger concern of a theory of semantic variation. Finally there are the members of my family who have struggled, I hope not always in vain, to produce a more readable text.

The publishers and Basil Bernstein would like to thank the following for permission to reprint material in this volume:

Academic Publications for 'Sociolinguistics: a personal view' in *The early days of sociolinguistics, memories & reflection*, (Eds) Paulston, C.B. & Tucker, G.R.

The British Journal of the Sociology of Education for: 'Codes and Their Positioning: a case study in misrecognition', 'Vertical and Horizontal Discourse: an essay', and 'Bernstein Questioned by Joseph Solomon'.

Routledge for permission to base chapter 2 of this volume on sections of *Class, Codes and Control*, Vol IV: *The Structuring of Pedagogic Discourse*.

Introduction to the Revised Edition

There have been a number of changes which distinguish this revised edition from the original book. These changes show new developments and applications of the theory. Briefly there are three new chapters and one paper in the original edition has been removed. I have omitted chapter 9, 'Discourses, Knowledge Structures and Fields: some arbitrary considerations'. This chapter introduced the concepts of Vertical and Horizontal discourses in the context of distinguishing my approach from more 'Bourdieuan' perspectives[1]. However, the original chapter tried to do too much and as a consequence became too dense. In this new chapter I have simplified the aims and this has allowed me to spell out in greater detail the central arguments. It also enabled me to show how the analysis related to previous work. In the case of earlier work on elaborated and restricted codes and their modalities of realisation, I was now able to discuss the *production* of these discourses themselves, as well as the social context of their reproduction, circulation and change. I could also show their interaction in the informal pedagogy of the family and community and that of formal education. This new chapter also advanced the argument in chapter 7 on 'Research and Languages of Description', where I discussed problems of empirical research resulting from the weak powers of empirical description of social theory. In this new chapter, 'Vertical and Horizontal Discourses: an essay', I developed a critique against the dominance of the specialised languages of sociology in the forming of consciousness and orientation of the profession—a dominance at the expense of the requirements of the empirical research process and its position in the intellectual field. My view has always been that both a conceptual *and* an empirical imagination are necessary and both should be recognised as such. The empirical imagination allows the theory to validly describe its objects, the contingencies of their realisation and reveals the entailed processes. I have placed this chapter in part III.

There is a new second chapter (chapter 4) 'Official Knowledge and Pedagogic Identities: the politics of recontextualisation'. The analysis here, as in all my research, builds on and develops previous work. In chapter 3 of the original edition

('Pedagogising Knowledge: studies in recontextualising') I had concluded with a discussion of the contemporary emerging of local identities. These identities were distinguished in terms of the temporal orientation of the resources used for their social construction. These temporal orientations translated into 'retrospective' (based on the past), 'instrumental' / 'therapeutic' (based on the present), and 'prospective' (based on the future). However, in the original analysis there was no corresponding model for describing the orientation of contemporary educational reforms, and for distinguishing the pedagogic identities these reforms projected. In the new analysis, chapter 4, I interpreted contemporary official state educational reforms as a means of managing economic, technological and cultural change by their projection of pedagogic identities. Different educational reforms projected different pedagogic identities. Any one reform was seen as a struggle between groups to impose a particular pedagogic identity/identities. It is as if a pedagogic palette was available for the construction of such pedagogic identities, pure or mixed forms, analogous to the selected colours on an artist's palette; but the analogy should not be pushed far. Basically, I constructed a model which enabled the interaction between official pedagogic identities and local identities to be analysed through the use of the same concepts. The tensions between macro projections and emerging micro projections could be analysed in terms of the potential for change arising out of such interaction.

Finally I have included in this revised volume an interview by Dr. Joseph Solomon, Reader in the Sociology of Education, University of Athens. The inclusion of this interview is not an act of self-indulgence. Dr. Solomon's questioning raised fundamental issues and revealed what was implicit or inadequately formulated. Thus it became important to clarify what was meant by 'pedagogic relation' and its various modes of realisation. A beginning had been made on this issue (see chapter 4, note) but in dealing with this question I was able to distinguish three modes (explicit, implicit and tacit) and explore mass media as a pedagogic discourse. Further, I was also able to articulate the various levels of operation of the theory, showing, perhaps for the first time, the transformation of its levels from macro to micro. It is possible to confine research activity to any one level. There is no need to 'buy into' all the levels; a certain democracy of access.

Dr. Solomon's questioning also drew attention to the deep structure of the conceptual language and perhaps also to its limitations. It is possible that at the heart of theoretical work in sociology, and other disciplines, is a metaphor operating at a deep level, which drives the language of the theory. In the social sciences this tacit metaphor, initially and, perhaps, terminally unknown to the theorist, condenses and focuses the biographical experience of the mode of social existence. The metaphoric level I am trying to articulate here, operates at a different, deeper level than the surface metaphors of the concepts themselves. The metaphor (or metaphoric level) is the outcome of unique psychic experience embedded in, arising out of, the history of the mode of social existence. This tacit metaphor shapes the language of the theory, its particular representation of empirical 'realities' and even perhaps the potential conceptual power of the language. I am not here referring to ideological assumptions, 'misrecognitions', for these are, from this point of view, surface features fairly accessible to inspection, if not by the theorist! Such assumptions, 'misrecognitions', biases and emphases represent the bias of the language and in some form or other are present in all social theory.

The deep metaphor, I am referring to, resonates with other levels of experience and undergoes processes of translation (transformation) as a function of the mode of final realisation, visual or graphic, *and* as a function of the presentational criteria and the rules of a particular mode.

These transformations attenuate the psychic distance from the original source and mask its generating content. This raises the issues of how can one be true to what one does not apparently know. And what does it mean 'to be true'? Independent of failures in their empirical power, all theories reach an inbuilt terminal stage when their conceptual power ceases to develop. This is when the generating tension of their language fails to develop new more powerful sentences. I am inclined to believe this is when the possibilities of the initiating metaphor is exhausted. And some metaphors get exhausted sooner than others. At this stage of inner termination, defensive strategies are often employed: disguised repetition, concern with technicalities becomes a displacement strategy, omnipotence to preserve a position acts as a denial strategy, restricting the intellectual 'gene' pool by controlling disciples. This is only a temporary strategy as it leads eventually to enlargement of the 'gene' pool through dissent (or treason?). Being 'true' to the metaphor is recognising the signs of its exhaustion. In a sense the generating metaphor is known more by its absence than its presence.

The interview with Dr. Solomon made it clear to me that the tacit metaphor operating in my case is 'boundary' (inside/outside, intimacy/distance, here/there, near/far, us/them). The crucial metaphorising is *what the boundary signifies.* Condensing the past but not a relay for it, rather a tension between the past and possible futures. The boundary is not etched as in copperplate nor as ephemeral as in quicksand, and is sometimes more enabling than disabling. I have been concerned with how distributions of power are realised in various, and often silent, punctuations of social space which construct boundaries. I have been equally concerned with how these boundaries are relayed by various pedagogic processes so as to distribute, shape, position and opposition forms of consciousness.

However, engaging with such a metaphor as boundaries, whilst opening possibilities at the same time limits them. It is important to know when this limit is reached.

NOTE

1. In chapter 5 of *Class, Codes and Control*, vol. IV (1990) I commented on Bourdieu's theory of cultural reproduction and proposed that this theory is more concerned with 'relations to' than 'relations within'. This was in a context of a discussion of the theory's inability to describe the process of construction, organisation and transmission modes of pedagogic discourse. Li Puma (1993) addressed a similar point but in a more general way, and with greater insight he proposed that there were three uses of 'arbitrary' (relations within) in Bourdieu's project. First, any particular cultural manifestation is arbitrary from an across-culture perspective. Second, there is what Li Puma calls a formal arbitrariness within culture, e.g. the high but arbitrary valuation of 'upper-class' culture or any one of its distinguishing features, taste, etc. Li Puma maintains there is a third far more thorough going use of the term. Bourdieu, according to Li Puma, holds 'an absolute substantive theory of arbitrariness'. Thus 'any feature, accent, aesthetic judgement, text can have served as the same function in the historical evaluation of bourgeois distinction'. It is this which is perhaps responsible for Bourdieu's disinterest in the inner constitution of a specific signifier of distinction, that is of 'relations within'. There is no need to show that any one specific exemplar has a determinate content. *Homo academicus* is less about the internal construction and distinguishing characteristics of various modes of academic discourses, their various forms of transmission and regulative functions, but is more about power games, positioning, position taking, strategies of various forms of capital accumulation and dissipation. This necessarily follows from Bourdieu's relational field analysis.

The first edition of this book appeared under the imprint of a series edited by Alan Lukes called *Critical Perspectives on Literacy and Education*, as a consequence the location of the book in the development of my own work was not clear. I was very pleased when Rowman & Littlefield agreed to publish this revised edition in the *Class, Codes and Control* series as volume 5.

Introduction

This volume, unlike the previous volumes of *Class, Codes and Control,* does not comprise a series of papers showing the temporal development of the thesis. Rather the main purpose is to illustrate the research possibilities of the thesis, and to engage both directly and indirectly with criticisms. A continuous criticism has been the level of abstractness of the writing and the lack of assistance to reading because of the absence of illustrations and examples which, above all, it is said, characterize volume IV.

Walford writes, 'Since that first paper, Bernstein has developed these ideas considerably (Bernstein, 1990), but unfortunately his exposition of these developments is virtually unreadable, and the complexity is such that the original illuminative nature of the concepts has been obscured. The opacity of Bernstein's writing is also partly responsible for the continued criticism to which it has been subjected. In fact, since the original formulation, criticisms appear to have been more plentiful than examples of use. One prominent critic is King (1976, 1981) who argued against the concepts on empirical and theoretical grounds. Another is Pring (1975) who questioned the theoretical structure of Bernstein's dichotomous categories. Gibson (1977, 1984) extended this critique and claimed that it is 'an exercise in mystification' and that the original 'paper actually distorts, and directs attention away from the sociological thesis it sets out to demonstrate' (p. 118). The attack thus focused particularly on the lack of clarity and the ambiguity of concepts employed, both at the theoretical and operational levels. In spite of Bernstein's (1990) attempts to deal with this criticism, much of it is undoubtedly justified. However, it must be recognised that Bernstein (1975) himself originally saw this part of his work as "a search for the basic concepts themselves" (Walford, 1994, p. 193). Edwards (1987, p. 246), in a little less vigorous vein, states 'even that high level of abstraction has been rising as readers of Bernstein's more recent work on pedagogic discourse will confirm'.

Whilst I cannot argue against what others find difficult to read, my own intention has always been to have worked towards formulations which offer clearer, more concise and more explicit guides to research. As I have remarked elsewhere, the research itself has been published separately by their authors in journals, monographs and books (with the exception of the research papers which appeared in *Class, Codes and Control*, vol. II, 1973). It is this dislocation of research using the theory which perhaps has been responsible for some of the comments on the style of presentation of the thesis. However, I am not too sure that this is the only or the major reason.

There is a considerable difference in perspective between those who write textbooks and those who do extensive research. First, they are usually, but not always, different individuals with different interests. Textbook writers need to place the thesis in a more general narrative and that narrative often decides how a particular theory is to be positioned. Such positioning can be regarded as discursive fieldwork: a necessary intellectual function. In this case the research potential of the theory, or the research it has guided, is not as relevant as its apparent epistemological position or potential. Sociological textbooks rarely give detailed discussion of empirical research. They are more concerned with general issues of methodology than with the specifics of research. Researchers, on the other hand, are faced with different issues: How can I get a clearer specification of my research problem(s)? How do I formulate, theoretically, the research object and recognise it unambiguously, empirically? How do I recognise the realisation of this empirical object under different regulations? How can I make a valid, reliable, systematic description of what I wish to describe? How do I interpret the results of my description? How do I relate my description and interpretation, horizontally, to similar studies, and vertically to other levels of sociological analysis? From this, rather different perspective, a different view of a theory may well arise.

It is also possible that a theory which attempts to integrate macro and micro levels of analysis, that is, interactional levels, institutional levels and macro-institutional levels, necessarily constructs a language which integrates those levels, or rather attempts such an integration. The forms of description which such a language generates may well create specialised descriptions which do not satisfy the requirements of differently orientated research or interests. Thus, in the case, for example, of classroom research, the forms of descriptions generated by the principles of code modalities $\pm C^{ie}/\pm F^{ie}$ are clearly not exhaustible of the potential classroom realisations. But because this is not the case it is no grounds for criticising such a formulation on the ground of omission.

The initial chapter in part I sets out developments of the classification and framing conceptualisation, and shows how the concepts which formulate different modalities of pedagogic practice provide for acquirers the principles for the production of what counts as the legitimate text. The legitimate text is *any* realisation on the part of the acquirer which attracts evaluation. Part II also includes a discussion of some empirical research based on classification and framing. There seems to be a difference between these coding principles as they function in the theory and how they are, often, employed in research. In the theory, classification strength (Cie) is the means by which power relations are transformed into specialised discourses, and framing (F^{ie}) is the means whereby principles of control are transformed into specialised regulations of interactional discursive practices (pedagogic relations) which attempt to relay a given distribution of power. However, in much research and textbook discussion, classification and framing are used only as the means of distinguishing and describing forms of classroom practice or curricula. This is a good example of the use of concepts for the purpose of a researcher's requirement rather than of the author's intention. It does show, however, that the formulation has research relevance independent of its functions in the theory. The first chapter attempts to set out clearly, with illustrations, the logic of these concepts. However, if only from my point of view, it would be a loss if the paper (Bernstein, 1981), which set out the theory more formally and with greater powers of generality, was bypassed.

I have some qualms about introducing chapter 2, 'The Pedagogic Device', into this volume, as much of it is to be found as a section of chapter 5 in *Class, Codes and Control*, vol. IV. The theorising of the pedagogic device enabled the integration of macro levels of analysis with institutional and interactional levels. The classification and framing analysis assumed what at the time was not available: the analysis of the construction of pedagogic discourse. While code modalities translated distribution of power and principles of control into forms of pedagogic communication and their contextual management, it was not entirely clear whose power and control was translated. Although the expected class regulation on code acquisition was explicit, it seemed to me that the following chapter (chapter 3), 'Pedagogising Knowledge: studies in recontextualising', would not be fully understandable unless it was placed in the perspective of the analysis of the pedagogic device and its fields of realisation. Chapter 3 is a long empirical illustration of chapter 2. It is also the case that the repeat from *Class, Code and Control*, vol. IV is not entirely identical. I have changed the introduction completely, so that the logical structure is, I hope, now clearer. I have also, in a number of places, attempted to make the paper more accessible.

Chapter 3, rather like the previous chapter, builds on and extends earlier more abstract formulations. Performance and competence models and their theoretical origins, which anchor the paper, have their roots in a series of papers on visible and invisible pedagogies (Bernstein, 1975, 1977, 1990). The institutionalising and change in these models and their various modes illustrates the more abstract formulation of the pedagogic device and its fields of practice. There is a clearer specification of the concept of field position in terms of three analytically distinguishable levels: author, actor and identity. I think this chapter shows how vacuous the comments are that see the theory only as a set of dichotomies. Despite several attempts to show that modalities are not simple dichotomies but oppositional forms, and that each has a range of realisations, this has had little effect. Perhaps this chapter (which shows three modes of competence models, three modes of performance models *and* the appropriation of competence for the purposes of performance) may contribute to a fresh perspective. The main drive of chapter 3, which I hope holds this wide-ranging analysis together, is towards an understanding of the critical changes now taking place in the pedagogising of knowledge, its management and the regulation on forms of pedagogic consciousness and identity.

I think this chapter is an example of how synthesis takes place. It is as if a prospective integration were adumbrated in features of previous work before that integration has taken place. Perhaps the drive to theoretical developments is motivated by a tacit metaphor whose actualisation is fragmented (metanymic chain?) and known only when the fragments resonate to produce an integration.

The final chapter in part I, although written before the previous chapter, argues that the end of the twentieth century is witnessing a dislocation between knowledge and the knower. That is, the production, distribution and circulation of knowledge are separated from inner commitments and dedications. The latter impedes the production, distribution and circulation of knowledge in response to external demands, i.e. the market. We are experiencing a truly secular concept of knowledge.

Part II has been written in order to show the very close relation between the development of the theory and empirical research. It is not unusual to find comments which lament the lack of empirical research (Edwards, 1987; Sadovnik, 1991). Rarely do textbook accounts refer to the extensive range of empirical research conterminous with the development of the theory. I have tried to set out in part II an account of the research with which I have been closely associated in order to show how models derived from the theory, at different stages of its development, provide principles of description and interpretation. The account makes it quite clear that the interaction between the theory and research has been vital for the development of both. Part II does involve some repetition of part I, because it is not possible to understand the significance of the research without some discussion of the concepts on which the research draws. I have added an appendix to this account which deals with recent research on the sociolinguistic level of the theory. This research, undertaken by Ruqaiya Hasan and her colleagues, involving studies of ongoing talk between mothers and their children, and teachers and children, described by Halliday's systemic functional grammar, has provided a more valid base for this level of the theory. Indeed Hasan has subsumed the original sociolinguistic thesis under the beginnings of a more general theory of semantic variation.

Part III is devoted to responses to critiques which extend responses to be found in *Class, Codes and Control*, vol. IV, ch. III and in *Pedagogy & Knowledge: the sociology of Basil Bernstein*, Ed. Sadovnik, A. The chapters give, I hope, sufficient detail for the reader to understand precisely the salient features of the various criticisms. I have tried to go beyond the specific criticisms and to use criticisms as a means of clarifying, and in some cases developing, the original text. For example, the notions of vertical and horizontal discourses were first introduced as a response to a paper in Sadovnik's book. These notions were further developed as an appendix to the paper 'Codes and Their Positioning: a case study in misrecognition', when it was published in the *British Journal of the Sociology of Education*, 1995. In this book they are developed further in the chapter 'Discourses, Knowledge Structures and Fields: some arbitrary considerations' in order to clarify differences between Bourdieu's perspective and my own.* Perhaps the most extensive and wide-ranging response to criticisms can be found in Sadovnik (1995, pp. 383–422).

There is some danger in the rather specialised focus of this volume and previous volumes that larger concerns of education are removed to the background or are apparently ignored. In a sense this is an inevitable consequence of any research of this kind. It might therefore be relevant to consider here some issues arising out of the relation between *education and democracy* which lie beneath the surface of this research.

Education is central to the knowledge base of society, groups and individuals. Yet education also, like health, is a public institution, central to the production and reproduction of distributive injustices. Biases in the form, content, access and opportunities of education have consequences not only for the economy; these biases can reach down to drain the very springs of affirmation, motivation and imagination. In this way such biases can become, and often are, an economic and cultural threat to democracy. Education can have a crucial role in creating tomorrow's optimism in the context of today's pessimism. But if it is to do this then we must have an analysis of the social biases in education. These biases lie deep within the very structure of the educational system's processes of transmission and acquisition and their social assumptions.

I am going to start with some assumptions about the necessary and effective conditions for democracy. These are minimum conditions and they may seem both simple and naïve to a political scientist or social theorist. However, these assumptions are adequate to my purpose here. I will derive from these assumptions of the conditions for a democracy a set of pedagogic rights for evaluating democracy in education which will provide principles for examining schools. I will then briefly look at inequalities in schools with respect to the distribution of valued images, knowledge and resources. This will be followed by a discussion of the mythological discourse of the school which attempts to contain the consequences of the relation between stratification of social groups in the wider society. At this stage I will present some empirical research showing inequalities in the orientation towards, and distribution and transmission of, pedagogic knowledge. Finally I will raise some fundamental questions about the limitations on democracy in education.

*Omitted from this edition; see Introduction to the Revised Edition.

DEMOCRACY AND PEDAGOGIC RIGHTS

First of all, there are the conditions for an effective democracy. I am not going to derive these from high-order principles, I am just going to announce them. The first condition is that people must feel that they have a stake in society. Stake may be a bad metaphor, because by stake I mean that not only are people concerned to receive something but that they are also concerned to *give* something. This notion of stake has two aspects to it, the receiving and the giving. People must feel that they have a stake in both senses of the term.

Second, people must have confidence that the political arrangements they create will realise this stake, or give grounds if they do not. In a sense it does not matter too much if this stake is not realised, or only partly realised, providing there are good grounds for it not being realised or only partly realised.

I want to translate those conditions in terms of the school, any school. We can translate them in this way. Parents and students must feel that they have a stake in the school and confidence that the arrangements in the school will realise or enhance this stake or, if not, good grounds are to be given as to why not. I have thus translated the initial conditions into a proposition about the school.

I want to suggest that if these conditions are to be realised in the schools then we will need to ensure that we have institutionalised three interrelated rights. These rights will set up a model against which I can compare what happens in various educational systems. I will first give the long version of these rights and then the short version. The first right is the right to individual enhancement.

I think I should put a gloss on 'enhancement' because it is a very ambiguous word. I see 'enhancement' as a condition for experiencing boundaries, be they social, intellectual or personal, not as prisons, or stereotypes, but as tension points condensing the past *and* opening possible futures. Enhancement entails a discipline. It is not so much about creativity, although that may be an outcome; enhancement has to do with boundaries and experiencing boundaries as tension points between the past and possible futures. Enhancement is not simply the right to be *more* personally, *more* intellectually, *more* socially, *more* materially, it is the right to the means of critical understanding and to new possibilities. I want to suggest that this right is the condition for *confidence*. Where that right is not met then neither students nor teachers will have confidence, and without confidence it is difficult to act. This right is a condition for confidence, and operates at an individual level.

The second right is the right to be included, socially, intellectually, culturally and personally. Now this right to be included is complex because to be 'included' does not necessarily mean to be absorbed. Thus the right to be included may also require a right to be separate, to be autonomous. Inclusion is a condition for communitas and this right operates at the level of the social.

The third right is the right to participate. I think one should be very clear about the word participation. Participation is not only about discourse, about discussion, it is about practice, and a practice that must have *outcomes*. The third right, then, is the right to participate in procedures whereby order is constructed, maintained and changed. It is the right to participate in the construction, maintenance and transformation of order. Participation is the condition for *civic practice*, and operates at the level of politics.

We can now show diagrammatically rights, conditions and levels.

Rights	*Conditions*	*Levels*
Enhancement	Confidence	Individual
Inclusion	Communitas	Social
Participation	Civic discourse	Political

We can now measure education against this model of rights and see whether *all* students receive and enjoy such rights or whether there is an unequal distribution of these rights.

I am going to look at, initially and briefly, distributive principles of the school with reference to the images they project, the knowledge made available and the resources.

Distribution of Images

A school metaphorically holds up a mirror in which an image is reflected. There may be several images, positive and negative. A school's ideology may be seen as a construction in a mirror through which images are reflected. The question is: who recognises themselves as of value? What other images are excluded by the dominant image of value so that some students are unable to recognise themselves? In the same way, we can ask about the acoustic of the school. Whose voice is heard? Who is speaking? Who is hailed by this voice? For whom is it familiar?

In this sense there are visual and temporal features to the images the school reflects and these images are projections of a hierarchy of values, of class values.

Distribution of Knowledge

If we look at the knowledge the school transmits we shall find that it is based on a distributive principle such that different knowledges and their possibilities are differentially distributed to different social groups.

This distribution of different knowledges and possibilities is not based on neutral differences in knowledge but on a distribution of knowledge which carries unequal value, power and potential.

Resources

The distribution of material resources tends to follow the distribution of images, knowledges and possibilities so that there is an inverse relation between resources and the hierarchy of images and knowledges. For those at the top there is more, for those at the bottom there is less, with respect to *their needs and conditions of effective support*. This maldistribution of resources, certainly outside the school and often within it, affects access to and acquisition of school knowledge.

Access

There can be no effective formal education where there is no adequate provision of types of schools of equivalent value, where there is no developed pre-school system for those for whom such provision is appropriate and where there is ineffective provision of supportive agencies—medical, social, vocational etc.

Acquisition

Acquisition requires effectively trained, committed, motivated *and* adequately salaried teachers with career prospects, sensible to the possibilities and contribution of *all* their pupils, operating in a *context* which provides the conditions for effective acquisition, and an education which enables reflection on what is to be acquired and how it is to be acquired.

I have been suggesting so far that there is likely to be an unequal distribution of images, knowledges, possibilities and resources which will affect the rights of participation, inclusion and individual enhancement of groups of students. It is highly likely that the students who do not receive these rights in the school come from social groups who do not receive these rights in society.

This raises the question of how the school deals with the correspondence between the hierarchy of social groups and their differential power external to the school and the hierarchies of knowledge, possibility and value within the school. How does the school attempt to deal with external issues of social order, justice and conflict?

Bourdieu proposes that the school accomplishes this trick by appearing neutral, by pretending that the hierarchy within the school is created by different principles from those of the hierarchy outside the school.

In this way the school disguises and masks the way power relations, external to the school, produce the hierarchies of knowledge, possibility and value within the school. In disconnecting its own hierarchies from external hierarchies, the school legitimises inequalities between social groups deriving from differential school attainments. This is the essence of what Bourdieu calls 'la violence symbolique'. Whilst not denying the explanation, I am not sure whether the trick works only in this way. I feel very confident that some social groups are aware that schooling is not neutral, that it presupposes familial power both material and discursive, and that such groups use this knowledge to improve their children's pedagogic progress. It may be that they have to rationalise their children's success by believing that their children *deserve* such success while others do not.

I would like to propose that the trick whereby the school disconnects the hierarchy of success internal to the school from social class hierarchies external to the school is by creating a mythological discourse and that this mythological discourse incorporates some of the political ideology and arrangement of the society.

First of all, it is clear that conflict, or potential conflict, between social groups may be reduced or contained by creating a discourse which emphasises what all groups share, their communality, their apparent interdependence.

By creating a fundamental identity, a discourse is created which generates what I shall call *horizontal solidarities* whose object is to contain and ameliorate vertical (hierarchical) cleavages between social groups. All schools make massive attempts to create horizontal solidarities among their staff and students, irrespective of the political ideology and social arrangement of the society. The discourse which produces horizontal solidarities or attempts to produce such solidarities from this point of view I call a mythological discourse. This mythological discourse consists of two pairs of elements which, although having different functions, combine to reinforce each other. One pair celebrates and attempts to produce a united, integrated, apparently common national consciousness; the other pair work together to disconnect hierarchies within the school from a causal relation with social hierarchies outside the school.

Myths of National Consciousness and Integration

In all modern societies the school is a crucial device for writing and rewriting national consciousness, and national consciousness is constructed out of myths of origin, achievements and destiny. Essentially national consciousness transforms a common biology into a cultural specific in such a way that the specific cultural consciousness comes to have the force of a unique biology. Nationalisms are inseparable from the state and from the struggle to become an autonomous state.

It is inevitable under these conditions that education becomes a crucial means and an arena for struggle to produce and reproduce a specific national consciousness. In turn the horizontal solidarity produced by such national consciousness creates fundamental and culturally specific identities. There are ranges of school practices, rituals, celebrations and emblems which work to this effect and of course there are also the crucial discourses of language, literature and history.

The second myth paired with the first, which works towards an integrated national consciousness, is the myth that society is an organism in which groups within a society, but not necessarily groups *between* societies, relate to each other through *interdependence* of specialised functions. In this way the contribution of each is as necessary and of as much importance and value as the contribution of another.

Thus all functions have *equivalence of value* despite differences in power, resources and potential: equivalence though difference. In explicit, but often in implicit and covert ways, the myth of society as an organism justifies and maintains gender relations. Gender relations are supposed here to complement each other through their differences: differences which allegedly have their basis in biology.

Myths of Hierarchy

I now want to look at two ways in which the school attempts to disconnect its own stratification features from stratification principles external to the school. The school's basic principle for stratifying groups is age. School stratification is thus based on an apparent non-arbitrary principle, unlike the arbitrary relation produced between social groups by class, race, religion, region. Age-groups within the school are given differential treatment and privilege according to age seniority. Thus age-groups form hierarchically arranged bands of horizontal solidarity. Yet age carries no cultural necessity and there are other forms of banding possible. The temporal progression of students in the school is therefore legitimised by an apparent non-arbitrary principle.

The school necessarily produces a hierarchy based on success and failure of students. This hierarchy both within the school, and its consequences for occupational class hierarchies outside the school, is potentially and actually highly divisive and so a major threat to horizontal solidarities. The school must disconnect its own internal hierarchy of success and failure from ineffectiveness of teaching within the school and the external hierarchy of power relations between social groups outside the school. How do schools individualise failure and so legitimise inequalities?

The answer is clear: failure is attributed to inborn facilities (cognitive, affective) or to the cultural deficits relayed by the family which come to have the force of inborn facilities.

Education preserves structural relations between social groups but changes structural relations between individuals. These changes in the structural relation between individuals are sufficient to create the impression of a general and probable movement. This enhances aspiration, motivation and commitment but failure, especially early school failure, can deaden these attributes. With such failure and personal damage there is resistance and alienation on the one hand and reinforced peer group loyalties and class solidarities on the other. But these solidarities and resistances may be contained in the context of the mythological discourses of education. And in this way perhaps orientation is displaced towards national consciousness and struggle rather than class consciousness and its conflicts.[1]

The mythological discourse of schools has its roots in a spurious biology or biological metaphors. Concepts of national consciousness and the organic society mythologise biology, and the legitimisation of the hierarchy of the school also rests on a mythological discourse to create horizontal solidarities. Thus mythical communities of common identities and interests are produced.

However, this mythological discourse and the horizontal solidarities it attempts to engender are often not effective enough to prevent the cleavages and contradictions within the school.

I started with a simple, if not naïve condition for effective democracy and translated that condition into pedagogic democratic rights of 'enhancement', 'inclusion' and 'participation' as the basis for *confidence, communitas* and *political practice.*

Despite clear indications of improvements in working class/race/gender educational chances, social class is a major regulator of the distribution of students to privileging discourses and institutions.[2] If we are going to talk about democracy, culture and education, and if we are serious, then we have to consider the constraints and grip of class-regulated realities. Further we have to consider their interactions with underlying structural pressures arising out of the changing complexity of the division of labour.

Class cultures act to transform micro differences into macro inequalities and these inequalities raise crucial issues for the relation between democracy and education. It may be that the serious question becomes one of what shortfall, what limitation of pedagogic democratic rights, for whom and where, is a given society prepared to tolerate and, at any one time, accept. Those subject to this shortfall, this limitation of pedagogic democratic rights, must be given good reason (and possibly other rights) if they are to have any confidence in the present and belief in the future.

This requires us to have an understanding of the *intrinsic* stratification features of modern educational systems and of the social groups upon whom these stratification features are likely to be inscribed.

Whereas much of my empirical research has been devoted to showing from this particular perspective this process of class inscription, the theoretical work has been increasingly concerned with general questions of pedagogic communication as a crucial medium of symbolic control. To understand the workers and workings of such control is probably more important today than at any other period. To know whose voice is speaking is the beginning of one's own voice.

Finally, a word about the title of this book: *Pedagogy, Symbolic Control and Identity.* The previous volumes on which this present volume depends were under the aegis of a different title: *Class, Codes and Control.* The latter title was an accurate representation of how I saw my endeavour in 1971. Yet *Class, Codes and Control,* Vol. I ended with an analysis of forms of school-based pedagogic practice. It has certainly become clear since the publication of that volume that the focus has shifted, although the fundamental problematic has not changed. What has changed is my realisation of what it is. There has been a tension in the papers between an understanding of the social class regulation on families and schools and more general issues of symbolic control. My approach is too limited to deal with large questions of culture and symbolic control; rather I have been exploring the processes whereby symbolic control and its modalities are realised: how power relations are transformed into discourse and discourse into power relations. The process whereby this transformation takes place, formally and informally in families and education, is to my mind essentially a pedagogic process and, in more generalised and diffuse forms, by the public media within the context of the arenas of power of state-managed societies. Collectivism may have been weakened, the market may have greater autonomy, but the devices of symbolic control are increasingly state regulated and monitored through the new techniques of de-centred centralisation.

Book titles are generally retrospective, that is referring to the contents. However, the title of this book is rather more prospective, referring to work that is to come and for which this volume, especially chapter 3 ('Pedagogising Knowledge: studies in recontextualisings'), is a trailer. *Pedagogy, Symbolic Control and Identity* is concerned with understanding the social processes whereby consciousness and desire are given specific forms, evaluated, distributed, challenged and changed. Perhaps this volume and its predecessors are a step towards such understanding.

NOTES

1. I am thinking here of racial oppression by some students in schools where the students seem more receptive to nationalist myths than to multicultural/race discourse.

2. Apple, amongst others, has remarked that class analysis has been disappearing in research in education as the focus has shifted to race, gender, region and indigenous groups. The effervescence of so-called post modernist analysis celebrates, on the one hand, the local, the blurring of categories, the contextual dependencies of subjectivity, and, on the other, announces the end of grand narratives. I might add further reasons. To a very great extent the foregrounding of discourse as the crucial centre of gravity of social analysis by Foucault and other Parisians had made these authors the new definers of the social. Thus the concept of the 'social' is being rewritten by non-sociologists and taken over by sociologists. It is not simply the evacuation from the use of social class but the evacuation from *sociological* analysis. The latter as a distinct category of analysis is now more and more the invisible basis of other forms of analysis, e.g. cultural studies etc. The privileging of discourse in these analyses tends to abstract the analysis of discourse from the detailed empirical analysis of its basis in social structure. The relationships between symbolic structures *and* social structures are in danger of being severed. (On the evacuation of class analysis, see Apple, 1995; Bernstein's Response, 1995; Lynch and O'Neil, 1994.)

Part I

Towards a Sociological Theory
of Pedagogy

Chapter 1

Pedagogic Codes and Their Modalities of Practice

INTRODUCTION

The models that I develop here should be able to describe the organisational, discursive and transmission practices in all pedagogic agencies and show the process whereby selective acquisition takes place. I also want to make it very clear that my concept of pedagogic practice is somewhat wider than the relationships that go on in schools. Pedagogic practices would include the relationships between doctor and patient, the relationships between psychiatrist and the so-called mentally ill, the relationships between architects and planners. In other words, the notion of pedagogic practice which I shall be using will regard pedagogic practice as a fundamental social context through which cultural reproduction-production takes place. Operating with this rather wide definition of pedagogic practice, the models of description that I shall try to create necessarily have a certain generality in order that they can cope with the differentiation of the agencies of cultural reproduction.

I want to make it clear that I will not here consider in any great detail the macro-institutional regulations on education systems, neither will I be concerned with any major discussions of the changes in the orientations of contemporary knowledge systems. Indeed, I have made a deliberate choice to focus sharply upon the underlying rules shaping the social construction of pedagogic discourse and its various practices. I am doing this because it seems to me that sociological theory is very long on metatheory and very short on providing specific principles of description. I shall be concentrating very much on being able to provide and create models, which can generate specific descriptions. It is my belief that, without these specific descriptions, there is no way in which we can understand the way in which knowledge systems become part of consciousness. Many of the models that we have, I think, are highly general; very important, but highly gen-

3

eral. They often do not serve to provide the necessary rules for the specific examination of specific agencies and transmission processes. I am not really apologising for lowering the academic level of the discussions which will take place.

The major theories of cultural reproduction which we have, essentially of the Parisian version, are limited by their assumptions and focus, and so are unable to provide strong principles of description of pedagogic agencies, of their discourses, of their pedagogic practices. This, I suggest, is because theories of cultural reproduction view education as a carrier of power relations external to education. From this point of view, pedagogic discourse becomes a carrier for something other than itself. It is a carrier of power relations external to the school, a carrier of patterns of dominance with respect to class, patriarchy, race. It is a matter of great interest that the actual structure which enables power to be relayed, power to be carried, is itself not subject to analysis. Paradoxically, what is missing from theories of cultural reproduction is any internal analysis of the structure of the discourse itself, and it is the structure of the discourse, the logic of this discourse, which provides the means whereby external power relations can be carried by it (chapter 2).

I suggest that theories of cultural reproduction essentially see education, and in particular the school, as a site of social pathology and that their concern is to diagnose education as essentially a pathological device. In these analyses, clearly, social class is necessarily—and crucially—foregrounded. But in this analysis social class will not be foregrounded. What will be, I hope, will be an explication of the inner logic of pedagogic discourse and its practices. If we want to understand how pedagogic processes shape consciousness differentially, I do not see how this can be done without some means of analysing the forms of communication which bring this about. I shall be more concerned to analyse how a pedagogic text has been put together, the rules of its construction, circulation, contextualisation, acquisition and change. It is these matters that I wish to address. I will mainly be concerned with three interrelated problems:

- First, how does a dominating distribution of power and principles of control generate, distribute, reproduce and legitimise dominating and dominated principles of communication?
- Second, how does such a distribution of principles of communication regulate relations within and between social groups?
- Third, how do these principles of communication produce a distribution of forms of pedagogic consciousness?

In summary, how does power and control translate into principles of communication, and how do these principles of communication differentially regulate forms of consciousness with respect to their reproduction and the possibilities of change?

POWER AND CONTROL

I shall start with the discussion of power and control. The distinction I will make here is crucial and fundamental to the whole analysis. In this formulation, power and control are analytically distinguished and operate at different levels of analysis. Empirically, we shall find that they are embedded in each other. Power relations, in this perspective, create boundaries, legitimise boundaries, reproduce boundaries, between different categories of groups, gender, class, race, different categories of discourse, different categories of agents. Thus, power always operates to produce dislocations, to produce punctuations in social space.

From this point of view, then, power always operates on the relations *between* categories. The focus of power from this point of view is on the relations *between* and, in this way, power establishes legitimate relations of order. Control, on the other hand, from this point of view, establishes legitimate forms of communication appropriate to the different categories. Control carries the boundary relations of power and socialises individuals into these relationships. We shall see, however, that control is double faced for it carries both the power of reproduction and the potential for its change.

To summarise this distinction between power and control: briefly, control establishes legitimate communications, and power establishes legitimate relations between categories. Thus, power constructs relations *between*, and control relations *within* given forms of interaction. The forms of interaction in which I am interested are those of pedagogic practice and the category relations in which I am interested are those of pedagogic discourse, its agents and its context. Now, in order to show formally how dominant power and control relations are realised as forms of pedagogic communications. I shall have to develop a special language. This language must be capable of recovering macro relations from micro interactions.

The language must also reveal both the process of interaction and the potential for change. It must be capable of providing general principles from which specific descriptions may be derived of the major agencies of cultural reproduction and their processes of transmission and acquisition.

CLASSIFICATION AND FRAMING

I will now proceed to define two concepts, one for the translation of power, of power relations, and the other for the translation of control relations, which I hope will provide the means of understanding the process of symbolic control regulated by different modalities of pedagogic discourse. And, perhaps, one can add a note here. The models that are created must be capable of generating a range of modalities of pedagogic discourse and practice. And the models must also be capable of generating pedagogic discourse and practices which at the moment do not exist.

I shall start first with power. We have said that dominant power relations establish boundaries, that is, relationships between boundaries, relationships between categories. The concept to translate power at the level of the individual must deal with relationships between boundaries and the category representations of these boundaries. I am going to use the concept of *classification* to examine relations between categories, whether these categories are between agencies, between agents, between discourses, between practices.

This may seem a somewhat bizarre use of the concept of classification because normally classification is used to distinguish a defining attribute which constitutes a category; but here classification refers to a defining attribute not of a category but of the relations *between* categories. Thus, if I take a series of categories, concretely we could think about the categories of discourse in the secondary school: physics, geography, language, etc. They need not be discursive categories within the school. They could be the categories which constitute the division of labour in the field of production: unskilled, skilled, clerical, technological, managerial (Bernstein, 1981, Appendix).

Consider a series of categories, the discourses of a secondary curriculum. Let us call them A, B, C, D. These categories may be considered to be a social division of labour of discourse. Now, if these discourses are differently specialised, then they must have a space in which to develop their unique identity, an identity with its own internal rules and special voice. It could be French, German, history if one thinks of the school.

But I want to argue that the crucial space which creates the specialisation of the category—in this case the discourse—is not internal to that discourse but is the space between that discourse and another. In other words, A can only be A if it can effectively insulate itself from B. In this sense, there is no A if there is no relationship between A and something else. The meaning of A is only understandable in relation to other categories in the set; in fact, to all the categories in the set. In other words, it is the insulation between the categories of discourse which maintains the principles of their social division of labour. In other words, it is silence which carries the message of power; it is the full stop between one category of discourse and another; it is the dislocation in the potential flow of discourse which is crucial to the specialisation of any category.

If that insulation is broken, then a category is in danger of losing its identity, because what it is, is the space between it and another category. Whatever maintains the strengths of the insulation, maintains the relations between the categories and their distinct voices. Thus, the principle of the relations between categories, discourses—that is, the principles of their social division of labour— is a function of the degree of insulation between the categories of the set we are considering. If this insulation changes its strength, then the principles of the social division of labour—that is, its classification—changes.

What preserves the insulation? What preserves the space between? What preserves the regions of silence? What preserves the dislocations? What preserves the insulation is *power*. Attempts to change degrees of insulation reveal the power relations on which the classification is based and which it reproduces.

We can distinguish between strong and weak classifications according to the degree of insulation between categories, be these categories of discourse, categories of gender, etc. Thus, in the case of strong classification, we have strong insulation between the categories. In the case of strong classification, each category has its unique identity, its unique voice, its own specialised rules of internal relations. In the case of weak classification, we have less specialised discourses, less specialised identities, less specialised voices. But classifications, strong or weak, always carry power relations.

The arbitrary nature of these power relations is disguised, hidden by the principle of the classification, for the principle of the classification comes to have the force of the natural order and the identities that it constructs are taken as real, as authentic, as integral, as the source of integrity. Thus a change in the principle of classification here is a threat to the principle of integrity, of coherence of the individual.

We can say, then, that the insulation which creates the principle of the classification has two functions: one external to the individual, which regulates the relations between individuals, and another function which regulates relations within the individual. So insulation faces outwards to social order, and inwards to order within the individual. Thus, externally, the classificatory principle creates order, and the contradictions, cleavages and dilemmas which necessarily inhere in the principle of a classification are suppressed by the insulation. Within the individual, the insulation becomes a system of psychic defences against the possibility of the weakening of the insulation, which would then reveal the suppressed contradictions, cleavages and dilemmas. So the internal reality of insulation is a system of psychic defences to maintain the integrity of a category.

However, these psychic defences are rarely wholly effective and the possibility of the other, the unthinkable, the yet to be voiced, is also rarely silenced.

CLASSIFICATION: SOME EXAMPLES

I want now to give some examples of classificatory principles. I want first of all to take a very brutal look at two different organisations of knowledge, one in the medieval university, the second in the twentieth century, in order to illustrate the significance of classificatory principles. In the first case, there is a strong classification, and in the second case, an example of a weakening classification.

If we look at the organisation of knowledge in the medieval period, there are two distinct differently specialised organisations of knowledge, one for mental practice and one for manual practices, strongly classified, with strong insulation between these two, between mental practice and manual practice. The relays which transmit mental practice and manual practice, have their own internal rules and their own carrier. Some individuals see the exclusion of manual practice as some kind of nasty capitalist plot. But the crucial point is that manual practice was never integrated into formal public systems of knowledge and transmission. Manual practice was relayed through the family and guild.

I want to look at the system for mental practice, and I want to look deeply at the organisation of knowledge. In the medieval university, we find the first fracturing, the first dislocation, the first classification of orders of knowledge in the relationship between the *trivium* and the *quadrivium*. It was the case, of course, that not all medieval universities had both knowledge systems. Some university systems may have had only the trivium. But whether the university had a quadrivium or not is beside the point for the purposes of this argument, because the trivium always presupposes the quadrivium.

If we look at this organisation very quickly, we know that the trivium is concerned with logic, grammar and rhetoric. And we know that the quadrivium is concerned with astronomy, music, geometry and arithmetic. We know also that the trivium is studied first and that the quadrivium is second. There is no quadrivium without the trivium. But the trivium, from this point of view, symbolises the limitations of the possibilities of the word, and the word is God. The quadrivium is concerned with abstract formulations about the fundamental structure of the world, of the physical world. There is a dislocation between two languages: linguistic (trivium) and mathematics (quadrivium).

Strongly classified, the word and the world are integrated through God. It is the principle of integration. The strong classification does not create dislocation because of its relation to God. Further, it is socialisation into the word that makes the abstract exploration of the world safe. The trivium comes first. The trivium is very much the regulative discourse. The trivium establishes a legitimate form of consciousness which can then be realised in other explorations.

I want to take it one stage further. So far we have looked very much at the surface, but it could be argued that the trivium is concerned with the construction of the inner, the inner consciousness. The quadrivium is concerned with the abstract structure of the outer. From this point of view, the trivium–quadrivium signifies a dislocation between inner and outer, a dislocation between inner and outer which finds a productive synthesis through the particular concept of God, the particular theological relationship of Christianity (see chapter 4).

From this point of view, the trivium–quadrivium, inner–outer, is symbolic of a dislocation which Christianity itself inserted, a dislocation between inner and outer as a means of a possibility and transformation of total experience. I would suggest that this is the first moment of pedagogic classification. It is clear that this dislocation between inner and outer becomes a fundamental problematic of all European philosophy and social science. What we have here, at another level, is the dislocation between inner and outer with respect to the individual, inner and outer with respect to the relationship between the individual and the society. This becomes a doxic principle of European consciousness, a principle that we do not find in the Orient. This is an example of the use of classification, of strong classification, in the medieval period and the power on which it was based and relayed—the Church.

I want to give another example, and this time I want to take the example from the restructuring of European knowledge in the twentieth century. Here I want to make a distinction between discourses as singulars and discourses as regions.

A discourse as a singular is a discourse which has appropriated a space to give itself a unique name. So for example physics, chemistry, sociology, psychology are, for me, singulars. And the structure of knowledge in the nineteenth century was, in fact, the birth and development of singulars. These singulars produced a discourse which was about only themselves. These discourses had very few external references other than in terms of themselves and they created the field of the production of knowledge. But the field of the production of knowledge was not only about knowledge.

In the twentieth century, particularly in the last five decades, there has been a change. The very strong classification of singulars has undergone a change and what we now have, I may suggest, is a *regionalisation of knowledge*. By that I mean the following: a region is created by a recontextualising of singulars. So, for example, in medicine, architecture, engineering, information science, we can see the development of the regionalisation of knowledge. But any regionalisation of knowledge implies a recontextualising principle: which singulars are to be selected, what knowledge within the singular is to be introduced and related?

The regionalisation of knowledge is a very good index of the technologising of knowledge, because regions are different from singulars. Singulars address only themselves. Singulars are intrinsic to the production of knowledge in the intellectual field. Regions are the interface between the field of the production of knowledge and any field of practice and, therefore, the regionalisation of knowledge has many implications. This is a change in the classification of knowledge.

The classification has become weaker and we shall see that, as the classification becomes weaker, we must have an understanding of the recontextualising principles which construct the new discourses and the ideological bias that underlies any such recontextualising. Every time a discourse moves, there is space for ideology to play. New power relations develop between regions and singulars as they compete for resources and influence (see chapter 3).

I have been discussing classification at the macro level. I want to move to the level of institutions; I want to look at an example of strong and weak classification at the level of any educational agency: it could be a school, it could be a university. I think it is easier if we think about it as a school.

If we take the letters in Figure 1.1, these represent discourses. They could be French, physics, chemistry, etc. These are departments. The strong lines indicate strong classifications. The first thing we notice in this diagram is that there is a

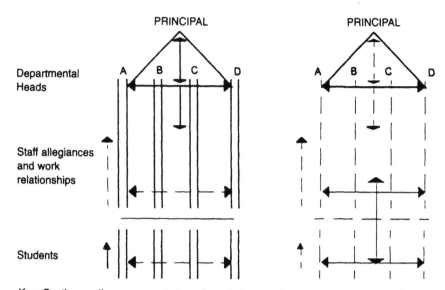

Key: Continuous lines represent strong boundaries, continuous arrows represent direction
of strong relationships. Dotted lines represent weak boundaries and dotted line
arrows represent direction of weak relationships.
Collection code type = strong classification: strong frames
Integrated code type = weak classification: weak frames

Figure 1.1: Ideal typical organizational structures

very strong classification between the inside of the institution and the outside. If
there is a very strong classification between inside and outside, then the knowledge here is given a special quality of otherness. If there is a strong classification
between inside and outside, then there is a hierarchy of knowledge between the
so-called common sense and the so-called uncommon sense. If we look at the diagram, we can see that the staff are tied to their departments. We can offer two
reasons. First, the department is symbolic of their category and therefore of their
internal cohesion, that is, the sacred reason. The main reason, however, is that
promotion only comes by appropriate activities in the department. The staff are
necessarily tied to their category and its organisational base. This means that, in
this system, the staff cannot relate to each other in terms of their intrinsic function, which is the reproduction of *pedagogic discourse*. Where the lines of communication between staff are established by a system of this kind, there will be
weak relations between staff with respect to pedagogic discourse, as each is differently specialised. Thus, their contents are not open to public discussion and
challenge.

It is also the case that the heads of the departments will relate to each other.
Here we will have the Principal, and power will be directed downwards. If we
now look at the left-hand side of the diagram, the diagram is a symbolic representation of the origin of the discourse; it is a temple. This is a representation of

what I call a *collection code*; the visual representation shows also its origin, its mixture of Greek philosophy and the Church. This is an example of strong classification.

In Figure 1.1 we also have a model of weak classification on the right-hand side of the diagram. There are weak lines which show that the boundaries are permeable. A model like this is highly vulnerable because communications from the outside are less controlled. Its identities are not established by the organisational structure because of the weak classification, but the staff are part of a strong social network (or it *must* be strong if the transmission is to work) which should be concerned with the integration of difference. And this is no easy activity.

Further, the relations between staff within a weakly classified system cohere around knowledge itself. The new organisation of staff made possible by weak classification establishes an alternative power base, so the power lines in such an organisation are more complex. Here, with weak classification, there is a re-ordering of specialised differentiation and this can provide a new social basis for consensus of interest and opposition. These are examples of strong and weak classifications at the level of the school.[1]

I want to look next at classification of the distribution of knowledge in the school. Although it is not *logically* necessary, strong classification of discourse at the level of the school is likely to produce a particular temporal dislocation of that knowledge. Strong classification of discourse is likely to lead empirically to a dislocation in the transmission of knowledge because, with strong classification, the progression will be from concrete local knowledge, to the mastery of simple operations, to more abstract general principles, which will be only available later in the transmission. Thus there is an internal classification and distribution of forms of knowledge. When children fail at school, drop out, repeat, they are likely to be positioned in a factual world tied to simple operations, where knowledge is impermeable. The successful have access to the general principle, and some of these—a small number who are going to produce the discourse—will become aware that the mystery of discourse is not order, but disorder, incoherence, the possibility of the unthinkable. But the long socialisation into the pedagogic code can remove the danger of the unthinkable, and of alternative realities.

There are two basic rules that are sufficient to generate this whole section of the model. Where we have strong classification, the rule is: things must be kept apart. Where we have weak classification, the rule is: things must be brought together. But we have to ask, in whose interest is the apartness of things, and in whose interest is the new togetherness and the new integration?

FRAMING

So far, I have discussed classification and the translation of power relations into principles of classification, and the relationships between these principles of classification and the metaphoric structuring of space. We can see that classification constructs the nature of social space: stratifications, distributions and locations. We have shown how power relations translate into principles of strong and weak classifications, and how these principles establish social divisions of labour, how these principles establish identities, how these principles establish voices. We have seen how these classifications disguise the arbitrary nature of power relations, create imaginary identities, replace the contingent by the necessary, and construct psychic systems of defence internal to the individual. And when I say *psychic systems of defence*, I do not simply mean at the conscious level.

I want to turn to pedagogic practice, to the forms of communication where classificatory principles—whether strong or weak—form consciousness in the process of their acquisition. That is, I am going to look at the form of control which regulates and legitimises communication in pedagogic relations: the nature of the talk and the kinds of spaces constructed. I shall use the concept of framing to analyse the different forms of legitimate communication realised in any pedagogic practice. The concept of framing must be capable of being taken to any pedagogic relation.

As an approximate definition, framing refers to the controls on communications in local, interactional pedagogic relations: between parents/children, teacher/pupil, social worker/client, etc. If the principle of classification provides us with our voice and the means of its recognition, then the principle of framing is the means of acquiring the legitimate message. Thus, classification establishes voice, and framing establishes the message; and they can vary independently. There is more than one message for carrying any one voice. Different modalities of communication can establish the same voice. Different modalities of framing can relay the same voice (identity).

The principle of the classification provides us with the limits of any discourse, whereas framing provides us with the form of the realisation of that discourse; that is, framing regulates the realisation rules for the production of the discourse. Classification refers to *what*, framing is concerned with *how* meanings are to be put together, the forms by which they are to be made public, and the nature of the social relationships that go with it.

In this way, framing regulates relations, within a context. In defining control, our first statement was that control regulates relations within. We now find that framing does exactly this; it regulates relations within a context, it refers to relations between transmitters and acquirers, where acquirers acquire the principle of legitimate communication.

Framing is about *who* controls *what*. What follows can be described as the *internal logic* of the pedagogic practice. Framing refers to the nature of the control over:

- the selection of the communication;
- its sequencing (what comes first, what comes second);

- its pacing (the rate of expected acquisition);
- the criteria; and
- the control over the social base which makes this transmission possible.

Where framing is strong, the transmitter has explicit control over selection, sequence, pacing, criteria and the social base. Where framing is weak, the acquirer has more *apparent* control (I want to stress apparent) over the communication and its social base. Note that it is possible for framing values—be they strong or weak—to vary with respect to the elements of the practice, so that, for example, you could have weak framing over pacing but strong framing over other aspects of the discourse.

We can distinguish analytically *two* systems of rules regulated by framing. And these rules can vary independently of each other, that is, their framing values can change independently. These are rules of *social order* and rules of *discursive order*.

First, the rules of social order refer to the forms that hierarchical relations take in the pedagogic relation and to expectations about conduct, character and manner. This means that an acquirer can be seen as a potential for labels. Which labels are selected is a function of the framing. Where the framing is strong, the candidates for labelling will be terms such as conscientious, attentive, industrious, careful, receptive. Where the framing is apparently weak, then conditions for candidature for labels will become equally trying for the acquirer as he or she struggles to be creative, to be interactive, to attempt to make his or her own mark. The actual labelling of the acquirer varies with the nature of the framing.

Second, there are the rules of discursive order. The rules of discursive order refer to selection, sequence, pacing and criteria of the knowledge. We shall call the rules of social order *regulative discourse* and the rules of discursive order *instructional discourse*. And we shall then write this as follows:

$$\text{framing} = \frac{\text{instructional discourse}}{\text{regulative discourse}} \quad \frac{ID}{RD}$$

In other words, the instructional discourse is always embedded in the regulative discourse, and the regulative discourse is the dominant discourse (Bernstein, 1990).

I have suggested that the strengths of framing can vary over the elements of instructional discourse. The strengths of framing can also vary between instructional and regulative discourse, for example, with weak framing of regulative discourse and strong framing of instructional discourse. It is very important to see that these discourses do not always move in a complementary relation to each other. But where there is weak framing over the instructional discourse, there must be weak framing over the regulative discourse.

In general, where framing is strong, we shall have a visible pedagogic practice. Here the rules of instructional and regulative discourse are explicit. Where framing is weak, we are likely to have an invisible pedagogic practice. Here the rules of regulative and instructional discourse are implicit, and largely unknown to the acquirer. Perhaps that is why such framings are called progressive (Bernstein, 1990).

I am now in a position to write pedagogic codes, but first I have to make the concepts of classification and framing more sensitive.

PEDAGOGIC CODES

So far, we have the following: the pedagogic code exists in this form:

$$+/- \text{ are the strengths of classification and framing } \pm C/F$$

This simple formulation can generate a very great range of modalities, both of discourse and practice.

However, we have to introduce internal and external features to complete the delicacy of this description. Classification always has an external value because it is concerned with relations. But classification can also have an internal value. There is a certain classification of dress, of posture, of position. This is part of the internal classification. The internal classification refers to the arrangements of the space and the objects in it. In a classroom with strong classification, there is a specialisation of spaces.[2] This is internal classification. Similarly, framing can have both an internal and an external value. The external value of framing refers to the controls on communications outside that pedagogic practice entering the pedagogic practice.[3] There is a great difference if you go to see a doctor when you pay and when you do not. And one of the major differences between the two is in the framing. If you are not paying, it is no good telling a long story about your particular problem, because the doctor is almost certainly not interested in that. Here the pacing is very strong, there are many to see and it is unlikely that the doctor will count this as legitimate communication. The external value of the framing can strip you of your identity and biography outside that context or it can include it.

In the case of framing, then, the external feature refers to the controls over communication outside the pedagogic context entering pedagogic communication within that context. Where framing is strong, that is when the external (e) feature is strong, social class may play a crucial role. Where the external framing is strong, it often means that the images, voices and practices the school reflects make it difficult for children of marginalised classes to recognise themselves in the school.

Now we can construct the basic code. We can write the code:

$$\frac{E}{\pm C^{i\text{-}e}/\pm F^{i\text{-}e}}$$

Under E (elaborated orientation) we have the values + or – and then the functions Cie/F^{ie}. In this way we can show how the distribution of power and the principles of control translate themselves in terms of communicative principles and spatial arrangements which give the elaborated orientation its particular modality. *Changes in the Cs and Fs will produce different modalities of elaborated codes.*

CODES AND CHANGE

I want to briefly look at *change*. We have put together classification and framing, and we can state that classification and framing provide the rules of the pedagogic code, that is, of its practice, but not of the discourse. As *Cs* and *Fs* change in values, from strong to weak, then there are changes in organisational practices, changes in discursive practices, changes in transmission practices, changes in psychic defences, changes in the concepts of the teacher, changes in the concepts of the pupils, changes in the concepts of knowledge itself, and changes in the forms of expected pedagogic consciousness.

The potential of change is built into the model. Although framing carries the message to be reproduced, there is always pressure to weaken that framing. There is very rarely a pedagogic practice where there is no pressure to weaken the framing because, in this formulation, pedagogic discourse and pedagogic practice construct always an arena, a struggle over the nature of symbolic control. And, at some point, the weakening of the framing is going to violate the classification. *So change can come at the level of framing.*

Although classification translates power into the voice to be reproduced, we have seen that the contradictions, cleavages and dilemmas which inhere in the principles of classification are never entirely suppressed, either at the social or individual level. Finally, one of the problems of theories of culture reproduction, amongst many, is that any theory of cultural reproduction should have strong rules which enable the theories to say that this is the same, this is an elaboration, this is a change. What is quite remarkable about theories of cultural reproduction is that, mostly, they lack such rules.

I suggest the following: if a value changes from strong to weak, or vice versa, if framing changes from strong to weak or the classification changes from strong to weak, there are two basic questions we should always ask:

* which group is responsible for initiating the change? Is the change initiated by a dominant group or a dominated group?
* if values are weakening, what values still remain strong?

CODES AND CONSCIOUSNESS

So far, we have tried to examine the internal logic by means of which pedagogic practice is constructed and have discussed classification and framing as they regulate modalities of pedagogic practice and, more generally, modalities of *official elaborated codes*. But we have only hinted at the relationship between these codes of transmission and the shaping of the pedagogic consciousness of the acquirer. We have a model that can generate modalities of transmission, whether these modalities of transmission are realised in the family, in the school, in the hospital, in the prison (a crucial agent of cultural reproduction). But there is no linkage between the model of transmission and the process of acquisition. I want now to turn to develop the general model so that I can show the biasing of the pedagogic consciousness of the acquirer and transmitter. In this discussion of the consciousness of the acquirer no reference is made to ideology. And the reason why ideology has not been mentioned is for the reason that this system constructs ideology. Ideology, here, is a way of making relations. It is not a content but a way in which relationships are made and realised.

TRANSMISSION AND ACQUISITION

The model in Figure 1.2 does not introduce any new concepts. It simply puts together all the concepts that we have developed and shows their dynamics. This model is going to refer to the process of acquisition within a given framing relation. It refers to the model of acquisition within any pedagogic context.

First of all, I want to show the relation between the principle of the classification, strong and weak, and the development of what I have called *recognition*

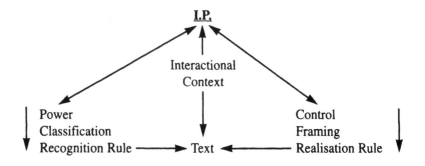

Figure 1.2: Transmission Context

I.P. = Interactional Practice

rules. These recognition rules are at the level of the acquirer. I shall argue that changes in classification strength change the recognition rules by means of which individuals are able to recognise the specialty of the context that they are in. We should remember that classification refers always to relations between contexts, or between agents, or between discourses, or between practices.

The classificatory principle, strong or weak, will indicate how one context differs from another. The classificatory principle provides the key to the distinguishing feature of the context, and so orientates the speaker to what is expected, what is legitimate to that. An example here might help. It is frequently the case that when I give a seminar it is made up of members covering a range of disciplines and practices. Yet the members share a common recognition rule which orientates the members to the speciality of this context. This rule determines what the context demands and enables the 'reading' of the context. Members not sharing this common pedagogic communication may well remain silent or offer what other members would consider inappropriate talk and conduct. From my point of view, replying to questions from such a diverse group is complex, for often it is not possible to infer the discursive context from which the questions issue and so produce an appropriate answer. This weakly classified context can create ambiguity in contextual recognitions.

From this point of view, the classificatory principle at the level of the individual creates recognition rules whereby the subject can orientate to the special features which distinguish the context. The classificatory principle regulates recognition rules, recognition rules refer to power relations. Certain distributions of power give rise to different social distributions of recognition rules and, without the recognition rule, contextually legitimate communication is not possible. It may well be, at the more concrete level, that some children from the marginal classes are silent in school because of the unequal distribution of recognition rules: power, classification and recognition rules. Power is never more fundamental as far as communication is concerned than when it acts on the distribution of recognition rules.

However, we may have the recognition rule which enables us to distinguish the speciality of the context but we may still be unable to produce legitimate communication. Many children of the marginal classes may indeed have a recognition rule, that is, they can recognise the power relations in which they are involved, and their position in them, but they may not possess the realisation rule. If they do not possess the *realisation rule*, they cannot then speak the expected legitimate text. These children in school, then, will not have acquired the legitimate pedagogic code, but they will have acquired their place in the classificatory system. For these children, the experience of school is essentially an experience of the classificatory system and their place in it.

The recognition rule, essentially, enables appropriate realisations to be put together. The realisation rule determines how we put meanings together and how we make them public. The realisation rule is necessary to produce the legitimate text. Thus, different values of framing act selectively on realisation rules and so on the production of different texts. Simply, recognition rules regulate what meanings are relevant and realisation rules regulate how the meanings are to be put together to create the legitimate text.

We now can see how the distribution of power and the principles of control translate into classification and framing values which select out recognition and realisation rules to create contextually appropriate text. In the model, the pedagogic context is essentially an interactive one.

The *interactional practice* is defined by classification and framing procedures. The classification and framing procedures act selectively on the recognition rules and on the realisation rules. These recognition and realisation rules, at the level of the acquirer, enable that acquirer to construct the expected legitimate text. However, the text that is constructed may be no more than how one sits or how one moves. In this system a text is anything which attracts evaluation. The *definition of a text* is anything which attracts evaluation, and this can be no more than a slight movement. Evaluation condenses into itself the pedagogic code and its classification and framing procedures, and the relationships of power and control that have produced these procedures.

However, the text is not something which is mechanically reproduced. The text which is produced can feed back on the interactional practice. There can be a dynamic relation between the text that is produced and the interactional practice. The text itself, under certain conditions, can change the interactional practice. But what does it mean to say 'change the interactional practice'? It means change in classification and framing values. Here, the text has challenged the interactional practice and the classification and framing values upon which it is based.

CODES AND RESEARCH

I want to turn to two pieces of research which illustrates the use and relevance of recognition and realisation rules as functions of classification and framing. More examples are given in part II. In one particular study (Holland, 1981), I was interested in how apparently similar contexts and tasks elicited different readings by children from different social backgrounds. I was even more interested in whether children's readings could be changed through their *tacit* reading of a series of tasks presented in interview. It is very difficult to create classificatory tasks which have similar significance to children coming from different class backgrounds. However, all the children ate lunch at their primary school. We constructed a series of cards showing pictures of the food that was on offer: potatoes, ice cream, fish fingers, milk, eggs, etc. We made a total of 24 pictures to be sorted into groups by 29 working-class and 29 middle-class children of 7 years of age. After ensuring each child could recognise the pictures on the cards, we said 'Here are some pictures of food. What we would like you to do with them is put the ones together you think go together. You can use all of them or you can use only some of them'. The characteristics of the instruction appeared to be as follows:

$$- C^{ie}/-F^{ie}$$

(You are free to choose any picture you like, you can choose to put them together in any way you want and for any reason you like.) After each child had made their groups, we then asked them about each grouping of pictures, as to why they had selected the cards. We found that we could distinguish two very different kinds of reasons, both equally valid. One type of reason for the classification referred the groupings to something in the child's life context, e.g. 'I have this for breakfast', 'I cook this for my mum', 'I don't like these'. The other type of reason referred to something the pictures had in common, e.g. 'They come from the sea', 'They're vegetables'. The difference between these reasons should not be seen as just simply that of abstract/concrete. To do this would be to lose sight of the social basis of the difference. One classification refers to a principle which had a direct relation to a specific material base. The reason is embedded in a local context, in a local experience. The other type of reason references an indirect relation to a specific material base. In sociological terms we are looking at a selection of classifying principles, each of which has a different relation to a material base. What we found *initially* was that the middle-class children were much more likely to offer reasons which had an indirect relation to a specific material base and that the working-class children were much more likely to offer reasons which had a direct relation to a specific material base.

However, this is not the most interesting finding. After the children had made their first sort of the cards we said 'What we would like you to do now is take the pictures and put them together another way'. We then asked the children, as before, to give their reasons for each grouping. This time a significant number of the middle-class children switched their reason to that offered by working-class children, that is, they referred their groupings to a local context or a local experience or local practice (e.g. 'I have them for breakfast', etc.). The working-class children continued to give the same type of reason as they had given on the first sort.

Hence, we concluded that the middle-class children had *two* principles of classification, which stood in a hierarchic relation to each other. One was privileged and came first. The questions which then arose were: why did the middle-class children select one type of reason first, and why did the working-class children offer only one type of reason?

In the case of the working-class children, I suggest the coding instruction is taken at its face value, $-C^{ie}/-F^{ie}$. The children, from their point of view, select a non-specialised recognition rule which, in turn, regulates the selection of non-specialised contexts. From the children's perspective, these are domestic or peer group contexts. This contrasts with the middle-class children, who *initially* recognised the context as specialised. Thus, for the middle-class children, $-C^{ie}$ is transformed into $+C^{ie}$ that is, this context is a specialised context and must be treated in a particular way. In other words, the recognition rule marks the context as having an intrinsic specialty, i.e. the $-F^{ie}$ is transformed into $+F^{ie}$. Thus $-F^{ie}$, that is 'talk about the grouping in any way you want to', is transformed into a realisation rule which selects a very *particular* orientation to meanings on the basis of the recognition rule. Thus the middle-class children transformed $-C^{ie}/-F^{ie}$ into $+C^{ie}/+F^{ie}$. But the recognition by the middle-class 7-year-old of the strong classification between home and school is itself based on the dominance of the official pedagogic practice and meanings over local pedagogic practice and meanings in this child's home. Such a dominance creates a position of relative power and privilege for the middle-class child and much less so for the working-class child.

I want now to turn to a very different research enquiry. Whitty, Rowe and Aggleton (1994a) investigated how secondary schools responded to requirements of the 1988 Educational Reform Act to introduce cross-curricular themes which related to the opportunities, responsibilities and experiences of adult life. The cross-curricular themes (economic and industrial understanding, education for citizenship, community understanding, environmental education, health education, careers education and guidance) were partly a response to criticisms of the narrowly subject-based curriculum as being an inadequate preparation for the world beyond school. The students were expected to synthesise the learning from a range of subjects and apply this to life beyond school.

The researchers were interested in how students talked about the themes. Did some students 'describe themes according to the convention of subject discourse, using abstract principles, while others [would] describe them according to topic orientation, which tended to be in the form of concrete example'? A short questionnaire was constructed and given to year 10 students (71) in four schools. A coding scheme, which distinguished between context-dependent and context-independent descriptions of themes, was applied to the students' responses (see Table 1.1). On the basis of prior information, the students were divided into non-manual and manual groups. The total non-manual group responses across the five themes were distributed as follows: 117 context dependent and 67 context inde-

Table 1.1: Student responses to themes

	Across all themes		Across health/economic and industrial themes	
	Total no. of responses	% context independent	Total no. of responses	% context independent
Non-manual	184	36	67	36
Manual	127	20	46	15

pendent. The distribution for the manual group, in contrast, was 102 context dependent and 25 context independent. However, the greatest difference between the two class groups occurred with the themes of health education and economic and industrial understanding, where the total for the non-manual group was 43 context dependent and 24 context independent, whereas the total for the manual group was 39 context dependent and 7 context independent.

It is not clear from the paper why the total number of responses is different. However, there was a school effect. Most of the students from one school, B, which, as the authors describe, 'relied largely on teaching themes through highly academic subject based curriculum', described economic and industrial understanding in terms of concepts derived from economics. Pupils in other schools were more likely to characterize this theme in context-dependent terms. Although the authors do not mention this, it may well be that there is an interaction between the social class of the students and the 'highly academic subject based curriculum' school. It seems that, in school B, the recognition and realisation rules, which its strong classification and framing generated in the students, defined the theme solely in terms of another academic subject, so defeating the purpose of the theme as a construct of an integration of subjects focusing on the world beyond school.

If themes were to fulfil their function, then their discourse would have to interact with the common-sense world of daily practice. But to do this the classification between official school knowledge and everyday knowledge would have to be weakened. This could lead to a perception on the part of the student that themes were not really official pedagogic discourse, as the researchers found when discussing personal and social understanding in a focused interview with students (Whitty, Rowe and Aggleton, 1994a, p. 175):

Researchers: Where do you discuss issues like moral issues?
Pupil I: We do this in PSE (Personal and Social Education) but it's much more boring (than RE). In PSE no one takes it seriously . . . fall asleep.
Pupil II: Depends on the teacher. Mr. Y they take the mick out of him. He talks and talks and never stops.
Pupil III: PSE is a catch all lesson. It takes in everything.
Researchers: What is the difference between PSE and English?
Pupil X: English is more down to earth.
Pupil IV: Whereas in subject area . . . like English.
Pupil II: It's more depth in a subject really, you go into it more.[4]

It is very clear that students are conscious of very specific subject-based recognition and realisation rules (p. 173):

Researcher: Right now when you talk in science is there any difference be-
                tween the way you talk in science and the way you talk in En-
                glish?

Pupil I: Yes, because the teachers restrict you, they say don't you know
                try to talk about anything else other than what you're working
                on so if you talk about what you're working on it's got to be dif-
                ferent from what you're working on in English.

Pupil II: Well in English you come up, you try to come up with creative
                ideas, so you can talk in a creative manner in science you talk in
                a more logical manner . . . analytical.

The different classification and framing values of Science and English create different specialised talk on the basis of different recognition and realisation rules.
The authors conclude 'Yet those pupils who had successfully learnt to differentiate subjects according to whether or not and in what way oral work was legitimate were actually inhibited from making thematic links across subjects by their
very success in recognising the distinctions between the different subject discourses' (p. 173).

I hope that these two illustrations from research give some idea of the empirical relevance of the models presented in this chapter.

CONCLUSION

I have developed a model for showing how a distribution of power and principles
of control translate into pedagogic codes and their modalities. I have also shown
how these codes are acquired and so shape consciousness. In this way, a connection has been made between macro structures of power and control and the micro
process of the formation of pedagogic consciousness. Of importance, the model
shows how both *order* and its *change* inhere in codes. The models make possible
specific descriptions of the pedagogising process and their outcomes.[5] What is
now required is a model for the construction of pedagogic discourse and to this
we shall attend in the next chapter.

NOTES

1. It is also the case that such a structure, integrated, can facilitate greater centralisation and weaker solidarities. The reduction in the number of departments, each with its
own head, may make the system more manageable by the centre. The new groupings consist of individuals with different interests in new competitive relations. As a consequence,
internal solidarities are likely to be weaker than in the case of a collection code organisation. It therefore becomes crucial to know the source of the motivation to change, whether
from the top or the bottom of the institution.

2. In a classroom, we may be concerned with, for example, the absence or presence of images on the wall, the form they take, the seating arrangements, the distribution of tasks among the pupils. This is internal classification.

3. The external value of the framing (F^x) is itself based on the classification between others' knowledge and the otherness of knowledge, between official pedagogic practice and local pedagogic practice.

4. Whitty, Rowe and Aggleton show that the form of communication may, itself, be subject to recognition and realisation rules which index pedagogic communication as referencing official pedagogic communication. Students refer to 'discussion' when referring to official pedagogic communication and 'talk' or 'just talk' when they describe communicative interaction in some themes. 'Talk' signifies extra pedagogic or non-pedagogic communication and so regulates their perception and response.

5. I should point out that the concepts of classification and framing should be treated as conceptually independent with respect to the specification of pedagogic codes. Variations in the values of classification and framing, as the text indicates, give rise to different code modalities. To consider as some commentators have that each concept only logically entails its opposite is to misunderstand the conceptual work these concepts *together* perform. Further, as Cie/F^{ie} values change we do not have dichotomies but different *modalities of regulation and challenge*. From this point of view visible and invisible pedagogies are not dichotomous but *opposing* modalities *within* the potential of the pedagogic code. Thus specific codes can develop incorporating features of different modalities. We need to know the processes whereby particular code modalities are constructed, institutionalised, distributed, challenged and changed (see chapter 3).

APPENDIX: PEDAGOGIC CULTURE AND PEDAGOGIC CODE

A criticism that has been made of the theory is that the code theory does not generate organisational or administrative descriptions. Ball raised the question of a fourth message system to supplement curiculum, pedagogy and evaluation messages of the original 1971 formulation (Bernstein, 1971). In a sense the organisational order can be regarded as the container and the transmission order the contained. From this point of view the container becomes the primary condition without which no transmission can be stable and reproduced. The container appears to refer to the management of the agency with respect to its administration of staff and resources, their relation to each other and the management of the agency with respect to its external responsibilities and interests. The contained would refer to the transmission and of its social relations. This formulation invites the question of the relation between the container and the contained.

The social division of labour of discourses, transmitters and acquirers (classificatory principle), and the social relations (framing), effect what we could call the *shape* of the container. As Cie/F^{ie} change their values, administrative units, relations within and between these units, and in particular their governance, also change, and therefore effect the shape of the container. But the pedagogic code modality does not only effect the shape of the container, but also its stability or rather the management of the stability (reproduction). As code modalities change so do problems of conflict and consensus, and of order and reproduction. As a consequence, the form of the management of stability and its strategies, and also strategies of resistance and solidarity, change. If we keep to the metaphor of the container and the contained then the pedagogic code modality has consequences for both the shape and the stability of the container.

However the management of resources, that is the *economy* of the container, is itself not necessarily related to the code modality, although different code modalities may make different demands on resources: symbolic, human, material. But the same code modality may be associated with different economies.

There is a further regulator of the pedagogic code realisations which is not intrinsic to the code modality. This regulator is extrinsic to the code, it is an external bias(es) imposed by some power (e.g. State) external to the code modality. This bias may well effect *both* the container and the contained. This external bias imposed from without effects the criteria the agency has to meet. This bias may well effect not only the focus of code realisations but also expected management orientation, control over intake and staff (the bias of marketisation). This external bias may well be differently contextualised depending upon the mandatory characteristics of the bias.

The picture now has become so complex that the metaphor of the container and the contained is no longer useful as a mode of thought. Whereas shape, stability and economy operate on the same level and fit with the notion of container, bias operates at a different level as it mediates between some external power and the internal regulation of the agency. It therefore seems better to change the metaphor, as it has exhausted its usefulness, but to retain the parameters to which it has given rise: bias, shape, stability, economy. I shall exchange the metaphor for a concept which embraces the outcome of these features.

A first step towards such a concept would be to understand that both shape and economy are realisations of distributive rules; in the former case, discourses, transmission and acquirers, and in the latter case, resources. But such distributive rules are essential features of regulative discourse although economy is not intrinsic to the code. The management of stability (reproduction) is also a basic feature of regulative discourse (order, relation, identity). Further, bias is an external regulative discourse even if it is restricted to the focus upon instructional discourse. Shape and stability are intrinsic to code modality, bias and economy are not, but all four are components of the regulative discourse of the agency and its external regulation. Thus we need to have a concept whose relations are dependent upon the pedagogic code but which also regulates the code. This concept would embrace the fundamental regulation of the *mode of being* of the agency. I propose the concept of pedagogic culture. We can now also consider the inter-relations between the pedagogic culture and the pedagogic code. Pedagogic culture is the mode of being of the agency's social relations as they cope with its bias, shape, stability and economy.

Chapter 2

The Pedagogic Device

INTRODUCTION

My question is: are there any general principles underlying the transformation of knowledge into pedagogic communication, whether the knowledge is intellectual, practical, expressive, or official knowledge or local knowledge?

The question may at first sight seem to be unnecessary. We have studies of educational systems in a number of different societies under different economic, historical and ideological conditions. We have a growing understanding of the complex interrelationships of educational systems with other systems, economic and cultural, national and international. We have a plethora of studies showing the function of education in the reproduction of inequalities; class, gender, race, region, religion. Classrooms have been subject to numerous descriptions, including their role in legitimising some identities and delegitimising others.

From all these perspectives pedagogic communication is often viewed as a carrier, a relay for ideological messages and for external power relations, or, in contrast, as an apparently neutral carrier or relay of skills of various kinds.

In terms of my questions, whether there are any general principles underlying the pedagogising of knowledge and what makes pedagogic communication possible, most studies have studied only what is *carried* or *relayed*, they do not study the constitution of the relay itself. We have studies of pedagogic messages and their institutional and ideological base, but we have not many studies of the *social grammar*, without which no message is possible. Therefore, I would like to explore the possibilities of constructing the sociological nature of pedagogic knowledge: official or local knowledge.

Initially I want to make clear the distinction between *a relay* and *the relayed*. To do this I am first going to compare the language device and what I shall call the pedagogic device. Second, I will outline the rules of the pedagogic device. Third, I will give an account of each of the three rules and their interrelation and implications.

THE LANGUAGE DEVICE AND THE PEDAGOGIC DEVICE

If we look at the language device, this device is a system of formal rules which govern various combinations that we make when we speak or write. The device operates at a number of different levels. There is some controversy about the origins of this device. Some argue, from a Chomskyan base, that the device has its basis in two facilities: a built-in sensitivity to *acquisition* of the rules of the device, and an *interactional* facility. Without the latter, acquisition is not possible.

Notice that from this controversial Chomskyan perspective, the rules of this device, the acquisition of this device, and its creative possibilities are independent of culture. In other words, it exists at the level of the social but not at the level of the cultural. From an evolutionary point of view why this is the case is because we could not leave a device as critical as this to the vagueness and vicissitudes of culture. We can say from this viewpoint that the *acquisition* of this device, which is fundamental, is ideologically free, but *not* its rules, as we shall see.

The model shown in Figure 2.1 says very simply that there is a meaning potential outside the language device, and this meaning potential activates the device, and the result is communication. Additionally, the communication has a feedback on the meaning potential, either in a restricted or in an enhancing fashion.

The rules that we indicate to provide an understanding of communication in its context are necessarily contextual rules. For instance, the distinctive rules of communication that we would have if we were having a drink or if we were talking to a teacher, would vary with the context. So *contextual* rules are required to understand the local communication which the device makes possible.

However, the rules which constitute the device are relatively stable, but they are not entirely stable over periods of time. These are not fundamental changes,

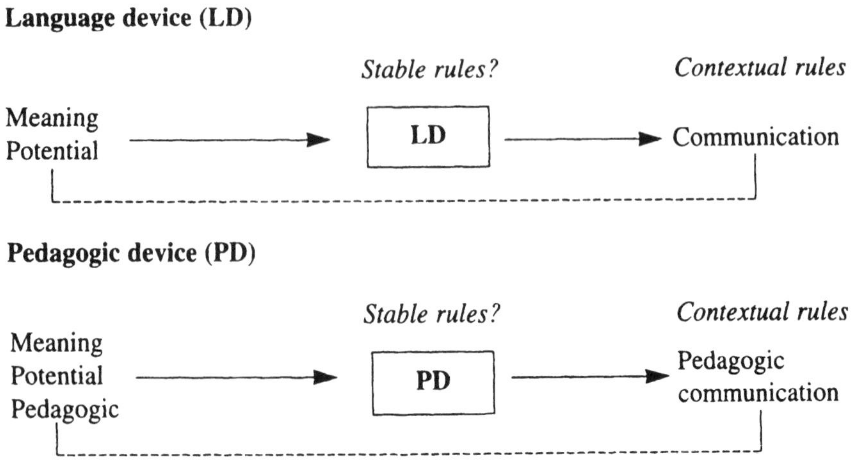

Language device (LD)

Pedagogic device (PD)

Figure 2.1

but a series of minor changes. The rules of the device are relatively stable, and the rules that regulate the communication that comes out of the device are contextually regulated.

This raises a very interesting question: is the language device in itself neutral, is the system of rules that constitute this device neutral with respect to the meaning potential and therefore neutral in respect to what comes out of it? The question really becomes: are the rules and the classifying systems built into the device in some way regulating what comes out of it? And if this were to be the case, then the carrier of communication, in some fundamental way, is regulating what is carried.

Halliday (1978, 1993) argues strongly, and I agree, that the *rules* of the language device are not ideologically free, but that the rules reflect emphases on the meaning potential created by dominant groups. Thus, from this point of view, the relative stability of the rules may well have their origin in the concerns of dominant groups. Language and speech should be considered as a system of dialectically interrelated systems.

I will not go into the intricacies of this problem because it is very complex and there are contradictory views about it. However, it raises the point that the device is not neutral, and that the device itself may have some intrinsic regulatory function.

At the most mundane level it clearly has, because the device has built into its system some very fundamental classifications, in particular gender classifications. For instance, the opposition to gender is made difficult by the classification system of the language itself. It can be very difficult to suspend or replace the classification distributions made in the language. The word 'mastery' is not easy to substitute for a less gendered term.

We have made a distinction between '*the carrier*' (or relay) and '*the carried*' (what is relayed). 'The carrier' consists of relatively stable rules and 'the carried' consists of contextual rules. Neither set of rules is ideologically free.

In a similar manner, I want to introduce a pedagogic device. This device has internal rules which regulate the pedagogic communication which the device makes possible. Such pedagogic communication acts selectively on the meaning potential. By *meaning potential* we simply mean the potential discourse that is available to be pedagogised. The pedagogic device regulates fundamentally the communication it makes possible, and in this way it acts selectively on the meaning potential. The device continuously regulates the ideal universe of potential pedagogic meanings in such a way as to restrict or enhance their realisations.

Although there are differences, the pedagogic device resembles the language device in a umber of ways. Its formal structure (see Figure 2.1) is similar. The pedagogic device makes possible a great potential range of communicative outcomes similar to the language device. The forms of realisation of the pedagogic device, like the forms of realisation of the language device, are subject to rules which vary with the context.

The variable forms of realisation of the pedagogic device can restrict or enhance the potential discourse available to be pedagogised. The intrinsic rules of the pedagogic device, like the intrinsic rules of the language device, I shall argue, are relatively stable. *These rules, like the rules of the language device, are not ideologically free.* Indeed, the rules of the pedagogic device are essentially implicated in the distribution of, and constraints upon, the various forms of consciousness.

Both the language device and the pedagogic device become sites for appropriation, conflict and control. At the same time, there is a crucial difference between the two devices. In the case of the pedagogic device, but not in the case of the language device, it is possible to have an outcome, a form of communication which can subvert the fundamental rules of the device.

THE RULES OF THE PEDAGOGIC DEVICE

As a start, I will suggest that the pedagogic device provides the intrinsic grammar of pedagogic discourse (i.e. *grammar* in a metaphoric sense). I will then consider the intrinsic grammar of pedagogic discourse that the device provides, essentially through three interrelated rules: *distributive rules, recontextualising rules* and *evaluative rules.*

These rules themselves stand in a particular relationship to each other. That is, these rules are hierarchically related, in the sense that recontextualising rules are derived from the distributive rules, and evaluative rules are derived from the recontextualising rules. There is a necessary interrelationship between these rules, and there are also power relationships between them. I shall very briefly say what these three rules are.

First, the function of the distributive rules is to regulate the relationships between power, social groups, forms of consciousness and practice. Distributive rules specialise forms of knowledge, forms of consciousness and forms of practice to social groups. Distributive rules distribute forms of consciousness through distributing different forms of knowledge.

Second, recontextualising rules regulate the formation of specific pedagogic discourse.

Third, evaluative rules constitute any pedagogic practice. Any specific pedagogic practice is there for one purpose: to transmit *criteria*. Pedagogic practice is, in fact, the level which produces a ruler for consciousness. I will go through these three rules step by step.

Distributive Rules

Distributive rules distinguish between two different classes of knowledge that I will argue are necessarily available in all societies. I believe that these two classes of knowledge are intrinsic to language itself; it is the very nature of language that makes these two classes of knowledge possible. I will term them the *thinkable* class and the *unthinkable* class.

Thus, in all societies there are at least two basic classes of knowledge; one class of knowledge that is *esoteric* and one that is *mundane*. There is the *knowledge of the other* and there is *the otherness of knowledge*. There is the knowledge of how it is (the knowledge of the possible), as against the possibility of the impossible.

The line between these two classes of knowledge is relative to any given period. What is actually esoteric in one period can become mundane in another. In other words, the content of these classes varies historically and culturally.

A brief comparison between small-scale non-literate societies with simple divisions of labour and literate societies which have complex divisions of labour will illustrate this point. If we look at these small-scale societies with simple divisions of labour, there is a division between the thinkable and the unthinkable. The unthinkable in small-scale non-literate societies is managed and controlled by their religious systems, agencies, agents, practices and the cosmologies to which they give rise.

In modern society today (this is indeed a very brutal simplification which I will develop later), the control of the unthinkable lies essentially, but not wholly, in the upper reaches of the educational system. This does not mean that the unthinkable cannot take place outside the educational system, but the major *control and management* of the unthinkable is carried out by the higher agencies of education. On the other hand, the thinkable in modern complex societies is managed by secondary and primary school systems. This is, however, a very rough and very crude simplification.

I want to suggest that there is a very profound similarity between simple societies and complex societies. This does not imply the same patronizing comparisons that some people suggest in saying that 'simple' societies have complex knowledge systems and navigational procedures, despite the fact that they are simple and non-literate. But I want to suggest that there is a fundamental similarity in the very structuring of meaning both in very 'simple' societies and in very complex societies.

This similarity refers to a particular order of meanings. However, this particular order of meanings should not be considered only as abstract. Clearly it is abstract, but it is inappropriate to say abstract as opposed to concrete. All meanings are abstract; it is not the *fact* of the abstraction but the *form* that the abstraction takes.

I will suggest that the form that the abstraction takes, and which unites 'simple' societies and complex societies, is a form of abstraction which postulates and relates two worlds. It relates the material world and the immaterial world, it relates an everyday mundane world to a transcendental world. This is a very interesting specialisation of meaning, which creates two worlds and relates them, for example religion.

When we look at this order of meaning more closely, the form that these meanings takes must be a form with an indirect relation between meanings and a specific material base. And the reason for this is very clear: if meanings have a direct relation to a material base, these meanings are wholly consumed by the context. These meanings are so embedded in the context that they have no reference outside that context. These meanings are not simply context dependent, they are necessarily context bound: and meanings which are context bound cannot unite anything other than themselves. They lack the power of relation outside a context because they are totally consumed by that context.

In this sense, the meanings which create and unite two worlds must always be meanings where there is an indirect relation between these meanings and a specific material base: there is a specific social division of labour and a specific set of social relationships within that division of labour.

If these meanings have an indirect relation to a specific material base, the meanings themselves create a gap or a space. If meanings are consumed by the context and wholly embedded in the context, there is no space. But if these meanings have an indirect relation to a specific material base, because they are indirect, there must be a gap. Intrinsic to these meanings is the potential of a gap, (a space) which I will term a *potential discursive gap*. It is not a dislocation of meaning, it is a gap.

What is it a potential of? I want to suggest that this gap or space can become (not always) a site for alternative possibilities, for alternative realisations of the relation between the material and the immaterial. The gap itself can change the relation between the material and the immaterial. This potential gap or space I will suggest is the site for the unthinkable, the site of the impossible, and this site can clearly be both beneficial and dangerous at the same time. This gap is the meeting point of order and disorder, of coherence and incoherence. It is the crucial site of the *yet to be thought*.

Any distribution of power will attempt to regulate the realisation of this potential. I will suggest that part of the reason why the rules of this device are stable is that this gap will always be regulated. The modes of the regulation will differ, but the gap will always be regulated. Any distribution of power will regulate the potential of this gap in its own interest, because the gap itself has the possibility of an alternative order, an alternative society, and an alternative power relation.

For 'simple' societies, of course, this regulation is affected by the religious system and the cosmologies to which it gives access and control. Historically, in the medieval period, this gap was regulated by religious systems in the first institutionalisation of knowledge.

Once there is a system of meanings, which has this potential of creating relationships between two worlds, the gap can produce different relations between these worlds. This is a paradox. The distributive rules attempt to regulate those who have access to this site, and in this way control alternative possibilities but, paradoxically, the device cannot do this effectively.

The control over access to the site is accomplished by a selection of the agents who have previously been legitimately pedagogised. But in such a process, the contradictions and dilemmas are rarely totally suppressed. Further, the very pedagogic process reveals the possibility of the gap, and shapes the form of its realisation. Thus, in controlling or attempting to control the realisations of the gap, it must necessarily reveal the modes which make connections between the two worlds. The power relations, for which the distributive rules are the relay, are then necessarily subject to change.

Power relations distribute the unthinkable and the thinkable, and differentiate and stratify groups accomplished by the distributive rules (see Figure 2.2). It should be possible to see that the distributive rules translate sociologically into *the field of the production of discourse*. Sociologically speaking, the distributive rules create a specialised field of production of discourse, with specialised rules of access and specialised power controls. This field is controlled more and more today by the state itself. We can now move from rules to structures, or fields.

Recontextualising Rules: Pedagogic Discourse

Recontextualising rules were said to constitute specific pedagogic discourses. The distributive rules mark and distribute who may transmit what to whom and under what conditions, and they attempt to set the outer limits of legitimate discourse. Pedagogic discourse itself rests on the rules which create specialised communications through which pedagogic subjects are selected and created. In other words, pedagogic discourse selects and creates specialised pedagogic subjects through its contexts and contents.

What is pedagogic discourse? First of all, I will describe it, and then I will try to explain how it arises. Initially, I will define *pedagogic discourse* as a rule which embeds two discourses; a discourse of skills of various kinds and their re-

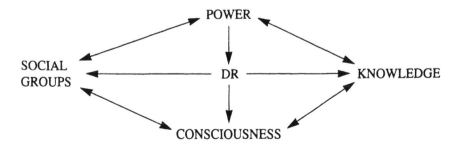

Figure 2.2

lations to each other, and a discourse of social order. Pedagogic discourse embeds rules which create skills of one kind or another and rules regulating their relationship to each other, and rules which create social order.

We shall call the discourse which creates specialised skills and their relationship to each other *instructional discourse*, and the moral discourse which creates order, relations and identity *regulative discourse*. We can write it as follows:

$$\frac{\text{INSTRUCTIONAL DISCOURSE}}{\text{REGULATIVE DISCOURSE}} \qquad \frac{ID}{RD}$$

This is to show that the instructional discourse is embedded in the regulative discourse, and that the regulative discourse is the dominant discourse. Pedagogic discourse is the rule which leads to the embedding of one discourse in another, to create one text, to create *one* discourse.

Often people in schools and in classrooms make a distinction between what they call the transmission of skills and the transmission of values. These are always kept apart as if there were a conspiracy to disguise the fact that there is only one discourse. In my opinion, there is only one discourse, not two, because the secret voice of this device is to disguise the fact that there is only one. Most researchers are continually studying the two, or thinking as if there are two: as if education is about values on the one hand, and about competence on the other. In my view there are not two discourses, there is only one.

From one point of view, pedagogic discourse appears to be a discourse without a discourse. It seems to have no discourse of its own. Pedagogic discourse is not physics, chemistry or psychology. Whatever it is, it cannot be identified with the discourses it transmits.

Then what is the nature and principle of this discourse? As a start, I will suggest that pedagogic discourse is a principle, not a discourse. It is the principle by which other discourses are appropriated and brought into a special relationship with each other, for the purpose of their selective transmission and acquisition. Pedagogic discourse is a principle for the circulation and reordering of discourses. In this sense it is not so much a discourse as a principle. We shall see later that this principle does give rise to a specialised discourse. At this stage, however, it is seen only as a principle for delocating a discourse, for relocating it, for refocusing it, according to its own principle.

Now, in this process of delocating a discourse (manual, mental, expressive), that is, taking a discourse from its original site of effectiveness and moving it to a pedagogic site, a gap or rather a space is created.

As the discourse moves from its original site to its new positioning as pedagogic discourse, a transformation takes place. The transformation takes place because every time a discourse moves from one position to another, there is a space in which ideology can play. No discourse ever moves without ideology at play.

As this discourse moves, it is ideologically transformed; it is not the same discourse any longer. I will suggest that as this discourse moves, it is transformed from an actual discourse, from an unmediated discourse to an imaginary discourse. As pedagogic discourse appropriates various discourses, unmediated discourses are transformed into mediated, virtual or imaginary discourses. From this point of view, pedagogic discourse selectively creates *imaginary subjects*.[1]

Before defining *pedagogic discourse* more specifically, let us take an example. When I was at school I spent three years in a large room with wooden benches and with side benches with saws and hammers and chisels. After three years, I had a pile of wood chippings as high as the bench itself. But what was I doing? Well, what I was doing was this: *outside* pedagogy there was carpentry, but *inside* pedagogy there was woodwork. In other words, here was a transformation of a real discourse called carpentry into an imaginary discourse called woodwork. This is just an example of this movement, in the same way that physics in school is an imaginary physics, which I will come to later.

I want to sharpen the concept of the principle which constitutes pedagogic discourse, by suggesting, formally, that *pedagogic discourse is a recontextualising principle*. Pedagogic discourse is constructed by a recontextualising principle which selectively appropriates, relocates, refocuses and relates other discourses to constitute its own order. In this sense, pedagogic discourse can never be identified with any of the discourses it has recontextualised.

We can now say that pedagogic discourse is generated by a recontextualising discourse, in the same way that we said distributive rules translate, in sociological terms, into fields of production of knowledge with their own rules of access. The recontextualising principle creates recontextualising fields, it creates agents with recontextualising functions. The recontextualising functions then become the means whereby a specific pedagogic discourse is created. Formally, we move from a recontextualising principle to a recontextualising field with agents with practising ideologies.

The recontextualising field has a crucial function in creating the fundamental autonomy of education. We can distinguish between an *official recontextualising field* (ORF) created and dominated by the state and its selected agents and ministries, and a *pedagogic recontextualising field* (PRF). The latter consists of pedagogues in schools and colleges, and departments of education, specialised journals, private research foundations. If the PRF can have an effect on pedagogic discourse independently of the ORF, then there is both some autonomy *and* struggle over pedagogic discourse and its practices. But if there is only the ORF, then there is no autonomy. Today, the state is attempting to weaken the PRF through its ORF, and thus attempting to reduce relative autonomy over the construction of pedagogic discourse and over its social contexts (see later chapter).

The Domination of the Regulative Discourse

Fundamental to my argument is that the regulative discourse is the dominant discourse. In one sense, this is obvious because it is the *moral* discourse that creates the criteria which give rise to character, manner, conduct, posture, etc. In school, it tells the children what to do, where they can go, and so on. It is quite clear that regulative discourse creates the rules of social order.

However, I also want to argue that regulative discourse produces *the order in the instructional discourse*. There is no instructional discourse which is not regulated by the regulative discourse. If this is so, the whole order within pedagogic discourse is constituted by the regulative discourse.

With physics as an example, we will distinguish between physics as activities in the field of production of a discourse, and physics as a pedagogic discourse. It is quite possible to look at the activities of physicists in the field in which physics is produced, and sometimes it is difficult to believe that what everyone is doing in physics.

This is not the case with physics as a pedagogic discourse. A textbook says what physics is, and it is obvious that it has an author. The interesting point, however, is that the authors of textbooks in physics are rarely physicists who are practising in the field of the production of physics; they are working in the field of recontextualisation.[2]

As physics is appropriated by the recontextualising agents, the results cannot formally be derived from the logic of that discourse. Irrespective of the intrinsic logic which constitutes the specialised discourse and activities called physics, the recontextualising agents will select from the totality of practices which is called physics in the field of production of physics. There is selection.

There is a selection in how physics is to be related to other subjects, and in its sequencing and pacing (pacing is the rate of expected acquisition). But these sections cannot be derived from the logic of the discourse of physics or its various activities in the field of the production of discourse.

Irrespective of whether there is an intrinsic logic to physics, the rules for its transmission are *social facts*. And if they are social facts, there are principles of selection. These will be activated by a component of the regulative discourse. That is, the rules of order of physics in the school (selection, relation, sequence and pace) are a function of the regulative discourse. Therefore, I argue that the regulative discourse provides the rules of the internal order of instructional discourse itself. If this argument holds, much can be derived from the notion that we have *one discourse* and that *the regulative discourse is dominant*.

Finally, the recontextualising principle not only recontextualises the *what* of pedagogic discourse, what discourse is to become subject and content of pedagogic practice. It also recontextualises the *how*; that is *the theory of instruction*. This is crucial, because the selection of the theory of instruction is not entirely instrumental. The theory of instruction also belongs to the regulative discourse, and contains within itself a model of the learner and of the teacher and of the relation. The model of the learner is never wholly utilitarian; it contains ideological elements. The recontextualising principle not only selects the *what* but also the *how* of the theory of instruction. Both are elements of regulative discourse.

Evaluative Rules

We have now constructed pedagogic discourse as instructional discourse embedded in regulative discourse. Our next problem is to transform this discourse into a pedagogic practice. I will do this by a series of transformations, starting at the most abstract level and then moving in steps to the level of the classroom itself.

At the most abstract level, pedagogic discourse specialises time, a text and a space, and brings these into a special relationship with each other (see Figure 2.3). Therefore, pedagogic discourse specialises meanings to time and space. This discourse may construct very fundamental category relations with implications for the deepest cultural level. Everything from this level downwards will have a cognitive and cultural consequence. This level of specialisation of time, text and space marks us cognitively, socially and culturally.

LEVEL 1

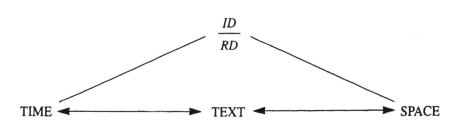

Any pedagogic discourse will punctuate *time*, it will dislocate time. Sometimes, it will dislocate it in perhaps only two periods. Sometimes it will produce a very fine punctuation, from pre-copulation to post-resurrection. Time transforms into age. Every pedagogic discourse will produce a punctuation in time so that we will have age stages, which are wholly imaginary and arbitrary.

Text is transformed into a specific content, and *space* will be transformed into a specific context. It is important from this point of view to understand that behind this more obvious real level stands the abstract first level.

LEVEL 2

AGE ◄──► CONTENT ◄──► CONTEXT

Finally, we can transform age, content, context, to the level of the social relations of pedagogic practice and the crucial features of the communication. Age is
transformed into acquisition. Content is transformed into evaluation. Context is
transformed into transmission. Thus:

LEVEL 3

ACQUISITION ◀━━━▶ EVALUATION ◀━━━▶ TRANSMISSION

We can see that the key to pedagogic practice is continuous evaluation. If we
place horizontal and vertical relations together, we obtain *pedagogic practice* (see
Figure 2.3).

This is what the device is about. Evaluation condenses the meaning of the
whole device. We are now in a position where we can derive the whole purpose
of the device. The purpose of the device is to provide a symbolic ruler for consciousness. Hence we can see the religious origins of the device: religion was the
fundamental system for both creating and controlling the unthinkable, the fundamental principle for relating two different worlds, the mundane and the transcendental. I think we can see the origins of the pedagogic device in this last stage of
the analysis.

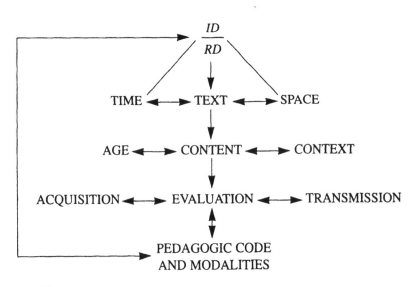

Figure 2.3

From a structural point of view we can bring out the homology between the religious field and the educational field. Following Max Weber we can see a paral-
lel between the positions in the religious field and in the pedagogic field.

RELIGIOUS FIELD   PEDAGOGIC FIELD
     Prophet   Producers
      Priest   Reproducers
        Laity   Acquirers

The religious field is constituted by three positions which stand in various relations of complementarity and opposition. In the religious field, we have the prophets, we have the priests, and we have the laity. The rule is that one can only occupy one category at a time. Priests cannot be prophets, and prophets cannot be priests, and the laity cannot be either. There is a natural affinity between prophets and laity, and there is a natural opposition between prophets and priests. These are the lines of opposition structuring the religious field.

If we look at the structure of the pedagogic field, we also have basically three positions that provide analogues to the prophets, priests and laity. The 'prophets' are the producers of the knowledge,[3] the 'priests' are the recontextualisers or the reproducers, and the 'laity' are the acquirers.

Thus, we have the structure of the pedagogic field.

CONCLUSION

In the model shown in Figure 2.4 I have tried to put together the relation between the formal rules of the device and the sociological structure, practices and processes to which they give rise.

The pedagogic device acts as a symbolic regulator of consciousness; the question is, whose regulator, what consciousness and for whom? It is a condition for

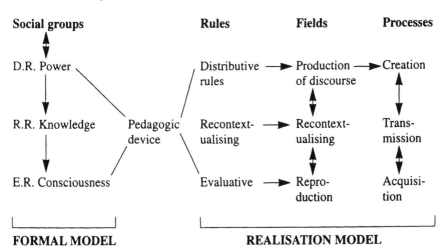

Figure 2.4: The device and its structurings

the production, reproduction and transformation of culture. However, the device is not deterministic in its consequences. The effectiveness of the device is limited by two different features.

1. *Internal:* It is not deterministic for a reason which is intrinsic to the device: I have mentioned this before. Although the device is there to control the unthinkable, in the process of controlling the unthinkable it makes the possibility of the unthinkable available. Therefore, internal to the device is its own paradox: it cannot control what it has been set up to control.
2. *External:* The external reason why the device is not deterministic is because the distribution of power which speaks through the device creates potential sites of challenge and opposition. The device creates in its realisations an arena of struggle between different groups for the appropriation of the device, because whoever appropriates the device has the power to regulate consciousness. Whoever appropriates the device, appropriates a crucial site for symbolic control. The device itself creates an arena of struggle for those who are to appropriate it.

I have tried to expose the *intrinsic grammar* of the device, and to expose what might be called the *hidden voice* of the pedagogic discourse. I have suggested that the grammar of the device regulates what it processes; a grammar whose realisation codes order and position and yet contain the potential of their own transformation.

NOTES

1. The distinction between the 'real' and the 'imaginary' is a distinction made to draw attention to an activity unmediated by anything other than itself in its practice and an activity where mediation is intrinsic to practice. The discourse carpentry in the practice of carpentry is only mediated by itself but pedagogic discourse is mediated by a recontextualising procedure. When a discourse moves, through recontextualising, from its original site to a pedagogic site the original discourse is abstracted from its social base, position and power relations.
2. Attempts are made to break down the strong classification between the field of the production of discourse and the recontextualising field, but there is rarely an institutionalised circulation between the fields. A notable exception was the circulation of staff between university and the *lycée* in France in the case of the philosophy class. Recontextualisers are rarely the producers of the knowledge, although there are important anomalies here. One notable case where the producers of knowledge are recontextualisers is generally at the higher levels of the university, where the recontextualiser may also be the producer of the knowledge. However, with recent developments in higher education teaching and research may well go on in different institutions.
3. It is important to show that the texts produced in the field of the production of knowledge, as the texts constructed in the recontextualising field, are imaginary in crucial

respects. In the case of texts in the field of the production of discourse the inner-textuality of the discourse is transformed into intra-textuality. A text in this field is expected to be original to have the highest renown. Ideally, it should be the first text of its kind and be the product of a single mind or a single dominating mind or joint minds (as in science). This text endeavours to proclaim its uniqueness and may contain strategies which mask, blur or differently position its antecedents. In this way inter-textuality is transformed into intra-textuality in the process of constructing unique authorship.

Chapter 3

Pedagogising Knowledge:
Studies in Recontextualising

INTRODUCTION

Titles are worthy of study in their own right, not simply as aesthetic forms, but as signifiers of the play of positions in the intellectual field. Thus it is possible that the title of this paper in the 1950s might well have been 'Knowledge and Social-isation: the case of education' with pronounced structural functional overtones. In the 1970s a more fitting title might well have been 'Knowledge and Cultural Reproduction' with an Althusserian resonance. But in the 1980s perhaps we would have had 'The Pedagogic Construction of the Subject: a technology', a clear Foucault choice. Today in the 1990s 'Knowledges and Subjectivities: a postmodern account' would surely be a winner. My title I admit seems to be somewhat of a compromise—perhaps an attempt to signify contemporary episte-mological ambiguities.

KNOWLEDGE, LOCATION AND AUTHORS

In the 1960s I want to suggest that a remarkable convergence took place in the field of the social and psychological sciences: a convergence which was perhaps unique with respect to the range of disparate disciplines involved. The conver-gence involved disciplines with radically opposed epistemologies, methods of in-quiry and principles of description. Such a convergence is worthy of special study by the sociology of knowledge. The paper begins with a discussion of a concep-tual convergence within the social psychological and linguistic fields during the early 1990s and proceeds to analyse the consequences of the recontextualising of this concept in the pedagogic recontextualising fields.[1] A complex typology of pedagogic modes and the identities these project is derived from two fundamen-

41

tal pedagogic models. The institutionalising of these modes and their change is traced and contrast is offered between the identities projected by the educational system and the new identity formations of what is called transitional capitalism.

However, the origin of this convergence is not the object of this paper, but rather its pedagogising consequence. Our analysis of the social logic of this knowledge may be helpful to a study of its origins. The knowledge concept I have in mind travelled across the major social sciences in one form or another, that is, the concept of competence. In one form or another in the 1960s and early 1970s this concept is to be found in the following.

Linguistics	: linguistic competence	(Chomsky)
Psychology	: cognitive competence	(Piaget)
Social Anthropology	: cultural competence	(Lévi-Strauss)
Sociology	: members competence (practical accomplishments)	(Garfinkle)
Sociolinguistics	: communicative competence	(Dell Hymes)

It may even be that the concept lurks in Wittgenstein's language games.

The concept refers to procedures for engaging with, and constructing, the world. Competences are intrinsically creative and tacitly acquired in informal interactions. They are practical accomplishments. The acquisition of these procedures are beyond the reach of power relations and their differential unequal positionings, although the form the realisations may take are clearly not beyond power relations. From this point of view the procedures which constitute a given competence may be regarded as social: the negotiation of social order as a practice, cognitive structuring, language acquisition and new cultural assemblies on the basis of old. These procedures are not the gift of any one culture, in the sense they are culture free. These procedures may rest on a biological base as in the case of Chomsky, Piaget, and Lévi-Strauss, but clearly not in the case of Garfinkle. However, this biological base does not give rise to fixed unchanging attributes, but rather points to variety and possibility: a 'progressive' biologism. Although not specifically entailed in the concept of competence, I shall argue later that it carries a potential antagonism to communication, specialised by explicit and formal procedures and their institutional base; a tendency to embrace populism (Jones and Moore, 1995).

COMPETENCE: ITS SOCIAL LOGIC

I want now to examine what could be called the social logic of this concept. By social logic I am referring to the implicit model of the social, the implicit model of communication, of interaction and of the subject which inheres in this concept. I would suggest that an analysis of the social logic of competence reveals:

1. an announcement of a universal democracy of acquisition. All are inherently competent and all possess common procedures. There are no deficits;
2. the subject is active and creative in the construction of a valid world of meanings and practice. Here there are differences but not deficits. Consider creativity in language production (Chomsky), creativity in the process of accommodation (Piaget), the *bricoleur* in Lévi-Strauss, a member's practical accomplishments (Garfinkle);
3. an emphasis on the subject as self-regulating, a benign development. Further this development or expansion is not advanced by formal instruction. Official socialisers are suspect, for acquisition of these procedures is a tacit, invisible act not subject to public regulation;
4. a critical, sceptical view of hierarchical relations. This follows from (3) as in some theories the socialisers' function should not go beyond facilitation, accommodation, and context management. Competence theories have an emancipatory flavour. Indeed in Chomsky and Piaget creativity is placed outside culture. It inheres in the working of the mind;
5. a shift in temporal perspective to the present tense. The relevant time arises out of the point of realisation of the competence, for it is this point which reveals the past and adumbrates the future.

Clearly these five features of the social logic do not apply equally to all usages of the concept, but most will. Further, the emphasis on one feature may be greater in one usage than another.

Summarising, broadly, according to competence theories there is an in-built procedural democracy, an in-built creativity, an in-built virtuous self-regulation. And if it is not in-built, the procedures arise out of, and contribute to social practice, with a creative potential.

However, this idealism of competence, a celebration of what we are in contrast to what we have become, is bought at a price; that is, the price of abstracting the individual from the analysis of distributions of power and principles of control which selectively specialise modes of acquisition and realisations. Thus the announcement of competence points away from such selective specialisations and so points away from the macro blot on the micro context.

However, it is not difficult to see the resonance of the concept of competence with the liberal, progressive and even radical ideologies of the late 1960s and their sponsors, especially those that dominated education. And to these I now wish to turn.

It is clear that competence theorists in the formation of these theories had little or no concern for education. Their texts created positions and addressed, usually, oppositionally, other texts in the intellectual field, which we have called the field of the production of discourse. These texts took their significance from their relation to other texts, e.g. Chomsky and IC grammars, Piaget and behaviourism, Garfinkle and structural functionalism, Lévi-Strauss's unconscious structures against the particularities of groups and individuals. Whilst it is the case that Chomsky, Piaget and Lévi-Strauss operated with varieties of structuralism, this certainly is not the case for Garfinkle and ethnomethodology, nor is it the case for Dell Hymes's communicative competence in sociolinguistics. Competence, then, has divorced, even opposed, epistemological roots. What probably united all the theorists was an anti-positivist position. What is at issue is how a concept which arose in the intellectual field, and whose authors had little or no initial connection with education, came to play such a central role in the theory and practice of education.

I have pointed to the convergence, within the field of the production of intellectual discourse, on the concept of competence by the disciplines of the social and psychological sciences. I have extracted what I take to be the underlying social logic of the concept. I have indicated that this social logic was particularly appealing to occupants of a specialised position in the pedagogic recontextualising field. Indeed the social logic was appealing to dominant members of the official recontextualising field as the Plowden Report (1969) *Children: Their Primary Schools* clearly testifies. The social logic of competence was dominant in both the pedagogic recontextualising field *and* the official pedagogic recontextualising field in the late 1960s, an unusual convergence.

Clearly not all the pedagogic disciplines were influenced by the same concept of competence. Piaget was more relevant to educational psychology and primary education;[2] Chomsky more relevant to psychology and language ethnomethodology and communicative competence to British sociology of education; communicative competence, Labov and Chomsky to language studies. Indeed in the latter case Halliday was recruited and his theory recontextualised to provide a concept of contextual competence or genre competence.

PEDAGOGIC MODELS: COMPETENCE AND PERFORMANCE

I now want to show how recontextualised 'competence' constructed a specific pedagogic practice essentially in primary and pre-school (see note 1). To do this I shall produce two contrasting models of pedagogic practice and context. I shall contrast a competence model with a performance model (see Table 3.1). Briefly, a performance model of pedagogic practice and context places the emphasis upon a specific output of the acquirer, upon a particular text the acquirer is expected to construct and upon the specialised skills necessary to the production of this specific output, text or product.

I shall discuss these models with reference to features which both models share:

Table 3.1: Recontextualised knowledge

	Competence models	Performance models
1. Categories: space time discourse	weakly classified	strongly classified
2. Evaluation orientation	presences	absences
3. Control	implicit	explicit
4. Pedagogic text	acquirer	performance
5. Autonomy	high	low/high
6. Economy	high cost	low cost

1. categories of time, space and discourse
2. pedagogic orientation to evaluation
3. pedagogic control
4. pedagogic text
5. pedagogic autonomy
6. pedagogic economy

1. Discourse

Competence models

Pedagogic discourse issues in the form of projects, themes, ranges of experience, a group base, in which the acquirers apparently have a great measure of control over selection, sequence and pace. Recognition and realisation rules for legitimate texts are implicit. The emphasis is upon the realisation of competences that acquirers already possess, or are thought to possess. Differences between displaces stratification of acquirers: classification is weak.

Performance models

Pedagogic discourse here issues in the form of the specialisation of subjects, skills, procedures which are clearly marked with respect to form and function. Recognition and realisation rules for legitimate texts are explicit. Acquirers have relatively less control over selection, sequence and pace. Acquirers' texts (performances) are graded, and stratification displaces differences between acquirers. Classifications are strong.

Space

Competence models

There are few specially defined pedagogic spaces, although facilitating sites (e.g. sandpits) may be clearly bounded. Acquirers have considerable control over the construction of spaces as pedagogic sites and circulations are facilitated by the absence of regulatory boundaries limiting access and movements. Classification is weak.

Performance models

Space and specific pedagogic practices are clearly marked and explicitly regulated. Interstices for acquirers to construct their own pedagogic space are restricted. Regulatory boundaries limiting access and distributing movements are explicit and well marked. Classification is strong.

Time

Competence models

Such models select the present tense as the temporal modality. Time is not explicitly or finely punctuated as a marker of different activities; as a consequence the punctuation of time does not construct a future. The present tense is thus emphasised. Further, the weak and implicit sequencing of different activities (no apparent progression) combines with weak pacing to emphasise the present tense. Inasmuch as the emphasis is upon what each acquirer is revealing *at a particular moment* (known only to the teacher), and that this is the signifier of what should be made available by the teacher, then the time dimension of the pedagogic practice is the present tense from the point of view of the acquirer.

2. Evaluation

Competence models

Here the emphasis is upon what is *present* in the acquirer's product. Consider a competence classroom where an acquirer has made an image. The teacher is likely to say 'What a lovely picture, tell me about it'. Criteria of evaluation of instructional discourse are likely to be implicit and diffuse. However, regulative discourse criteria (criteria of conduct and manner, and relation) are likely to be more explicit. See 'Control' for further discussion.

Performance models

Here the emphasis is upon what is *missing* in the product. Consider a performance classroom where the acquirer has completed a painting of a house. The teacher is likely to say 'What a lovely house, but where is the chimney'? Or if the acquirer has drawn a figure, the comment may well be 'Very good, but your man has got only three fingers!'. If the emphasis is upon what is *absent* in the acquirer's product, then criteria will be explicit and specific, and the acquirer will be made aware of how to recognise and realise the legitimate text.

3. Control

Competence models

As space, time and discourse do not give rise to explicit structures and classifications these cannot serve both to constitute and relay order. The absence of explicit structures and classifications makes both the possibility and use of positional control a low priority strategy. Further, such control militates against the concept of the transmitter, as a facilitator and acquirer, as self-regulating. Control, then, is likely to inhere in personalised forms (which vary with each acquirer), which are realised in forms of communication which focus upon the intentions, dispositions, relations and reflexivity of the acquirer. This is not to say that positional and imperative control modes will not occur, only that these are not favoured modes.

Performance models

Space, time and discourse do give rise to explicit structures and classification and, although these may become sites of contention, they do both constitute and relay order. Such structures and classifications are resources for positional control which in turn legitimises the structures and classifications. The mode of the instructional discourse itself embeds acquirers in a disciplining regulation where deviance is highly visible. The economy of performance models, set up by explicit rules, makes the use of personalised modes of control less favoured options, as these modes often entail lengthy communication upon an individual basis. I should make it clear that acquirers develop strategies to subvert order in both competence and performance modes, but the strategies are likely to be mode specific.

4. Pedagogic Text

Competence models

Here the text is less the product of an acquirer for this product indicates something other than itself. It reveals the acquirer's competence development, be this cognitively affective as social, and these are the foci. The teacher operates with a theory of reading through the product the acquirer offers (or does not offer) to the teacher. This theory of reading marks the professionalism of the teacher and is recontextualised from the social and psychological sciences which legitimise this pedagogic mode. The consequence is that the meaning of an acquirer's signs is not available to the acquirer, only to the teacher.

Performance models

Here the pedagogic text is essentially the text the acquirer produces, that is, the pedagogic text is the acquirer's performance. This performance is objectified by grades. The professionalism of the teacher inheres in the explicit pedagogic practice and in the grading procedures. Grading gives rise to a potential repair service and its diagnostic theory, practice and distribution of blame. I have stated previously that performance models relative to competence models emphasise the future. However, with reference to the production of the pedagogic text it can be said that performance models signify the past. The pedagogic practice which produces the text positions the acquirer, *invisibly,* in the past and its rituals which have produced the instructional discourse. Thus in the case of performance models, the future is made visible, but that which has constructed this future is a past invisible to the acquirer. In the case of competence models it is the *future* which is invisible to the acquirer (only known to the teacher) and the present which is continuously visible.

5. Autonomy

Competence models

Such models require a relatively wide area and range of autonomy, although teachers in any one institution are likely to have reduced autonomy over their pedagogic practice as this mode requires homogeneity of practice. Although the construction of a particular context and practice will show commonalities, any particular context and practice will also be dependent upon the particular features of acquirers and their contexts. As a consequence each institution requires a measure of autonomy for this to be realised. The pedagogic resources required by competency models are less likely to be pre-packaged as textbooks or teaching routines. The resources are likely to be constructed by teachers and autonomy is required for such construction. Competency models are less susceptible to public scrutiny and accountability, relative to performance models, as their products are more difficult to evaluate objectively. Finally, competence models are not geared to specialised futures and are therefore less dependent and less regulated.

Performance models

It is more difficult to discuss autonomy with respect to performance models as there are crucial differences in their modalities. Briefly it is possible to distinguish between performance futures which refer only to performances which I shall call, initially, introverted modalities, and performance futures which are dependent upon some external regulation which I shall call, initially, extroverted modalities. In the case of introverted modalities the future is the exploration of a specialised discourse itself as an autonomous activity. In the case of extroverted modalities the future is likely to be dependent upon some external regulation, for example, the economy or local markets. In the case of introverted modalities, whilst the specialised discourse constructs—is accorded—autonomy, any particular pedagogic practice and acquirer's performance is subordinate to external curriculum regulation of the selection, sequence, pacing and criteria of the transmission. It may be, because of the strong classification of discourse, space and time, that individual teaching practice (unlike in competence models) may vary within the limits of the expected performances of acquirers. In the case of extroverted performance modalities there clearly is less autonomy because of the external regulation on performance futures. However, here it is possible under some managerial conditions for institutions (or organisational units within institutions) to enjoy autonomy with respect to how they distribute their financial and discursive resources in order to optimise their market niche.

6. Economy

Competence models

The transmission costs of these models are likely to be higher than the costs of performance models. The costs of training the teachers are likely to be high because of the theoretical base of competency models. Selection of students is likely to be stricter as the qualities required are perhaps more restricted and tacit than in the case of teachers of performance models. Further, there is a range of hidden costs if the competence model is to be successful in its own terms. The hidden costs are time based. The teacher often has to construct the pedagogic resources; evaluation requires time in establishing the profile of each acquirer; and in discussing projects with groups, socialising parents into the practice is another requirement; establishing feedback on the acquirer's development (or lack of it) is a further time cost. Within the institution extensive interaction between teachers over the practice is required for purposes of planning and monitoring, as the structure is constructed rather than received. These hidden costs are rarely explicitly recognised and built into budgets, but charged to the individual commitments of teachers. This lack of recognition of hidden costs may lead to ineffective pedagogic practice because of the demands of the practice, or, if these are met, the lack of recognition may give rise to ineffectiveness because of the fatigue of the teachers.

Performance models

The transmission costs of these models are relatively less than in the case of competence models. Training in the case of performance models requires a much less elaborate theoretical base and so the provision of staff for such a base is less necessary. The explicitness of the transmission makes such modes less dependent upon personal attributes of the teacher and so their supply is less restricted. Accountability is facilitated by the 'objectivity' of the performance and thus outputs can be measured and optimised. Performance models may well entail packages and algorithms which reduce training costs and also increase teacher supply. In general performance models are more susceptible to external control and to the economies of such control. Finally, planning and monitoring do not give rise to hidden costs as is the case with competence models because of the explicit structures of the transmission and of its progression.

None of the above rules out the importance of the teacher's commitment, motivation and personal attributes, but these qualities operate within particular models.

MODELS AND THEIR MODES

I have indicated that there are competence models and performance models, but so far I have given only the general model for each modality. It will be useful to press a little further on the differences between these two general models before discussing their variations.

In the case of competence models there is a focus on procedural commonalities shared within a group. In the cases we have analysed the group is children but procedural commonalities may well be shared with other categories, e.g. ethnic communities, social class groups. From this point of view competence models are predicated on fundamental 'similar to' relations. Differences between acquirers are not subject to stratification but can be viewed as complementary contributions to the actualisation of a common potential. On this basis it is possible to distinguish three distinct modes of competence models. All three share a blend of emancipation and opposition, but to different degrees, and with different foci. I shall distinguish these modes in terms of the location of 'similar to' relations.

In the first mode (first historically), 'similar to' relations are located *within* the individual and refer to common procedures that all individuals share. This mode was opposed to what it considered were repressive forms of authority (usually male) in the family and school, and industry, and was emancipatory with respect to the new concept of child to be actualised by appropriate pedagogic practices and controls. This mode, which legitimised a new science of child development, professionalism of caretakers and professional careers for women, had implications for strong patriarchal modes of family authority. Essentially and briefly the focus of this mode was upon intra-individual potential which could be revealed by appropriate pedagogic practice and contexts. The mode could be called liberal/progressive. It was developed, sponsored and institutionalised by that fraction of the developing and developed new middle-class located in the field of symbolic control (Bernstein, 1975/1977/1990; Jenkins, 1990).

The second mode locates 'similar to' relations not within the individual but within a local culture (class, ethnic, region). The reference here is to the validity of communicative competences intrinsic to a local, usually dominated, culture. This second mode presupposes an opposition between a dominating official pedagogic practice and local pedagogic practices and contexts. The second mode presupposes a silencing of the latter by the former. The sponsors of this mode show or attempt to show that a group of competences—scientific, mathematical, linguistic, cognitive, medical—are generated by local communicative practices, but are ignored, unseen or repressed by members of official pedagogic fields. This mode I shall call a *populist* mode.

The third mode follows from the second in locating competence within a local dominated group or class, but this mode does not focus upon indigenous competence as does the second mode. Neither does it focus upon intra-individual procedures as does the first mode. The third mode focuses upon inter-class/group opportunities, material and symbolic, to redress its objective dominated positioning. The pedagogic practice and contexts created by this mode presuppose an emancipatory potential common to all members of the group. This can be actualised by the members' own exploration of the source of their imposed powerlessness under conditions of pedagogic renewal. I shall call this mode the radical mode. (Freire is a good example of a creator of this mode.) It is more often found in adult informal education.

Broadly speaking, all three competence modes focus on 'similar to' relations, albeit that these relations have different locations. All three emphasise difference rather than deficit. All three oppose stratification procedures, announce a common creativity—emancipation. All three operate with forms of an invisible pedagogy (Bernstein, 1975/1977/1990). However, within the pedagogic recontextualising field these modes are in opposing positions. The third mode, the radical mode, is absent from the official recontextualising field (ORF), and its presence as a position in the pedagogic recontextualising field (PRF) depends upon the autonomy of that field.

In the same way that different competence modes can be distinguished, so different performance modes can be distinguished. Performance modes differ from each other according to the mode of specialisation of their texts. Performance modes are based on different principles of text construction, on different knowledge bases and on different social organisations. Whereas competence modes are based on different locations of 'similar to' relations, performance modes are based on 'different from' relations. Competence modes are generally found regulating the early life of acquirers or in repair sections. Performance modes are empirically normal across all levels of official education. From this point of view competence modes may be seen as interrupts or resistances to this normality or may be appropriated by official education for specific and local purposes.

I will distinguish three performance modes according to their knowledge base, focus and social organisation.

Singulars

Singulars are knowledge structures whose creators have appropriated a space to give themselves a unique name, a specialised discrete discourse with its own intellectual field of texts, practices, rules of entry, examinations, licenses to practice, distribution of rewards and punishments (physics, chemistry, history, economics, psychology, etc.). Singulars are, on the whole, narcissistic, orientated to their own development, protected by strong boundaries and hierarchies.

Regions

Regions are constructed by recontextualising singulars into larger units which operate both in the intellectual field of disciplines and in the field of external practice. Regions are the interface between disciplines (singulars) and the technologies they make possible. Thus engineering, medicine, architecture are regions. Contemporary regions would be cognitive science, management, business studies, communications and media. Regionalisation in higher education has proceeded at a rapid pace in the new universities, as any glance at their brochures will testify. Which disciplines enter a region depends upon the recontextualising principle and its social base. Thus the singulars entering medicine have expanded to include the sociology of medicine. Regionalisation as a discursive procedure threatens pedagogic cultures dominated by singulars and raises issues of legitimacy for such cultures, e.g. journalism, dance, sport, tourism, as university studies. However, changes in the reproduction of singulars from course base to modular form facilitate regionalisation. Regionalisation necessarily weakens both the autonomous discursive base and the political base of singulars and so facilitates changes in organisational structures of institutions towards greater central administrative control. The regions have, perhaps, autonomy over their contents in order to be more responsive to, more dependent upon, the market their output is serving. Increasing regionalisation of knowledge is then a good indicator of its technologising, of centralising of administrative control and of pedagogic contents recontextualised according to external regulation. Increasing regionalisation necessarily is a weakening of the strength of the classification of discourses and their entailed narcissistic identities and so a change of orientation of identity towards greater external dependency: a change from introjected to projected identities (see later discussion).

It is a matter of interest that the organisation of discourse at the level of the school is firmly based in singulars, despite movements to regionalisation in higher education. Indeed the attempt to introduce themes cutting across singulars as laid down by the Education Reform Act 1988 has been ineffective (Whitty et al., 1994a). Perhaps the equivalent of regionalisation in higher education at the level of the school is the move to generic skills.

Generic

This performance mode is a recent construction and can be distinguished from other modes by the following:

1. *The recontextualising location*: Generic modes are constructed and distributed outside, and independently of, pedagogic recontextualising fields. These modes had their origin in the Manpower Services Commission (MSC) and the Training Agency (TA) under the aegis of the Department of Employment. As Moore and Hickox (1995) point out, the programmes were developed from earlier MSC/TA work with the job components inventories in association with the Youth Training Scheme (YTS) (MSC, 1977, 1981; TA, 1989). These programmes 'blossomed' into a distinctive 'competences' methodology realised in the National Council for Vocational Qualifications' use of functional analysis (Jones and Moore, 1995) in its standard programmes. (See also, Eraut 1994; Hyland, 1994.)

2. *Focus*: Generic modes are essentially directed to extra-school experiences: work and 'life'.

3. *Location*: Generic modes are predominantly, but not exclusively, found in Further Education (FE). Jones and Moore (1995) state: 'The impact of competency [here read generic performances] upon the FE sector where the influence is most pronounced has involved a major restructuring of the professional culture, working practices, college management style and conditions of service that has overturned both the liberal education and technical craft tradition'.

4. *Misrecognition*: Generic modes are produced by a functional analysis of what is taken to be the underlying features necessary to the performance of a skill, task, practice or even area of work. These underlying apparently necessary features are referred to as 'competences'. As Jones and Moore (1995) cogently analyse, these underlying tacit features, identified as 'competences', appropriate resonances of an opposing model, silence the cultural basis of skills, tasks, practices and areas of work, and give rise to a jejune concept of trainability. (See also Whitty, 1991.)

MODELS, OPPOSITIONS AND IDENTITIES

I am now in a position to construct the discursive potential of the recontextualising field which characterises the contemporary context. Which discourse is appropriated depends more and more today upon the dominant ideology in the official recontextualising field (ORF) and upon the relative autonomy of the pedagogic recontextualising field (PRF). These matters will be discussed in the following section where we will examine the initial shift from performance modes to competence modes and the reverse shift from competence modes to performance modes. Here I want to examine oppositions and identity constructions entailed in different models and modes.

The divisions within, the opposition between, competence and performance models created three competence modes: liberal/progressive, populist and radical; and three performance modes: singulars (specialist), regional and generic. Competence modes are considered here as therapeutic (but 'empowering' by their sponsors) although the goals of each mode are different, whereas most performance modes, at least regionalised and generic, serve economic goals and are considered here as instrumental.

It is possible to see that different modes of *both* models signify oppositional positions in the recontextualising fields. In the case of competence models, the liberal/progressive mode and populist mode are opposed because the latter accuses the former of abstracting the acquirer from her/his local cultural context. The radical mode is opposed to both, because both fail to position pedagogic discourse in political struggle and both fail to use this discourse as a means of political change of consciousness. In the case of performance modes there is a potential and often actual opposition between specialist (singular) modes and new regions. New regions are regarded as suspect mixed categories and as competitors for scarce resources.

All competence modes, despite oppositions, share a preoccupation with the development (liberal/progressive), the recognition (populist) and change (radical) of consciousness. Competence modes are therapeutic and are directly linked to symbolic control. Performance modes and *especially their change* are more directly linked to the economy although they clearly have symbolic control functions. However, the picture is more complex for these modes as we shall now see.

The evolution of a range of singulars, specialised knowledge structures of the division of discursive labour, is very much a phenomenon of the last century. The development of English was linked to the development of nationalism and Britain's international position at the end of the nineteenth century. The development of the University of London, with its specialised knowledge structures in specialised institutions (schools and institutes), was linked to the management of the Empire. The development of economics and the social sciences was linked to the new technologies of the market and the management of subjectivities.

Classics provided privileged access to the administrative levels of the Civil Service. The specialised sciences provided the basis for material technologies. However, despite these external linkages singulars are like a coin with two faces, so that only one face can be seen at any one time. The sacred face sets them apart, legitimises their otherness and creates dedicated identities with no reference other than to their calling. The profane face indicates their external linkage and internal power struggles. Organisationally and politically, singulars construct strong boundary maintenance. From this point of view singulars develop strong autonomous self-sealing and narcissistic identities. These identities are constructed by procedures of *introjection*.

Regions are recontextualisations of singulars and face inwards towards singulars and outwards towards external fields of practice. The 'classical' university regions, medicine, engineering, architecture, reflect this double position with professional bodies setting standards of practice and often creditation or additional creditation. If singulars were the modal form of discursive organisation in the 100 years between the mid-nineteenth century and the mid-twentieth century, then it may be that regions will become the modal form from the late twentieth century onwards. Identities produced by the *new* regions are more likely to face outwards to fields of practice and thus their contents are likely to be dependent on the requirements of these fields. Identities here are what they are, and what they will become, as a consequence of the *projection* of that knowledge as a practice in some context. And the future of that context will regulate the identity. The volatility of that context will control the nature of the regionalisation of the knowledge and thus the projected identity. If the procedures of introjection construct the identities produced by singulars then the procedures of projection construct the identities produced by the new regionalisation of knowledge.

The third performance mode, generic, is complex. It shares the fundamental features of all competence modes, that is, 'similar to' relations. However, what is 'similar to' in the case of competence modes is a common humanity (liberal/progressive mode), a common local culture (populist mode), a common position and opposition (radical mode). What is 'similar' in the case of generic modes is a set of general skills underlying a range of specific performances. Thus generic modes and the performances to which they give rise are directly linked to instrumentalities of the market, to the construction of what are considered to be flexible performances. From this point of view their identity is constructed by procedures of projection despite superficial resemblance to competence modes.

Figure 3.1 sets out the discursive possibilities of the recontextualising field on two axes: control and discourse. Control refers to the general function therapeutic and economic, and discourse refers to the pedagogic mode. The specialist (singular) performance mode is ambiguous with respect to identity construction and control. The 'autonomous' mode is ambiguous as the context acts selectively upon whether autonomy is emphasised and dependency masked or dependency is pragmatically embraced. Thus the identity here is split but manageable when introjected elements and projected elements can be actualised in discrete contexts, i.e. strongly classified. The dependent mode is clearer. Here the performance is dependent upon the economic and the discourse is explicitly applied. The economic exigencies, or what are considered to be exigencies, act selectively on the focus of the discourse.

Finally, I have been considering these models and their modes as discrete, and as giving rise to distinct forms. It is crucial to understand that this may not always

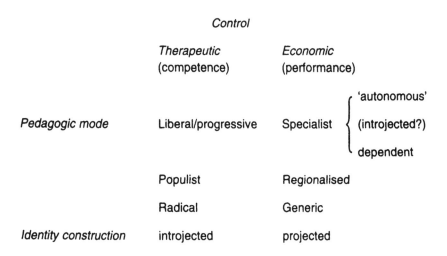

Figure 3.1: The Recontextualising Field

be the case. The models and modes may give rise to what could be called a pedagogic pallet where mixes can take place. A therapeutic mode may be inserted in
an economic mode, retaining its original name and resonances, whilst giving rise
to an opposing practice.

THE RECONTEXTUALISING FIELD AND ITS DYNAMICS

I have discussed the convergence in the field of the production of discourse on
the concept of competence and shown how it gave rise to the construction of a
general pedagogic modality underlying various modes: liberal progressive, populist and radical. It is clear that the liberal progressive mode had its origins much
earlier than the convergence (Jenkins, 1990), but its institutionalising in the official recontextualising field (ORF) did not take place until the Plowden Report
(1969) *Children: Their Primary Schools.*

I shall discuss here how competence modes became dominant positions in the
pedagogic recontextualising field (PRF) in the late 1960s. I have indicated earlier
that competence modes resonated with the ideologies of emancipation dominant
in this field, but this does not constitute an explanation. I outlined a generalised
performance model before discussing its various modes in anticipation of this
discussion. In the 1960s and early 1970s the British state had no *direct* control
over the pedagogic contents and modalities of transmission; these were more directly linked to the activities of the PRF. In other words, the PRF enjoyed at that
time a considerable autonomy with respect to the training of teachers. This training was the outcome of discursive pedagogic positions in that field, which regulated recontextualising principles. The major educational reform of the period,

comprehensivisation, changed only the *organisational form*; pedagogic discourse was not the subject of legislation. The change of form by the state under the impetus of the movement towards reducing arbitrary privilege (selective schools) created an autonomous local space for the construction of curriculum and the manner of its acquisition.

The abolition of selection, consequent upon the movement to comprehensivisation, removed a crucial regulator upon the organisation and curricular emphasis of the primary school. Thus both at primary and secondary levels a pedagogic space existed for appropriation by the activities of the PRF.

Performance modes were linked to and legitimised by the selective grammar schools and their discursive organisation, codes of singulars, collection codes. In turn this regulated the dominant pedagogic mode of the primary school: the performance mode. Thus the dominance of performance modes in the PRF was linked to the organisational and discursive structure of primary and secondary education. Performance modes focus upon something that the acquirer does not possess, upon an absence, and as a consequence place the emphasis upon the text to be acquired and so upon the transmitter. Performance modes select from the field of the production of discourse theories of learning of a behaviourist type which are atomistic in their emphasis. And this selection (recontextualisation) has consequences for behaviourist positions in the field of the production of discourse. This illustrates the symbiotic relation between this field and the PRF.

With the change in the organisational structure of secondary education towards weakening of classification, a space was now available for pedagogic appropriations at both secondary and primary levels, *not subject to direct state regulation.* How this space was filled was a function of the level of education: primary or secondary. At both levels there was a strong move to a competence modality and its modes, powerfully legitimised by the convergence in the field of the production of discourse.

In the PRF, with the weakening of the performance positions, previously subordinate, competence positions became dominant and new competence positions appeared. From the point of view of competence positions, performance modes were based on the concept of deficit, whereas competence modes were considered to be based on the concept of empowerment. Thus from this perspective, different from 'therapeutic' as identified earlier, the liberal-progressive mode was the basis of cognitive empowerment, the populist mode was the basis of cultural empowerment and the radical mode the basis for political empowerment. Each of these modes recontextualised different theories in the field of the production of discourse as outlined earlier.

Thus, in the 1960s and early 1970s, although the competence model was dominant, there were opposing modalities within the PRF: oppositions among liberal-progressive, populist and radical modes.

I have argued that a new space existed for the insertion of pedagogic models generated by the PRF. The weakening of the classification of discourses, acquirers and organisational contexts facilitated the dominance of competence modalities and their modes in *both* the ORF and the PRF, and so in the training of teachers (if not in their practice) both at primary and secondary levels. During the 1960s, as a consequence of the postwar population bulge working its way up the age-group, there was an expansion of colleges of education, with subsequent lesser control over staff and student selection. Further, there was a change in the discourse towards greater specialisation of the theoretical discourses and their greater dominance. A similar process occurred at the level of the secondary school, where teacher shortage shifted the power relations from the selective power of management to that of teachers. At the same time full employment moved the focus of schools to issues of social relations (multiculturalism, youth cultures) and leisure. Not only were there new spaces at all levels of education from higher education to the infant school, but *new agendas* were filling these spaces. Thus the move to institutionalise competence models and their modes was made possible at primary and secondary levels by the general weakening of classifications within and between levels, and by the introduction of new agents under conditions of autonomy of the PRF and ideological rapport between that field and the ORF: a unique set of conditions (see note 2).

Much has been written about the accelerating role of state intervention from the late 1970s and it is not the intention to discuss that literature here. The move of the state to control the content of education occurred before the late 1970s (school council), but the crucial impetus came under the Thatcher regime. At all levels of the educational system a combination of the decentralisation in respect of local institutions and their management, and centralisation with regard to their monitoring and funding, changed the culture of educational institutions, their internal management structures, criteria for staff appointments and especially promotions and their pedagogic practices. Survival and growth depended now upon optimising a market niche, upon objective productions, upon value-adding procedures. At the same time centralisation of the control over the contents of education, the denuding of the responsibilities of Local Education Authorities (LEAs), the setting up of minister-appointed and directed committees and authorities, reduced the autonomy of the PRF and changed the positions of dominance within it. It also introduced new discourses, e.g. management, assessment. The autonomy of the PRF was further weakened by the development of school-based training of teachers, which affected the theoretical pedagogic discourses and their research, by reducing their significance and moving their orientation towards practical and policy interests. The shift to performance models and their modes was initiated by the ORF which now more directly regulated pedagogic practices, contents and research. Clearly which performance modes regulated which practices depended upon the levels of education and curricular distribution within institutions within a level.

I want to turn to the construction and insertion of generic modes as the pedagogic basis of 'work' and 'life' experiences. Generic modes are not simply economic pedagogic procedures of acquisition but are based on a new concept of 'work' and 'life', a concept of 'work' and 'life' which might be called 'short-termism'. This is where a skill, task, area of work, undergoes continuous development, disappearance or replacement; where life experience cannot be based on stable expectations of the future and one's location in it. Under these circumstances it is considered that a vital new ability must be developed: 'trainability', the ability to profit from continuous pedagogic re-formations and so cope with the new requirements of 'work' and 'life'. These pedagogic re-formations will be based on the acquisition of generic modes which it is hoped will realise a flexible transferable potential rather than specific performances. Thus generic modes have their deep structure in the concept 'trainability'.

The concept of trainability places the emphasis upon 'something' the actor must possess in order for that actor to be appropriately formed and re-formed according to technological, organisational and market contingencies. This 'something', which is crucial to the survival of the actor, the economy and presumably the society, is the ability to be taught, the ability to respond effectively to concurrent, subsequent, intermittent pedagogics. Cognitive and social processes are to be specially developed for such a pedagogised future. However, the ability to respond to such a future depends upon a capacity, not an ability. The capacity to enable the actor to project him/herself *meaningfully* rather than relevantly, into this future, and recover a coherent past. This capacity is the outcome of a specialised identity and this precedes ability to respond effectively to concurrent and subsequent retraining. In this sense effective forming and re-forming rests upon something other than its own process. It rests upon the construction of a specialised identity. This identity, which is the dynamic interface between individual careers and the social or collective base, cannot be constructed by lifting oneself up by one's shoelaces. It is not a purely psychological construction by a solitary worker as he/she undergoes the transitions which he/she is expected to perform on the basis of trainability. This identity arises out of a particular social order, through relations which the identity enters into with other identities of reciprocal recognition, support, mutual legitimisation and finally through a negotiated collective purpose. There seems to be an emptiness in the concept of trainability, an emptiness which makes the concept self-referential and thus excluding.

If the identity produced by 'trainability' is socially 'empty', how does the actor recognise him/herself and others? By the materialities of consumption, by its distributions, by its absences. Here the products of the market relay the signifiers whereby temporary stabilities, orientations, relations and evaluations are constructed. The extension of generic modes from their base in manual practices to a range of practices and areas of work, institutionalises the concept of trainability as the fundamental pedagogic objective. The specialised recontextualising field produces and reproduces imaginary concepts of work and life which abstract such experiences from the power relations of their lived conditions and negate the possibilities of understanding and criticism.

THE STATE AND RECONTEXTUALISING

If we now consider the move to performance models and their modes in respect of the recontextualising process whereby these models and modes are imaginatively constructed into pedagogic discourses and practices, then we must first examine the form of official control over these recontextualising procedures. In the case of higher education there is no official recontextualising field (ORF) for the construction of an official higher education discourse. However, there is strong indirect regulation on the recontextualising process by the Higher Education Funding Council Executive (including the crucial research selectivity exercise) and by Research Councils, and in the case of some institutions by their industrial niche. Within these constraints higher education institutions have to optimise their outputs with regard to teaching and research. Whilst each institution has its own recontextualising field and particular management structure, each institution is in competition with significant others.[3] Thus the higher educational field takes on an internal stratification of institutions which provides its referent group for internal recontextualising.

Those at the top, or near the top, of this hierarchy may maintain their position more by attracting and holding key academic stars than by changing their pedagogic discourse according to the *exigencies of the market*. This is not to say, of course, that developments in the intellectual field are not provided for, and especially those which have a technological pay-off, but that they are less likely to regionalise their discourses.[4] On the other hand, those institutions which are much less fortunate in their position in the stratification are usually in no position to attract stars, and so will be more concerned with the marketing possibilities of their pedagogic discourse. Thus these institutions are likely to develop projected identities. What they are is a function of the exigencies of the market context which signifies the resources out of which their particular identity is constructed. Regionalisation here is likely to be a crucial recontextualising procedure, and the contents and names are likely to shift with what is taken to be the demand. If these institutions develop projected identities, then those near the top are perhaps able to maintain their traditional introjected identities, albeit rather more *ambiguous and ambivalent* now, owing to their more applied orientations. Thus in higher education not only is there a stratification of recontextualising contexts and of regionalisation but also a stratification of identities not only of institutions but also of staff and students.

The recontextualising process in higher education is therefore likely to generate a considerable diversity (through stratification) of pedagogic discourse on the basis of a probably common move to modularisation.

It is now very clear that performance modes dominate both primary and secondary levels. However, these modes are different from the modes in higher education, where I have suggested there are pronounced moves to regionalisation. In contrast, as a consequence of the National Curriculum (and its many revisions), there is a stronger classification, for this curriculum is a collection of singulars (subjects) where commonalities are not effective in practice (Whitty et al., 1994b). State monitoring of this curriculum through national testing and the structures of public examinations support this collection code. Framing, on the other hand, in respect of evaluation has weakened as a consequence of the growing significance of course-work assessment and the opportunities for students to repeat their course work if their grade is not as they wish. Schools may well exploit such weak framing over evaluation as a means of increasing their performance. Although the curriculum monitoring of schools has become centralised, the management structure has become decentralised. Schools now have greater autonomy over their budget and its distribution, and over their administrative location (opting-out potential). The management structure's major focus is upon the school's performance, with regard to attracting and retaining students, their conduct and their attainments. From this point of view, although pedagogic discourses are differently focused, the management focus of all institutions at all levels is similar. The management structure has become the device for creating an entrepreneurial competitive culture. The latter is responsible for criteria informing senior administrative appointments and the engaging or hiring of specialised staff to promote the effectiveness of this culture. Thus there is a dislocation between the culture of the pedagogic discourse and the management culture. The culture of the pedagogic discourse of schools is *retrospective*, based on a past narrative of the dominance and significance of disciplines, whereas the management structure is *prospective* pointing to the new entrepreneurialism and its instrumentalities. The state has therefore embedded a retrospective pedagogic culture into a prospective management culture. However, the emphasis on the performance of students and the steps taken to increase and maintain performance, for the survival of the institution, is likely to facilitate a state-promoted instrumentality. The intrinsic value of knowledge may well be eroded even though the collection code of the curriculum appears to support such a value.

CONCLUSION

Thus the state, through greater centralisations and new forms of decentralisation, has shifted pedagogic models and modes, management structures, and cultures of all educational institutions and sponsored generic modes. The reproduction of state-recognised and -rewarded forms is facilitated by the change in positions of dominance in the recontextualising fields (ORF, PRF), the introduction of new discourses and, of crucial importance, the dominance of new actors with new motivations.

We have examined changes in recontextualising processes at all levels of education and the new insertion into work and life. We have proposed that this process, with the exception of elite institutions, is shifting *official pedagogic identities where the codes have been acquired* from introjected modes to projected modes. We have seen that introjected modes are narcissistic, hierarchic and elitist and we have argued that the new forms of projected modes erode a collective base and replace inner commitments and dedications by short-term instrumentalities. The discourse so far has been entirely concerned with the construction and distribution of official pedagogic discourses, institutions and identities. While such discourse relays, or is expected to relay, politicised solutions and strategies of dominant groups and parties, it is by no means exempt from other influences, regulations and identity constructions to which we finally turn in the next chapter.

NOTES

1. A pedagogic recontextualising field is composed of positions (oppositional and complementary) constructing an arena of conflict and struggle for dominance. Any position can be examined at three analytically distinguished levels: author, actor and identity. Author refers to the authorative discourse, actors refer to the sponsors and identities are the outcome of pedagogic specialisations. A position in the field is a specialisation of discourse, specialisation of sponsoring actors and a specialised identity, which takes significance from opposition and complementary positions. From this point of view official recontextualising fields are arenas for the construction, distribution, reproduction and change of pedagogic identities. Pedagogic identities have a social base and a career. The social base is the principles of social order and desires, institutionalised by the state in its educational system. The career is moral, knowledge and locational. A pedagogic identity, then, is the embedding of a career in a social base. The questions become: whose social base, what careers and for whom?

2. It is important to note that during the late 1980s, and increasing in the 1990s, there was, as we have noted, a decline in the dominance of Piaget in the PRF subsequent to the official move to performance modes. However, in the same period a new author appeared with old sponsors in the PRF: Vygotskyism or post-Vygotskyism. Vygotskyism may be regarded as the salvation of the liberal/progressive position and permitted the retention in the PRF of previous Piagetian sponsors in the new performance culture. (Note here the move of Bruner from Piaget to Vygotsky.) Vygotskyism (that is, the recontextualising of Vygotsky by the Americans; Wertsch, 1985a, 1985b) enabled the introduction of a social base to developmental theories via the role of language, and foregrounded the active acquirer in a *pedagogic* relation. Thus there was an emphasis upon instruction, rather than an emphasis upon maturation, an emphasis upon pedagogic contents in a context where the pedagogised is an active partner, and where learning is an outcome of this relationship. Vygotsky could be integrated with Bakhtin to form once more a basis for empowerment (Daniels, 1994). The shift to Vygotskyism enabled the survival of the liberal/progressive position in the new performance culture.

3. 'The forty 'new' universities, the former polytechnics, freed from local authority control in 1989 and the 600 further education colleges which followed them into corporate independence a year ago (1993) have identically constructed governing bodies. Independent governors drawn principally from local businesses fill the majority of the 12–24

places, while representatives of lecturers and other staff have been marginalised. New university and college governors are modelled on boards of directors: they are meant to be agents of culture change dragging their institutions into the new age of (privatised) enterprise.' Bargh and Scott (1994), reporting their research in *The Times*, Monday 12 December.

4. I should point out that the effects of the state's monitoring of research publications through the Research Selectivity exercise every four years is altering the type of research and publication. Long-term basic research which may take many years (as in the humanities) and whose outcome is risky is not at a premium. It is likely to be replaced by short-term applied research, with low risks and rapid publication. Short-termism is facilitated by the activities of funding agencies, state and private. These changes in research and publications have consequences for the basis and orientation of teaching and thus the knowledge base and motivations of the students. Not only is the nature of research changed (Mace, 1995) it is reasonable to expect a reduction in the number of university committees, a reduction in their size and more appointed than elected members. Such changes act selectively on those who are appointed or preferred. In this way a new culture is created and reproduced by new actors with new motivations.

Chapter 4

Official Knowledge and Pedagogic Identities: The Politics of Recontextualisation

I want to share with you, on this occasion what is really no more than a sketch, no more than an embryonic outline, rather than a completed painting ready to be signed and framed. Unfortunately, within this sketch, the figures, their interactions, and their tensions may not all be recognised. However, despite the possible difficulty of recognising their relevance today, it may be that some of the figures, interactions and tensions will be recognised but in the future. Now this may be both a presumptuous and dangerous prediction. I can only hope you will not think it presumptuous. I have always lived somewhat dangerously, so I at least in academic terms cannot apologise for that.

'Official Knowledge' in the title refers to the educational knowledge which the state constructs and distributes in educational institutions. I am going to be concerned with changes in the bias and focus of this official knowledge brought about by contemporary curricula reform currently ongoing in most societies. I shall propose that the bias and focus, which inheres in different modalities of reform, constructs different pedagogic identities. From this perspective, curricula reform emerges out of a struggle between groups to make their bias (and focus) state policy and practice. Thus the bias and focus of this official discourse are expected to construct in teachers and students a particular moral disposition, motivation and aspiration, embedded in particular performances and practices. I shall develop a simple model of the official arena in which this struggle takes place. The model will generate four positions. These positions differ in their bias and focus, and so differ in the pedagogic identities they are projecting. I will apply this model particularly to the U.K. but also hint of its application to other societies. I will then use the same model to consider resources for the construction of local identities under today's conditions of cultural, economic and technological change. Finally I will look briefly at the relation between the official pedagogical identities of the state and the local identities available in communities and groups.

PEDAGOGIC IDENTITY

I want first to indicate how I am using the term pedagogic identity (see notes). From the point of view of this chapter a pedagogic identity is the result of embedding a career in a collective base. The career of a student is a knowledge career, a moral career and a locational career. The collective base of that career is provided by the principle of social order (or the ordering of the social if of a postmodern persuasion) expected to be relayed in schools and institutionalised by the state. The local social base of that career is provided by the orderings of the local context. It is commonplace today to say that over the last 50 years there have been major changes in the collective base of European societies, and major changes in the principles of social order. There also have been major changes in the contexts in which careers are enacted, whether these contexts be international, national, domestic, economic, educational or leisure. Curricula reform today arises out of the requirements to engage with this contemporary cultural, economic and technological change. The four positions I shall discuss in the official arena represent, through their different biases and focii, different approaches to regulating and managing change, moral, cultural and economic. And these different approaches to the management of change are expected to become the lived experience of teachers and students, through the shaping of their pedagogic identity (see diagram 1). I am proposing then an official arena of four positions for the projecting of pedagogic identities, through the process of educational reform. Any one educational reform can then be regarded as the outcome of the struggle to produce and institutionalise particular identities.

Two of these identities I shall discuss are generated by resources managed by the state: centreing resources. Two identities are generated from local resources where the institutions concerned have some autonomy over their resources: decentred resources. I shall consider first the identities constructed from centreing resources. These resources are drawn from some central, often considered national discourse. De-centred resources are drawn from local contexts or local discourses and focus upon the present, whereas centred resources focus upon the past.

RETROSPECTIVE PEDAGOGIC IDENTITIES (R.I.)

What are the resources which construct retrospective identities? Retrospective identities (or R.I.) are shaped by national religious, cultural, grand narratives of the past. These narratives are appropriately recontextualised to stabilise that past in the future. An important feature of the resources that construct R.I. is that the

Diagram 1

Modelling Pedagogic Identities
Classification

Restricted
Retrospective
(Old conservative)

Selected
Prospective
(Neo-Conservative)

Re-Centred State

Differentiated
De-Centred (Market)
(Neo-Liberal)

Integrated
De-centred (Therapeutic)
(Professionals)

In any one case there can be opposition and collaborations between these positions in the arena of reform, alternatively, some positions may be illegitimate and excluded from the arena.

discourse does not enter into an exchange relation with the economy. The bias, focus and management here leads to a tight control over discursive *inputs* of education, that is its contents, *not* over its *outputs*. R.I.s are formed by hierarchically ordered, strongly bounded, explicitly stratified and sequenced discourses and practices. What is foregrounded in the construction of the R.I. is the collective social base as revealed by the recontextualised grand narrative of the past. The individual careers is of less interest. What is at stake here is stabilising the past and projecting it into the future. We would expect to find the R.I. today strongly and fiercely projected and dominating the arena where the past is threatened by secular change issueing from the West, e.g. Middle East, North Africa. However, the position is active, but not dominant in most official arenas. We might find R.I.s projected in the official arenas of societies now fragmented or segmented after the collapse of totalising regimes, e.g. Russian Federation, Balkans.

PROSPECTIVE PEDAGOGIC IDENTITIES

These identities are formed like the retrospective from the past, but it is not the same past. The discursive base of prospective identities has a different focus and bias. It has a different focus and bias because this identity is constructed *to deal with cultural, economic and technological change*. Prospective identities are shaped by *selective* recontextualising of features of the past to defend or raise economic performance. For example in the case of Thatcherism features of the past were selected which would legitimate, which would motivate, and which would create what were considered to be appropriate attitudes, dispositions and performances relevant to a market culture and reduced state welfare. A new collective social base was formed by fusing nation, family, individual responsibility and individual enterprise. Thus prospective identities are formed by recontextualising *selected* features from the past to stabilise the future through *engaging with contemporary change*. Here, unlike retrospective identities where only the collective base is foregrounded, with prospective identities it is careers (that is dispositions and economic performances) which are foregrounded and *embedded in an especially selected past*. The management of prospective identities, because of the emphasis upon performances which have an exchange value, requires the state to control both *inputs* to education and *outputs*. I am grateful to Joseph Solomon, University of Athens, for his concise formulation).

We can consider Blair's New Labour's entry into the official pedagogic arena as launching a new prospective identity; an identity drawing on resources of a different past. An amalgam of notions of community (really communities) and local responsibilities to motivate and restore belonging in the cultural sphere, and a new participatory responsibility in the economic sphere. Thus the underlying collective of New Labour appears to be a recontextualising of the concept of the organic society. In this new potential official arena, the retrospective identity would be projected by 'old Labour'. The positions remain but the players change. Blair's New Labour, as with the New right, would control both inputs and outputs of education but in the service of a different prospective identity.

DE-CENTRED PEDAGOGIC IDENTITIES

I now want to turn to the resources for the construction of the two de-centred identities. These are the identities where the relevant institutions have some autonomy over their resources. In the case of the Therapeutic identity the autonomy of the institution is necessary to produce the features of this identity; an integrated modality of knowing and a participating, co-operative modality of social relation. In the case of the De-centred Market (D.C.M.), autonomy is necessary so that the institution and its units can vary their resources in order to produce a competitive output. Whereas the centreing resources of retrospective and prospective identities recontextualises the past, although different pasts, de-centreing resources construct the present although different 'presents'.

I call the identity "therapeutic" because this identity is produced by complex theories of personal, cognitive and social development, often labelled progressive. These theories are the means of a control invisible to the student. This identity is orientated to autonomous, non-specialised, flexible thinking, and socially to team work as an active participant. It is very costly to produce and the output is not easily measured: the position projecting this identity is a very weak position in all contemporary arenas so the social group which sponsors it has little power.

DE-CENTRED MARKET

I now want to turn to the resources which construct the D.C.M. identity. I think there will be difficulty in recognising this if this identity is not as yet an identity projected from a position in your official arena. Imagine an educational institution which has considerable autonomy over the use of its budget, the organisation of its discourse, how it uses its staff, the number and type of staff, the courses it constructs, provided: (1) it can attract students who have choice of institution, (2) it can meet external performance criteria and (3) it can optimise its position in relation to similar institutions. The basic unit of the institution, a department, or a group will also have autonomy over its own position in the market: that is to optimise its position with respect to the exchange value of its products, namely students. Thus the pedagogic practice will be contingent on the market in which the identity is to be enacted. The management system here is explicitly hierachial, small, non-elected committees, few in number, which will distribute resources to local units, according to their efficiency and their procedures of accountability. Management ideally reveals itself to distribute rewards and punishments. Management monitors the effectiveness of the local units, groups or departments in satisfying and creating local markets. The transmission here arises to produce an identity whose product has an exchange value in a market. The focus is upon those inputs which optimise this exchange value. We have here a culture and context to facilitate the survival of the fittest as judged by market demands. The focus is on the short term rather than the long term, on the extrinsic rather than the intrinsic, upon the exploration of vocational applications rather than upon exploration of knowledge. The transmission here views knowledge as money. And like money it should flow easily to where demand calls. There must be no impediments to this flow. Personal commitment and particular dedication of staff and students are regarded as resistances, as oppositions to the free circulation of knowledge. And so personal commitments, inner dedications, not only are not encouraged, but also are regarded as equivalent to monopolies in the market, and like such monopolies should be dissolved. The D.C.M. position constructs an outwardly responsive identity rather than one driven by inner dedication. Contract replaces covenant.

The resources which construct D.C.M. identities may also create a new stratification both of knowledge and identities. If we consider the university sector the outlines of this stratification are already perhaps becoming clear. Elite universities can maintain their position by buying in research leaders, and as a consequence will have *less* need to change their discourse or its organisation to maintain their power and position. This does not mean that such universities will not change their discursive organisation in the light of new technological knowledge and market potential, only that the *organisational* structure will still be essentially retrospective. Despite tensions from the change of focus to applied research (Mace, 1995, 1996) the identities formed in elite institutions are likely to be formed by introjection of knowledge. That is the identity finds its core in its place in an organisation of knowledge and practice. It is inwardly driven, although perhaps today more riven than driven. In the case of non-elite institutions, these do not have the resources (economic or symbolic) to attract high ranking scholars as a means of maintaining their powers of attraction, so we can expect here that the discursive organisation itself will be the means to maintain or improve competitive position. In these non-elite institutions the unit of discourse is likely to be a unit which with other units can create varying packages according to the contingencies of local markets. As these market contingencies change, or are expected to change, the 'new' permutations of units can be constructed. Here the identity of staff and students are likely to be formed less through mechanisms of introjection but far more through mechanisms of *projection*. That is the identity is a reflection of external contingencies. The maintenance of this identity depends upon the facility of *projecting* discursive organisation/practices themselves driven by external contingencies. The resources which produce D.C.M. identities, organisational and discursive have complex and profound consequences.

DE-CENTRED THERAPEUTIC IDENTITIES (D.C.T.)

Finally I want briefly to consider the D.C.T. position. I shall spend little time because it is not a strong player in any arena. The transmission here which produces this identity is against specialised categories of discourse and against stratification of groups. The transmission prefers weak boundaries, integration prefers to talk of regions of knowledge, areas of experience. The management style is soft, hierachies are veiled, power is disguised by communication networks and interpersonal relations. Whereas the D.C.M. position projects contingent, differentiated competitive identities, the D.C.T. position ideally projects stable, integrated identities with adaptable co-operative practices.

APPLICATION OF THE MODEL

If we now briefly consider the curricular reforms of the late 1980s and early 1990s of England and Wales, we can give some interpretations according to the diagram. In general, contemporary educational reforms aim to achieve control over both inputs and outputs of education, and this can be done effectively by tight and public evaluation over inputs. This requires standardisation of knowledge inputs if comparisons are to be made, and local autonomy (both of customers and suppliers) if institutions are to be competitively optimum. How did this work out in the official arena of the late 1980s out of which emerged the radical educational reforms?

Clearly there was a complementary relation between the prospective (neo-conservative) position and the D.C.M. market (the neo-liberal position) with respect to integrating a de-centralised device of management (evaluation and enterprise), embedded in a curriculum emphasising national enterprise (cultural, economic and political). However, this complementary relation was not without tension. Ideally the neo-liberal position would be against a centralised national curriculum. However, if we look at the contents and organisation of the educational reform this would appear to have emanated from the *retrospective* position, as it consisted (with an occasional new subject) of the segmented, serial array of subjects on the whole departmentally organised, typical of the past and included a focus upon 'basic skills'. There clearly have been vocational insertions in the curriculum stemming from the prospective position. The D.C.M. identity projected from the professionals of the pedagogic recontextualising field, and despite having some support among civil servants of the Ministry of Education itself was not a strong player and its proposals were severely restricted. The complex profiling forms of assessment of students were reduced to simple tests. Although thematic connection between the segments of the national array of separate subjects were written into the reform, these were rarely effective in practice (Whitty et al., 1991, 1994).

If we now look at the outcome of the play of positions in the official arena with respect to the radical educational reforms, it appears that the D.C.M. position has transformed the managerial structure of educational institutions, from primary school to university, and it has created an enterprise competitive culture. Whilst it has had little or no effect upon the curriculum, it introduced new discourses of management and economy in the training of heads of schools and so in the concept of leadership. Although the D.C.M. position had little effect on the institutional discourse of the school which was firmly sited in the retrospective position*, it can be said to have radically transformed the *regulative* discourse of *the institution as this affected its conditions of survival*. The D.C.M. oriented identities towards satisfying external competitive demands, whereas the segmental, serial ordering of the subjects of the curriculum orientated the identities towards the intrinsic value of the discourse. This tension between the intrinsic and the extrinsic is not, of course, new. What is new is the official institutionalising of the D.C.M. and the legitimising of the identity it projects. We have a new pathological position at work in education: the pedagogic schizoid position.

---

*Attempts are being made to modify the 'A' level examination taken at 17/18 years to vocational subjects with academic subjects on equal footing.

MODELLING LOCAL IDENTITIES

The analysis so far has been entirely concerned with the development of modelling resources, positions and identities in the struggle for dominance within the official arena of educational policy and reform. But these identity projections from the official arena are by no means exempt from the effects of identity constructions external to the official arena to which we now turn.

Much has been written about 'post modernism', 'late modernism', 'globalising capitalism', 'disembedding expert systems' and I have no wish to rehearse the literature here (Giddens, 1990; 1991, Harvey, 1988; O'Neil, 1995; Touraine, 1996). However, it does seem clear that, in the old speak, 'ascribed' identities, those identities which had a biological referent (age, gender and age relation) have been considerably weakened. These cultural punctuations and specialisations of time (age, gender, age relation) are today weak resources for the construction of identities with a stable collective base. To some extent these previously ascribed identities are now potentially achieveable by individual practice, contemporary resources and technologies. At the same time there has been a *contraction in the range of that life space which is socially significant.* At one extreme the young through style resources can project themselves as older, whilst individuals are now excluded from the labour market in their fifties and sometimes earlier. Time punctuations have shifted. Further, in the old speak, 'achieved' identities of class and occupation have also become weaker resources for stable, unambiguous identities. However, this should *not* be taken to mean that because of changes in oppositional working-class solidarities, consequent upon changes in technology, economy and state regulation, that unequal distributive consequences of class have weakened. So far then the punctuations of time and space have shifted. It is also the case that geographically movements of population, appropriated by the internationalising of labour, have created new sets of cultural pressures on generations and gender. The weakening of stable, unambiguous collective resources for the construction of identities consequent upon this new period of re-organising capitalism has brought about a disturbance and disembedding of identities and facilitated new identity constructions.

It should be noted here that the identity constructions to be discussed do not necessarily replace or displace the 'old' established formations of social identity. Simply the positions and oppositions in the identity field we will discuss take on a new valency under contemporary conditions of change. I want to use the same model for the construction of official pedagogic identities to model the emerging local identity field and its arenas of opposition. Basically I distinguished 'de-centred', 'retrospective', 'prospective' positions, resources and projections. 'De-centred' were constructed on the basis of local resources oriented to the present; 'retrospectives' were contructed on the basis of grand past narratives, national, religious, cultural; 'prospectives' were constructed from past narratives to create a re-centreing of the identity to provide for a new social base and to open a new future.

I shall now apply this model to the emerging identity field and its arenas of opposition (see diagram 2). I will first discuss de-centred identities, then centreing retrospective and finally re-centreing prospective.

DE-CENTRED IDENTITIES

I shall distinguish here an instrumental identity (in the previous model 'de-centred market') and a therapeutic identity. These are constructed from differently localised and oppositional resources. In one case the resources are market, and in the other they are sense-making resources to create internal coherence.

INSTRUMENTAL

These identities are constructed out of market signifiers. The identity arises out of a *projection* on to consumables. This projection relays to self and others the spatial and temporal attributes of the identity; that is, it's what, where, who and progression. Such constructions are stable only in their procedure of construction, *not* in their temporal realisations which are contingent. For these identities boundaries are permeable, and the past is no necessary guide to the present, let alone the future. The economic base of these identities orients their politics: anti-centralist.

THERAPEUTIC

These identities are also constructed from local resources but these are *internal*, unlike instrumental, which are external. If instrumental identities are produced by projection, then the therapeutic is produced by introjection. Here the concept of self is crucial and the self is regarded as a personal project. It is an internally regulated construction and relatively independent of external consumer signifiers. It is a truly symbolic construction. The identity takes the form of an open narrative which constructs a personal time. It shares some features with the oppositional instrumental. As with the instrumental, for the therapeutic, boundaries are permeable and the past is no necessary guide to the present or the future. If the instrumental is dependent upon the segmentations of the shopping mall, then the therapeutic is dependent upon internal making sense procedures the external segmentation. Both of these constructions are differently fragile. In the case of the instrumental, the identity depends upon economic resources, and when those are

Diagram 2

Contemporary Identity Field
Reorganising Capitalism

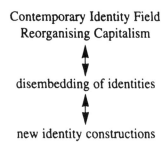

disembedding of identities

new identity constructions

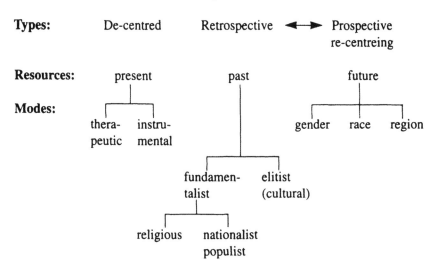

not available then a shift to other possible resources in the field is likely. In the case of the therapeutic the dependency here is upon internal sense making procedures, and if those fail then a shift to other resources is likely. Tentatively, instrumental may shift to retrospective (nationalist) and therapeutic to prospective, but these shifts may depend in turn upon age and context.

RETROSPECTIVE IDENTITIES

These identities use as resources narratives of the past which provide exemplars, criteria, belonging and coherence. In these respects retrospective identities are opposed to decentred identities. Both of these modes reject past narratives as the source for criteria, belonging and coherence for the present and future. For both of these de-centred modes boundaries are permeable. In the same way as we distinguished two opposing modes of de-centred identities, we shall distinguish two basic opposing modes of retrospective identity: fundamentalist and elitist.

FUNDAMENTALIST

As the diagram illustrates there are a number of subsets of this position but they all share a fundamentalist religious or nationalist, or combination, resource. This provides for an unambiguous, stable, intellectually impervious, collective identity. This consumes the self in all its manifestations and gives it a site outside of current and future instabilities, beyond current ambiguities of judgement, relation and conduct. In some contexts it produces a strong insulation between the sacred and profane, such that it is possible to enter the profane world without either being appropriated or colonised by it. Islamic fundamentalism enables the appropriation of western technologies without cultural penetration. Nearer home orthodox Jews in the 1920s, and even earlier, occupied small shops and business slots in the economy and retained their identity through strict orthodox practice. In the 1960s and onwards many British Asian Moslems occupied a similar economic and cultural context. The problem here for such retrospective identities is their reproduction in the next generation, and here we might expect a shift to prospective or even therapeutic positions. Age may well influence the expression of the retrospective identity through differential selection of resources. It may well be that the young are attracted to the current revival of charismatic Christianity with its emphasis upon the subjective, the emotional, upon intense interactive participation and upon oppositions to institutional orthodoxes. On a more anecdotal level I have been impressed with the revival of student fraternity rituals in Portugal, Norway and Germany. Finally we can consider nationalism and populism as subsets of retrospective fundamentalism, drawing on mythological resources of origin, belonging, progression and destiny (rise of the extreme right). Any weakening of the collective resource on which the fundamentalist identity draws and which minutely regulates conduct, belief and participation, as is likely in inter-generation reproduction, may entail a shift to re-centreing identities on the part of the young (see later discussion).

ELITIST

This is a retrospective identity entirely opposed to fundamentalist, indeed to all other possibilities in the field. It is constructed on the resource of high culture: an elitist appropriation. This narrative of the past is as consuming of the self as fundamentalist, and provides exemplars, canons, criteria and develops aesthetic sensibilities. It is an amalgam of knowledge, sensitivities, manners, of education and upbringing. However, it can be appropriated by education and social networks without the intervention of upbringing. It shares with fundamentalist identities strong classifications and internal hierachies, but unlike fundamentalist it refuses to engage in the market. Whereas fundamentalist identities (other than those resting on national or populist resources) allow for conversion and often actually encourage conversion, this is much less the case for elitist identities as these require a very long and arduous apprenticeship into the aesthetic mode. A mode which needs to be maintained without the intense solidarities in which fundamentalist identities are embedded. Perhaps narcissistic formations underlie and maintain elitist identities, whereas fundamentalist identities are maintained by strong super-ego formations and communalised selves.

PROSPECTIVE

These identities are essentially future oriented in contrast to the past of retrospective and the present of de-centred identities. They rest, as with retrospective identities, upon narratives but these narrative resources ground the identity not in the past but in the *future*. These are narratives of becoming, but a new becoming not of an individual but of a social category, e.g. race, gender or region. The narrative resources of de-centred identities announce distance from a collective, social base for these are individualised constructions. But the narratives constructing the new becoming of prospective identities create a new basis for social relations, for solidarities and for oppositions. In this respect prospective identities involve a *re-centreing*. Prospective identities are often launched by social movements, for example gender, race and region. They are in their takeoff stage evangelist and confrontational, and we shall see later have strong schismatic tendencies. Prospective identities share with fundamentalist the consummation of the self, in that the manifestations involve the whole self in the new becoming. De-socialisation procedures are necessary to erase the previous identity. New group supports facilitate this process, protect vulnerabilities and orient re-centreing. Prospective identities, as with fundamentalist, engage in economic and political activity to provide for the development of their potential. In the U.S.A., Islamic movements have created a new basis for black identity, for a revitalised politics and a new entrepreneuralism. Here is an example of a prospective identity arising out of a recontextualising of a retrospective narrative.

I have mentioned earlier that there is a strong schismatic tendency in the social base of the resources and relations which construct prospective identities. These resources are narratives of becoming other than the projections and impositions of others; a becoming which is so to speak a recovery of something not yet spoken, of a new fusion. But there may be more than one path to this new future. The identities of becoming are prone to heresy, to pollution, to waywardness, and require close supervision, delicate monitoring before recognition of authenticity and licensing. The group basis of prospective identities contain gatekeepers and licensers. It may well be that it is more accurate to conceive of each social category (gender, race, region) as giving rise to its own arena of positions, struggling to dominate the narrative resource for the construction of authentic becoming.

Implicit in the emerging identity field, and especially in its arenas, is perhaps the beginning of a change in the moral imagination. One of the momentous outcomes of the enlightenment was the announcement of universal rights but this was at the cost of the anonymity of the subject. All were entitled and guaranteed rights, but the very universalism de-contextualised the subject. Today we can query whether we are experiencing a *shrinking* of the moral imagination. Empathy and sympathy can only be offered and received by those who are so licensed to offer and receive. It may well be that the emerging identity field and its arenas facilitate the shrinking of the moral imagination, but, unlike the de-contextualised subject of the enlightenment, the subject is now no longer anonymous but eloquent in a new contextualising.

A caricature may help here. I am two and a half inches under the average height, losing ground with every dietary improvement, and subject to the projections and impositions of others which have produced a spoiled identity. To discover with others in my social category the possibility of a new becoming, a narrative resource (to interpret my past otherness, to discover authentic voice, to create a new language of participation and discovery) is developed on the basis of valid scholarship and research. Valid scholarship and research can only be valid if carried out by a licensed member of the social category. Only we can know us or is allowed the possibility of knowing us. Exemplars are found (perhaps Napoleon, Chaplin). A prospective identity has been constructed, criteria of membership, belief and practice developed, economic and political aims formulated; a new social category has been established. However, some years later a junior member of the group produces a more radical agenda, with new membership criteria on the basis of a new narrative resource. New membership criteria in the new narrative sets membership at three and half inches below average height. Most of my group are excluded and now seen as part of otherness. We have the first schism and a new shrinking of the moral imagination.

CONCLUSION

What appears to be happening at the end of the twentieth century is a weakening of, and a change of place, of the sacred. In the beginning of this century the sacred was centrally located and informed the collective social base of society through the inter-relation of state, religion and education. Today this collective base has been considerably weakened (more in some societies than others) as a resource for a centralised sacred. The sacred now reveals itself in dispersed sites, movements and discourses. It is less fragmentation of the sacred but more its segmentation and specialisation. From this perspective the diversity of local identities we have discussed (with the exception of the instrumental) may be less an index of cultural fragmentation as in some post modern stories, but more a general cultural resurgence of the rituals of inwardness in new social forms. In the first section of this paper we noted the growing pathology in educational institutions which we referred to as a pedagogic schizoid position. We are in the process of producing for the first time a virtually secular, market driven official pedagogic discourse, practice and context, but at the same time, there is a revival of forms of the sacred external to it.

There appears to be a reversal of the Durkheimian sites of the sacred and the profane, and a rusting of the bars of Weber's iron cage of dismal prophesy. There are new sources of tension, change and possibility in the relation between the official pedagogic identities and their contexts of transmission and acquisition, and the local identities of the emerging field. but this is not to say that all new local identities now becoming available are to be welcomed, sponsored or legitimated.

NOTES

Official Knowledge
The term 'official knowledge' is derived from Bernstein (1986) where he distinguished the Official Recontextualising Field. A state constructed field of agents concerned to produce official pedagogic discourse. On official pedagogic practice, see Bernstein (1990); also on Official Knowledge, see Apple (1993).

Re-centred State
This refers to new forms of centralised regulation whereby the state de-centralises and through (a) central setting of criteria and (b) the central assessment of outputs of agencies, financially (and otherwise), rewards success and punishes failures: 'choice', selection, control and reproduction.

Pedagogy
I should offer here a definition of pedagogy. Pedagogy is a sustained process whereby somebody(s) acquires new forms or develops existing forms of conduct, knowledge, practice and criteria from somebody(s) or something deemed to be an appropriate provider and evaluator—appropriate either from the point of view of the acquirer or by some other body(s) or both. We can distinguish between: institutional pedagogy and segmented (informal) pedagogy.

Institutional pedagogy is carried out in official sites (state, religious, communal), usually with accredited providers, and where acquirers are concentrated voluntarily or involuntarily as a group or social category. *Segmental pedagogy* is carried out usually in the face to face relations of everyday experience and practice by informal providers. This pedagogy may be tacitly or explicitly transmitted *and* the provider may not be aware a transmission has taken place. Unlike institutional pedagogy, the pedagogic process may be no longer than the context or segment in which it is enacted. Segmental, that is, *unrelated* competences result from such pedagogic action. For example, a child learning to dress, tie up shoes, count change in a supermarket are competences acquired through segmental pedagogies which may vary in their explicitness and in their code of realisation. Learning to be a patient, waiting room behaviour, doctor/patient conduct and report, is an example of a tacit mode of a segmental pedagogy where the provider(s) *may* be unaware that they are providers. What is of interest is the interactional consequences of the relation between institutional and segmental pedagogies legitimately put together (communicated). Framing relations regulate the acquisition of this 'voice' and create the 'message' (what is made manifest, what can be realised). The dynamics of the framing relations *initiated* by the acquirer can initiate change in the expected message and so in the governing 'voice'. Thus identity in the code theory is the outcome of the 'voice message' relations. With respect to the definition of pedagogic identity, the embedding of a career in principles of social order, acquisition would be regulated by the classification and framing relations ($\pm C^{ie}/\pm F^{ie}$) of the pedagogic practice.

Local Identity: social location
It is difficult to give the social location of the social identities as these vary with age, gender, social class, occupational field, economic or symbolic control. Further, as we have indicated in the text, these identities are not necessarily stable positions and shifts can be expected depending upon the possibility of maintaining the discursive or in some cases on the economic base of the identity. In Bernstein 1996, chapter 3, there are some tentative hypotheses. The present discussion is a development of that chapter. (See also The Lancaster Group, 1985; Giddens, 1990; Hay, O'Brian & Penna, 1993/4.)

Moral Imagination
This imagination is differently, and more dangerously, threatened by collective stereotyping stemming from fundamentalist retrospective positions. Thus what is at stake today is both the shrinking of the moral imagination (prospective positions) and the eroding of this imagination (fundamentalist retrospective positions).

Sources
The model of the four positions and the projected identities in the official arena had its origins in a response (Bernstein, 1995) to a paper by Tyler (1995). I have drawn on the research of Ball (1990), Dale (1994), Grace (1993) and Whitty (1991, 1994) on the origins, dynamics and consequences of the radical educational reforms of the late 1980s and 1990s initiated by the Conservative Government. I have enjoyed and benefitted from discussions and disputes with Wexler on the resurgence of the sacred (Wexler, 1995, 1996; Bernstein, 1995).

Chapter 5

Thoughts on the Trivium and Quadrivium: The Divorce of Knowledge from the Knower*

I am afraid that this will not be a paper in the usual sense of that term. It will not be a systematic presentation or exposition of a particular thesis, nor an account of research, nor an overview of a relevant section of the intellectual field. I thought I would take this opportunity to explore some ideas which have arisen out of some recent work on the nature of pedagogic discourse. I am not entirely sure I can present these ideas, these intuitions, rather than worked-out positions, in the orderly way to which you are accustomed. This is not said as an academic strategy of defence but as an accurate assessment of my present state of knowledge. You may well ask—well, why don't you keep it to yourself until you have got the story right? Who wants to listen to a script where the plot is not worked out and half the characters are missing? The only answer I can give is that sometimes a script needs a little help and perhaps that is what will happen here, even if it means the script will have to be abandoned. The problem started many years ago when I read Durkheim's magnificent analysis of the evolution of education in France. It started with his analysis of the discourse, social structure and social relations of the medieval university. Durkheim was concerned to show how the discourse of the medieval university contained within itself *a tension, even a contradiction*, which provided the dynamics of the development of the university. This tension or contradiction he saw as a representation of the two discourses upon which the medieval university was founded, that of Christianity and that of Greek thought. These two discourses, he argued, produced the tension between faith and reason which he saw as providing the dynamic of the development of the university.

*Originally public lecture given to the University of the Aegian.

81

Durkheim was also interested in the origin of the abstract nature of the knowledge and this should not have been a problem to him. For if you recontextualise Greek thought you must have an abstract, idealised, essentialist discourse. Of course Durkheim was clear about the rapport, the harmony between Christianity and selected forms of Greek thought. However, he did say something else which set me thinking. To many of you it will be obvious. Durkheim said that the Christian God was a god you had to think about. It was a god that not only was to be loved, but also to be thought about. And this attitude created an abstract modality to the discourse. I am not concerned whether Durkheim is right here. I think (by the way) he is right, but not for the right reasons. I think he is right but his analysis is not sufficiently fundamental. Like many abstract problems this one started with something which did not seem at first sight to be a real problem at all. The problem started with the first dislocation in official European knowledge. The first classification, the first, in Foucault's terms, archaeological flaw in the continuity of official knowledge. A dislocation which has had profound consequences for culture, a specialisation of two discourses to different time periods, the first progression, sequencing of official knowledge. I am of course referring here to that specialisation, that grouping of knowledge called the Trivium and that different specialisation of knowledge called the Quadrivium. The Trivium consisted of grammar, logic and rhetoric and the Quadrivium consisted of arithmetic, astronomy, geometry and music. Durkheim gives a very interesting account of how the emphasis on the elements of the Trivium changed with the development of a new bourgeoisie in the Renaissance. But this is not our concern here. Durkheim argued that this classification, dislocation, boundary, represented a split between the Trivium as exploration of the word and the Quadrivium as the exploration of the world; word and world held together by the unity of Christianity. Of course this is not quite right. It is not so much the Word but the means of understanding the principles behind the word and its realisation. Similarly it is not the World but the principles of understanding the material world. It was also the case that the Trivium was studied first and the Quadrivium second. Word before the World in Durkheim's terms. My version will be stronger, no world prior to the word. Durkheim, it seemed to me, had formulated and conceptualised a problem but had not explained it. Why was the Trivium first, what was the modality of the abstraction that Christianity gave to official discourse? And that was where I started.

Why was the Trivium first—it could be argued that the Trivium was first for material or pedagogic reasons; for example, you must first know how to think before you apply thought. It was also of interest that in the annual celebration it was the Quadrivium teachers who led the university parade and the Trivium teachers were last. A metaphoric realisation of the last shall be first. However, it was also the case that the Trivium dominated the university. The Trivium teachers had the power. Now, about the abstract orientation of the knowledge: is it enough to say:

if you teach the Greeks you teach abstraction—you teach that the word is empty and is but a pointer to a concept? I am not sure either of those explanations is adequate but I am also not sure whether the one I shall offer is wholly adequate either.

I shall start where Durkheim left off in his discussion of the Trivium/Quadrivium and carry his analysis a stage further. I shall propose that there is another level below that of word and world. I shall propose that the Trivium is not simply about understanding the word, the principles which lie behind it, the mechanics of language and reasoning, but is concerned to constitute a particular form of consciousness, a distinct modality of the self, to set limits to that form of consciousness, to regulate the modality of the self. To constitute that self in the Word, yes, but the Word of God. A particular god. The Christian God. In other words, the Trivium is there to create a particular form of the outer (the world). The dislocation between Trivium and Quadrivium, then, is a dislocation between inner and outer. A dislocation as a precondition for a new creative synthesis between inner and outer generated by Christianity. Perhaps more than this. The Trivium comes first, because the construction of the inner, the valid inner, the true inner, is a necessary precondition that the understanding of the world will also be valid, will also be true, will also be acceptable, will also be legitimate in terms of the discourse of Christianity. The sacredness of the world is guaranteed or should be guaranteed by the appropriate construction of the inner, the truly Christian self. Thus, whereas the apparent form of the discourse is Greek, the message is Christian. More than this, the deep grammar of the Trivium, Quadrivium, that is, its paradigmatic and syntagmatic features, is a metaphor of the new dislocation between inner and outer that Christianity itself introduced and resolved. I shall argue that it is this new mediated relation between inner and outer which is the origin of the necessary abstract orientation of Christianity, a Christianity which appropriated Greek thought for its own message.

It is possible to illustrate both this abstract orientation and prior dislocation of inner and outer, so essential to the formation of the Christian self, by examining the process of conversion. In the early stages of the development and dissemination of the faith, conversion did not require a change of nationality. It did not require a change of culture. It did not require even a change of practice. It required a revolution of inwardness, a turning to a recognition of Christ, the meaning of Christ. Note here that Christianity takes a point outside the culture and practice of those to be converted as the basis for this conversion and then colonises from within. Christianity drives a wedge between inner self and outer practice. It creates a gap which becomes the site for a new awareness. To think and feel outside your culture and practice is intrinsically an abstract orientation. Although clearly the new feeling and thinking will be confined to the terms of the new modality. Thus the dislocation of inner and outer, to open up a new existential self, is intrinsic to Christianity. It is not Greek. There are dislocations in Greek thought, individual/society issues of distributive justice, the word and the concept, the ideal form and the particular representation, but I would not suggest reflection upon the dislocated self and its new synthesis.

In order to highlight further these tentative propositions, I want to make some comparison between Judaism and Christianity which will bring me nearer to the title of this lecture.

The crucial feature of Judaism I would argue is less that it is a monotheistic faith but more that the God is invisible. The God can only be heard. The Judaic God, unlike the Christian, is temporal not visual. If the Judaic God is invisible, then the distance between God and people is maximal. There is no way in which people can become God and God become human. The distance is uncrossable by both. How do people relate to this invisible God? How is the uncrossable crossed? Through relating to an attribute of that God. Holiness. Then how does the holiness of this God become material, become palpable? The holiness becomes material, becomes palpable through the daily cycles of prayer, ritual and through the classifications of the law. The holiness is realised in prayer, ritual and classifications which establish the fundamental nature of the social bond between men, women and community. Holiness, the attribute of the invisible God, establishes the unity of God and people through the nature of the social bond. There is no dislocation of inner and outer in Judaism. This does not mean to say that Judaism does not speak to the inner—the Psalms are sufficient testimony here— only that there is no dislocation of the self. Instead there is the complete and perfect community established by prayer, ritual and classification. The perfect community is the ultimate realisation of the Judaic God. Let us take this matter further before comparing the discourse of Judaism and Christianity. A consequence of the Invisible Judaic God is that exemplars are not possible. You cannot have an exemplar of something that is invisible. Judaism, unlike Christianity, is a non-exemplary religion. The Judaic God does not want mediation through exemplary figures. It is an unmediated religion, there are only two terms: God and Man, whereas Christianity, later, provides a metaphor of three. If we consider the Old Testament, we find that narratives of the major figures Moses, David, Solomon, the major prophets Elijah, Elisha seem to be predicated on one rule— all shall be shown to be fallible. Every great figure of the grand narratives commits great errors of judgement and practice. The rule that all must be shown to be fallible is the other side of the rule. 'There shall be no exemplars'. Such a rule emphasises, declares there is only one perfection, that of the invisible God. However, there is an implication here—God is Absolute—Man is relative, no man holds the truth—God is the principle of all things.

I want now briefly to look at Judaism as discourse. In Judaism we have a non-exemplary religion but with an incomplete text. This requires some explanation. There is the written law, the Torah, which is not only a blueprint of the universe but is a guide to most mundane and minute details of life, in which every minute detail connects with the whole. The particular carries the sanctity of the whole.

Through proper interpretation, application and meaning, any contingency may be revealed. Thus the written law is subject to endless interpretation, interpretation which forbids generalisation, which proceeds from one particular to another. For generalisation, the holy principle is alive in every particular. Thus, in Judaism, a non-exemplary religion with an incomplete text, interpretation is through continuous elaboration of particulars and generalisation is abhorred. Such elaboration is only possible because of certainty of faith. Thus, in Judaism, we have a non-exemplary religion, an incomplete text but a *perfect* society, made perfect by the Torah. Christianity, on the other hand, is an exemplary religion, where the text is complete and perfect in Jesus, where generalisation and metaphor embrace the abstract. However, it is also a faith where faith cannot be taken for granted; it must be constantly re-won, revitalised, renewed. Thus the Christian self, unlike the Judaic self safe in its certainty, is subject to doubt, to questioning, to interrogation. In this sense Christianity creates a special modality of language, an interrogative mode which splits the self from its acts, intention from practice. At the same time language itself can both reveal and deceive. The very medium of communication can carry revelation or deception. No wonder language, communication, is so central to Christianity for it forms the authentic relation and its means of interrogation, and thus the true self in faith.

We can now at long last return to the Trivium/Quadrivium dislocation and Durkheim's insights. I have attempted to show that the abstract orientation and the dislocation of the two fundamental discourses of the medieval university have their roots in Christianity, in the original dislocation of the self which Christianity engendered as the prime condition for its own good news, the news of Christ. I have suggested that this dislocation of inner and outer, the condition for the establishment of the truly Christian self, is not a dislocation to be found in Greek thought. But Greek thought was selectively appropriated by Christianity and realised in a way to make Greek thought safe. In this it did not succeed.

Finally, I now want to make a rapid move from the principle of the organisation of discourse in the medieval period to the principles underlying the organisation of official discourse today. I have tried to show that in the medieval period we had two differently specialised discourses, one for the construction of the inner, one for the construction of the outer—the material world. The construction of the inner was the guarantee for the construction of the outer. In this we can find the origin of the professions. Over the next five hundred years there was a progressive replacement of the religious foundation of official knowledge by a humanising secular principle. I want to argue that we have, for the first time, a dehumanising principle, for the organisation and orientation of official knowledge. What we are seeing is the growing development of the specialised disciplines of the Quadrivium, and the disciplines of the Trivium have become the disciplines of symbolic control—the social sciences. In a sense the Trivium has been replaced by the social sciences for the management of feelings, thoughts, relations and practices. There is now less dislocation of knowledge. Genetic engineering and cognitive science reach across the natural, biological and social sciences. What of the principle underlying the new discourse? Today throughout Europe, led by the U.S.A. and the U.K., there is a new principle guiding the latest transition of capitalism. The principles of the market and its managers are more and more the managers of the policy and practices of education. Market relevance is becoming the key orientating criterion for the selection of discourses, their relation to each other, their forms and their research. This movement has profound implications from the primary school to the university. This can be seen in the stress on basic measurable skills at the primary level, vocational courses and specialisations at the secondary level, spurious decentralisation, and the new instruments of state control over higher education and research.

Of fundamental significance, there is a new concept of knowledge and of its relation to those who create it and use it. This new concept is a truly secular concept. Knowledge should flow like money to wherever it can create advantage and profit. Indeed knowledge is not like money, it *is* money. Knowledge is divorced from persons, their commitments, their personal dedications. These become impediments, restrictions on the flow of knowledge, and introduce deformations in the working of the symbolic market. Moving knowledge about, or even creating it, should not be more difficult than moving and regulating money. Knowledge, after nearly a thousand years, is divorced from inwardness and literally dehumanised. Once knowledge is separated from inwardness, from commitments, from personal dedication, from the deep structure of the self, then people may be moved about, substituted for each other and excluded from the market.

This orientation represents a fundamental break in the relation between the knower and what is known. In the medieval period the two were necessarily integrated. Knowledge was an outer expression of an inner relationship. The inner relationship was a guarantee of the legitimacy, integrity, worthwhileness and value of the knowledge and the special status of the knower as Christian. We know, however, how this special status in turn limited and distorted the knowledge, but this is not the point here. Today the market principle creates a new dislocation. Now we have two independent markets, one of knowledge and one of potential creators and users of knowledge.

The first dislocation between the Trivium and the Quadrivium constituted inwardness as a prior condition of knowing; the second dislocation, the contemporary dislocation, disconnects inner from outer, as a precondition for constituting the outer and its practice, according to the market principles of the New Right.

Durkheim stated that there was a contradiction at the heart of the medieval university, between faith and reason, and this was the key to the development both of knowledge and the university. Today perhaps there is not so much a contradiction as a crisis, and what is at stake is the very concept of education itself.

Part II

Theory and Research

Chapter 6

Codes and Research

INTRODUCTION

The three volumes of *Class, Codes and Control* represent the first stage in the development of a theory of pedagogic discourse and modalities of symbolic control. This is not immediately obvious in vols. I and II, but the direction is clearer in vol. III with its focus upon modalities of elaborated codes as pedagogic relays in schools. Originally the work arose out of two interdependent problems: the empirical problem of the explanation of class-regulated differential school success and the more general problem of what, in the late 1950s, was termed the process of socialisation. The latter, but not the former, was a very low-status area of study in sociological courses at the London School of Economics (LSE) in that period. I was dissatisfied with the then current theories of socialisation which in the end relied on some mystical process of 'internalisation' of values, roles and dispositions. I was attracted to Meadian symbolic interactionism and the early Chicago School because of the centrality of communication and their detailed ethnographic studies of marginalised cultures. Durkheim and Cassirer provided a Kantian perspective, though in different ways, which alerted me to the social basis of symbolic forms. Marx opened up the problem of the class specialisation of consciousness, and its relation to the social division and social relations of production. I linked the unlinkable—Durkheim's analysis of mechanical and organic solidarity to unspecialised, homogeneous occupational functions, on the one hand, and specialised interdependent functions, on the other, in relations of differential power. In this way different positions of power and specialisation created different modalities of communication differentially valued by the school, and differentially effective in it because of the school's values, modes of practice and relations with its different communities.

The first empirical studies of families, children and teachers were carried out by members of the Sociological Research Unit which I directed and issued in a number of papers and books reporting studies of elaborated and restricted codes *and* their modalities in families and children. Those early studies were criticised for their methods, questionnaires and interviews. However, later naturalistic studies of families, children and classrooms, carried out by researchers, confirmed the central propositions of the theory (see Appendix). The theory at this stage (the 1970s) was considered, in my opinion wrongly, as wholly a deficit theory and codes were trivialised and confused with dialect.[1] As a consequence the theory was viewed by some as biased against the lower working class and towards the middle class.[2] Further, the attempt of the theory to integrate macro/micro levels and disciplines often resulted in each discipline ignoring or misunderstanding the others. As a consequence bits of the theory were abstracted from the original integrated theory which mapped the semantic on to the linguistic and showed how both were generated and relayed by forms of context-specific social relations. The manner of the developments of the theory was unusual as it progressed through a series of papers. Papers were often taken out of their place in this development, regarded as terminal, and evaluated as such. A remarkable exception to this, from my point of view, is the set of research papers included in the book edited by Frances Christie (1999). These empirical papers, from different perspectives, e.g. learning contexts, early literacy education, culture, competence and schooling, language, knowledge and mathematics, genre-based literacy and preparation for literacy, provide strong evidence for the theory. This research using Bernstein's sociology and Halliday's linguistics show the viability of the theory in integrating semantic, linguistic and contextual levels in revealing reproductive processes in families, schooling and culture.

From the late 1970s and early 1980s, although empirical studies at the microsociological level were carried out by colleagues and PhD students, the focus shifted more and more to the various modalities of elaborated codes institutionalised in education, the principles of their description and their social assumptions. Finally the theory of elaborated codes was transformed into a more general account of the social structuring of pedagogic discourse and the shaping of its various practices as relays of a society's distribution of power and principles of control. In this way the theory returned to its partly Durkheimian origins in the nature of symbolic control.

CRITERIA FOR THE THEORY

Before going on to give a detailed account of the development of the conceptual language of the theory and the models this language generated, I think it would be relevant here to give first the criteria which the theory must satisfy. These criteria we can regard as internal to the theory, in the sense that they are criteria I hold, and which have influenced both the development of the theory and the research to which it has given rise. However, even assuming that the theory satisfies all the criteria (a doubtful assumption), it may well be that it fails to satisfy external criteria, that is the criteria held by others. It is useful to make explicit the internal criteria as these provide the rules of the approach and show the assumptions underlying the methodology.

1. The transition between different levels of the theory must be made through the use of concepts, which at each level describe the key relations of the theory as these are realised at each level. The concepts must be able to hold together and specify both interactional and structural relations. That is, macro-constraints must be made visible, by the conceptual language, in their power to shape interactions. At the same time the potential of interaction to shape macro-constraints must be capable of being described. The concepts must be able to distinguish between variation in, and change of, the agencies and fields of the empirical analyses. Further the concepts should be able to show how such variation and change occurs.

2. The theory must be capable of providing an explicit, unambiguous description of the objects of its analysis. The theory must not simply specify its objects at the theoretical level, but must provide the rules for their empirical recognition, description and modalities of realisation (that is the different forms the same object can take).

3. The theory must clearly specify not only the contexts which are crucial to its exploration *and* change, it must also specify the procedures for the description of these contexts and their interpretation. In other words the theory must lay down what is to be investigated, how it is to be investigated, how its data are to be investigated and described. It is important to add here that the descriptions or, rather, the rules which generate the descriptions, must be capable of realising all empirical displays to which the context gives rise. This is crucial if circularity is to be avoided; in which case the theory constructs at the *level of description* only that which lives within its own confines. Thus the principles of description, although derived from the theory, must interact with the empirical contextual displays so as to retain and translate the integrity of the display. Thus the principles of description are the key principles in bringing about a dynamic relation between theoretical and empirical levels. These principles must preserve the integrity of contextual displays and so preserve its original activities, relations and voices *and* at the same time show the nature of their relation to the theory and its models. Thus a theory is only as good as the principles of description to which it gives rise. Ideally the principles must have the *potential* of exhausting the possibilities of contextual displays. This means that they have the *potential* not only of describing imputed regularities to the displays but also of showing their diversities.

4. The substantive issue of the theory is to explicate the process whereby a given distribution of power and principles of control are translated into specialised principles of communication differentially, and often unequally,

distributed to social groups/classes. And how such a differential/unequal distribution of forms of communication, initially (but not necessarily terminally) shapes the formation of consciousness of members of these groups/classes in such a way as to relay both opposition and change. The crucial issue is the translation of power and control into principles of communication which become (successful or otherwise) their carriers or relays.

5. Explicit rules are required for:

   (a) writing these principles of communication, their social construction and institutional bases;

   (b) their modalities of transmission and acquisition as pedagogic discourse and their institutional bases;

   (c) identifying the *various* realisations of members of groups/classes and agencies as cultural displays of a specialised consciousness.

There is something misleading in the spelling out of these criteria if it is thought that they were present in the beginning of the research over 35 years ago, when clearly they were not. In an important sense the research has been a journey (often rather bumpy) into the consciousness of the criteria as regulators of the research endeavour. The issue of the source of these criteria seems to me to be inherent in the project itself, and the criteria become the motivators of the development of the project. It is interesting to compare this activity of internal development with external assessment. This takes the form of an epistemological botany, classifying a theory as determinist, functionalist, positivist, conservative, progressive, radical. Evaluation follows the classification. Apparently this theory is now pinned down as structuralist with strong Durkheimian roots, but how does this relate to the internal criteria of the theory's own construction and development? It seems to me that the epistemological exercise attempts to evaluate the image of the social that the theory is allegedly projecting. The exercise sees this image as having a self-fulfilling function as the theory becomes intellectually active as a set of concepts, as a research practice and, possibly, as an instrument for policy. For example, a theory's concept of subjectivity, and of its displays, may be a crucial determinant of that theory's classification, rather than the concept being viewed as a necessary limitation on the stories which can be told. Perhaps even more relevant than the classification of the theory are the theory's principles of description by means of which we are given access to the displays. Here we return to the internal criteria. Finally it seems to me that some theories, especially in their final development, do not permit too straightforward a classification. Indeed the ambiguity which lies at the heart of the social, the nature of social order, may well require representation in a theory. In the case of my theory this representation is realised in the concept of code, which at the same time as it relays ordering principles and their related practices necessarily opens a space for the potential of their change. Inherent in the concept of code is a choice about itself. Further, the pedagogic device, as this is conceptualised, creates an arena of conflict over its ownership and monopoly. We will return to these matters at the end of this account.

MODELLING FAMILIAL CONTROLS: EARLY CONCEPTS

In this section I want to move from the general outline of the project and the abstract discussion on methodology to a detailed account of the more specific relations between the conceptual language, principles of description and empirical research. Elsewhere I have shown these relations in respect of the realisation of elaborated and restricted codes in children and parents, so my discussion here will be limited (Bernstein, 1987, 1990).

In an important sense, the formulation of concepts for the description of modalities of elaborated codes institutionalised in education had their origin in the conceptualising of modalities of family systems and their principles of control. This focus was determined by our funded research which throughout the middle 1960s and early 1970s was concerned to study the social origins of codes in the family, their sociolinguistic realisations in children aged between 5 and 7 years, and the influence of the primary school on the initial codings that lower working-class children brought to the school. The pattern of the research, however, throughout the 35 years has always been the same: the theory, however primitive, has always come before the research. Thus by the time a piece of research *has been initiated* the theory has already been subject to conceptual clarification as it engages with the empirical problem. And by the time it has finished there have been further conceptual developments. From this point of view some of the papers represent pre-research stages, whilst others the post-research stage. One paper, in 1981, 'Code Modalities and the Process of Cultural Reproduction: a model', formalised conceptual development up to that point *and* pointed the way to future work on the nature of pedagogic discourse. In the case of the early 1960s–1970s family studies they were preceded by a conceptualising of family types and their modes of control. In 1963 I gave a paper to the International Conference on Cross Cultural Research into Childhood and Adolescence, held at the University of Chicago (itself based on an earlier paper, unpublished, originally written as part of my PhD), which analysed family types in terms of the division of labour of roles and the relations between different divisions (different degrees of role specialisation) and different modes of control of children. I introduced shorthand terms for these family types, positional (earlier termed status oriented) and personal. The sociolinguistic realisations of positional and personal modes of control were considered to be different. Here was the first appearance of the crucial role of the division of labour as a regulator on forms of communication. (I may add that different class positions in the social division of labour in the economy were correlated with different codes of communication.)

However, although the theoretical formulation of family types existed as early as 1963, even before that, briefly referred to in a 1962 paper, the major exposition did not appear in published form until 1971 ('A Sociolinguistic Approach to Socialisation: with some reference to educability').

In the interval there was considerable empirical research culminating in a strong language of description of modes of control. In 1963, when the parents of the children were interviewed, we included a series of questions on how the mother communicated to the child (tick schedules): the mother was asked a set of hypothetical questions on how she controlled the child and a set of questions invited the mother to explain how she would answer these questions if they were put to her by her own child (then aged 5 years). Two years later the child was posed the same question, originally put to the mother, and the child was asked how he/she would answer the same questions about control of children originally put to the mother. Our first attempt (Bernstein, 1971) to explore positional/personal control was the creation of an Index of Communication and Control. Based on interview schedules low scores were associated with positional, and high scores with personal control (total sample 379, drawn from predominantly middle- and working-class areas). We were able to show that *high* scores on this index *within the working class* correlated more strongly with two measures of the child's IQ than with the parent's social class. Further again, *within* the working class high scores on this index were strongly correlated with favourable estimates of the children after they had been in school for two years. This work has been dismissed because of the method (closed questionnaire), but I think this is too ideological a dismissal for we still have to account for the differential pattern within the working class *and* the external correlations with the teachers. There seemed to be some evidence within the working class for the link between reported communication and control and external measures (Brandis and Bernstein, 1974)— all as predicted. However, it could be said that the index was a very crude and indirect indicator of positional and personal modalities of control. The next step was to construct a more direct and sensitive measure. We had, as data, the mothers' *and* their children's reported modes of control as given by their answers to the same open-ended questions. As theory we had notions of imperative control, and what we called two modes of appeal, positional and personal, distinguished by the area of discretion which the appeals (reasons) made available to the child. Basically the controller could focus upon general attributes of the child (age, gender, age relation, etc.), or particular attributes unique to the child. In either case the child could be accorded high and low discretion (see Figure 6.1). From this very formal model, Jenny Cook-Gumperz and I generated complex principles of descriptions of the speech of parents and children (Bernstein and Cook-Gumperz, 1973).

Basically we conceived of control as consisting of a number of subsystems, each subsystem accessing a network of choices. Thus a *rationale system* accessed a network describing the controllers' justification of the control. A *strategy* system accessed a network of choices employed to avoid problems of future control.

A *concessional system* was concerned with diverse bargaining choices. A *punish-ment* system accessed a network of different forms of imperatives, verbal and non-verbal. An *appeal* system accessed a complex set of choices within positional and personal modes. A *reparation system* accessed a network of choices describing actions the controller takes to restore or repair the relationship with the controlled. A *motivational system* accessed a set of choices describing intention of both controller and controlled. There were basically seven systems, each accessing a network of choices. It was possible to analyse in terms of (a) which subsystems are taken up, (b) in what order and (c) with what choices. Each subsystem was a realisation of the formal model outlined earlier.

I have given a detailed explanation here of the principles of description in order to show what I mean by the relation between the theory and the principles of description to which it gives rise. Thus these principles of description give a stronger basis for classifying modes of control and also enable us to obtain a more

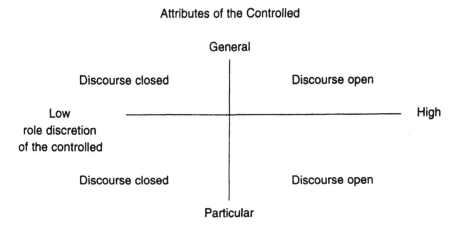

Figure 6.1: Model of control

delicate view of control than that given by the abstract formal model. The principles of description of modes of control are published in *Social Control and Socialisation* (Cook-Gumperz, 1973, pp. 48–73).

MODELLING SCHOOL STRUCTURES

Thus by the mid-1960s I had a simple language to describe control systems, consisting of their social division of labour → modes of control → communicative outcomes. In the same period (often disregarded by critics) I began an analysis of the school in terms of pupils' involvement in two interrelated systems of the

Table 6.1: Types of involvement in the role of pupil

		Instrumental		Expressive	
		means	ends	means	ends
1	Commitment	+	+	+	+
2	Detachment	+	+	+	−
3	Deferment	- -
4	Estrangement	−	+	+	+
5	Alienation	−	−	−	−

Notes: means: *understands* the means (+−: YES NO)
       ends: *accepts* the ends (+−: high/low involvement)

school, an instrumental order concerned with the transmission of specialised skills and an expressive order concerned with the transmission of conduct, character and manner (Table 6.1).

Table 6.1 shows the formal model. The model does not articulate contents of either of the two orders instrumental/expressive. However, this model provided the basis for an empirical study of a selective school, published as *Values and Involvements in a Grammar School* by King (1964). Two papers which followed attempted to provide contents for the instrumental and expressive orders and drew upon the notions of boundary and their relation to communication—notions conveyed by the earlier concepts of positional and personal modes of control. The paper 'Ritual in Education' (Bernstein et al., 1966) examined changes in the way in which the expressive order was transmitted, and argued that the shift from stratified to differentiated schools entailed a shift in the way the expressive order was transmitted. *Stratified* schools (or organisations) were schools where the units of organisation were based on fixed attributes or attributes thought to be fixed, e.g. age, gender, 'ability', categories of discourse (school subjects). It was thought that where units/categories were considered fixed then the school would develop explicit horizontal and vertical structures. These would provide an unambiguous basis for the ritualisation of boundaries and the celebration of consensus. However, where the basic unit/category was not a fixed, specialised unit (e.g. mixed groupings of pupils with varying membership, more integration of school subjects), the school structure was called *differentiated*. Here the expressive order was less likely to be relayed by extensive and intensive ritualisation as the social organisation provided weaker grounds for ritualisation. The expressive order in differentiated schools was expected to be relayed by elaborated forms of personalised communication; in the 1966 paper named 'Therapeutic Control'. It was of course possible to have sections of a school stratified and other sections differentiated. The latter organisation in the U.K. was thought to be more probable for the students considered to be 'less able'.

After this paper I read Mary Douglas, in particular her remarkable book *Purity and Danger* (1966). I wrote a short paper making more explicit concepts of boundary, insulations, social divisions of labour, with regard to the purity and mixing of categories of discourse and organisation. I placed the analysis firmly in Durkheim, suggesting that schools in the 1960s (at least at the level of ideology if not in fact) were moving from mechanical solidarity to organic solidarity as an integrating principle. Thus *stratified* schools now became Closed Types integrated through mechanical solidarity, whereas *differentiated* schools were integrated through organic solidarity (this view was later modified). The models in the two papers were combined to generate principles of description for empirical study of schools (see Figure 6.2) (Bernstein, 1967).

Here we can see again the translation of theory into explicit principles of description for empirical exploration. I did not personally carry out empirical research on the model, but R. King collected data on a range of schools and then tired to interpret his results in terms of the model. He concluded that there was only very weak evidence for the relations expected (King, 1976, 1981). However, Tyler (1988) criticises severely King's statistical treatment of the data.

So far I have tried to show how implicit in the sociolinguistic thesis and family forms of transmission were the concepts I used in the early work on forms of pedagogic transmission in the school. I have highlighted the importance of the conceptual language in its ability to generate strong principles of description for empirical studies. However, there were severe limitations of the theory. It was unable to conceptualise macro-constraints on micro-processes. The concepts used to analyse modalities of elaborated codes institutionalised in schools could not connect with the concepts used to explicate codes. No distinction was possible between power and control relation. Social class was not much more than a shadow concept, more hidden than revealed.

By 1970 the principles of analysis of the large research project, in which as many as 12 researchers were engaged, had been decided and so less of my focus was upon the complex problems of analysis of the data. Further, I was heavily engaged in teaching and supervision in the general area of the sociology of education. The specific sociolinguistic features of the theoretical project rarely were part of my teaching and supervision. Only *one* of over 30 completed PhDs has been upon the narrow sociolinguistic features of the thesis. My own focus had certainly changed from the study of primary socialisation in the origins of codes, to the forms of institutionalising of elaborated codes. During the period from the final collection of the data of the large study mentioned earlier (1966), until the present, I myself initiated only one study of coding orientation of children. This was published by Janet Holland (1981).

Mixing of Categories   *Purity of Categories*

Teaching groups: Heterogeneous—size and composition varied	**Teaching groups:** Homogeneous—size and composition fixed
Pedagogy: Problem setting or creating / Emphasises *ways of knowing*	**Pedagogy:** Solution giving / Emphasises *contents* or states of *knowledge*
Teachers: Teaching roles cooperative/inter-dependent / Duties *achieved* / Fluid points of reference and relation	**Teachers:** Teaching roles insulated from each other / Duties *assigned* / Fixed points of reference and relation
Curriculum: Subject boundaries blurred (inter-related) / Progression: deep to surface structure of knowledge / Common curriculum	**Curriculum:** Subject boundaries sharp (less inter-relation or integration) / Progression: surface to deep structure of knowledge / Curriculum graded for different ability groups
Pupils: Varied social groups reducing *group* similarity and difference—increased area of choice / Aspirations of the *many* raised / Fluid points of reference and relation	**Pupils:** Fixed and stable social groups emphasising *group* similarity and difference—reduced area of choice / Aspirations of the *few* developed / Fixed points of reference and relation

TYPE–OPEN —————————————————————————————————————— TYPE–CLOSED

(1) Ritual order celebrates participation/cooperation	(1) Ritual order celebrates hierarchy/dominance
(2) Boundry relationships with outside blurred	(2) Boundary relationships with outside sharply drawn
(3) Internal organisation: wide range of integrative sub-groups with active membership and success roles across ability ranges	(3) Internal organisation: narrower range of integrative sub-groups with active membership and success roles confined to high-ability range
If prefect system—wide area of independence from staff, but limited exercise of power	If prefect system—under staff control and influence, but extensive exercise of power
Range of opportunities for pupils to influence staff decisions, e.g. opportunities for self-government	Limited opportunities for pupils to influence staff decisions, e.g. limited opportunities for self-government
(4) Teacher–pupil authority relationships: Reward and punishment less public and ritualised / Teacher–pupil relationships of control—inter-personal	(4) Teacher–pupil authority relationships: Reward and punishment public and ritualised / Teacher–pupil relationships of control—positioned

Mixing of Categories   *Purity of Categories*

ORDERS: EXPRESSIVE

MODELLING PEDAGOGIC CODES

I was dissatisfied with the models of the transmission systems of the school. In particular I was dissatisfied because the relations generated did not bring me close to the basic principles of transmission/acquisition at the micro level of pedagogic practice. Nor was it within the potential of the models to do this. In other words, I had no language to write codes of transmission, pedagogic codes, and so no language to distinguish precisely between modalities of elaborated codes, and even less of a language for describing macro-contexts. In the previous models there was no separation of discourse from the form of its transmission and evaluation. This separation was crucial to the next step, which was influenced by Durkheim and symbolic interactionisms. From Durkheim I took *classification* and from the early symbolic interactions I took the concept of *framing*, although I defined both differently.

Classification was used to refer to the relations between categories, these relations being given by their degree of insulation from each other. Thus strong insulation created categories, clearly bounded, with a space for the development of a specialised identity, whereas the weaker the insulation, the less specialised the category. The key to the category relations, be these categories of discourses, practices or agencies, was insulation. For, once the insulation changed its strength, the category relations changed. I argued that power relations maintained the degree of insulation and thus the principle of the classification. In this way category relations are the relay for power relations. Classification could be strong $(+C)$ or weak $(-C)$, according to the degree of insulation. Classification could also apply to relations *within* a category. We could talk about the relation between objects, between tasks and between persons within a classroom. Here we could be referring to the internal classification $(\pm C^i)$ as distinct from the external classification $(\pm C^e)$, for example, between school subjects. In this way power relations gave rise to boundary rules and so to classificatory principles.

What about communication? Communication here referred to the means whereby legitimate messages could be constructed according to the boundary rules, that is, according to the principles of the classification. In other words, communication referred to the specific pedagogic practices necessary for the construction of legitimate messages or texts. In a school this practice refers to the relations of transmission and acquisition between teacher and taught. Framing referred to the locus of control over the selection, sequencing, pacing and criteria of the knowledge to be acquired. Thus with strong framing $(+F)$ control lies with the teacher, whereas with weak framing $(-F)$ control lies apparently with the student. We can, as with classification, distinguish between the *internal strength of framing* $(\pm F^i)$, that is framing within a given pedagogic context, and the *external strength of the framing* $(\pm F^e)$, that is, the strength of the framing between the pedagogic context and a context external to it; for example, between communication in the school and communication in the local communities to which the students belonged. Another example of external framing (F^{ie}) would be the controls on communication between school and work.

In short, the principle of the classification regulates *what* discourse is to be transmitted and its relation to other discourses in a given set (e.g. a curriculum). The principle of the framing regulates *how* the discourse is to be transmitted and acquired in the pedagogic context. Pedagogic codes can now be written as:

$$\frac{E}{\pm C^{ie}/\pm F^{ie}}$$

where E refers to the orientation of the discourse (elaborated): —— refers to the embedding of this orientation in classification and framing values. Thus variation in the strength of classification and framing values generates different modalities of pedagogic practice.

It might be useful to pause here and discuss the relation between the above formulation and earlier formulations. The fundamental notion of the relation between the social division of labour and forms of communication still underpinned the concept of classification, for the relation between categories (be these categories of discourse, practices, agents or agencies) refers to a given social division of labour. However, the principle of the classification attempts to establish, maintain and relay power relations. Classification holds together, in one concept, horizontal relations and vertical or hierarchical relations. Further the concept, as we will see, can relate macro-structural and micro-interactional levels of analysis. Framing at a very abstract level refers to the social relations of a given social division of labour. Framing, from this point of view, is the relay for the practices or, rather, the principle of the practices, which sustain a given social division of labour. Variations in framing refer to modalities of control over practices: in our analyses, pedagogic practices. Strong framing over these practices marks boundaries and makes them explicit, and so is a reformulation of the earlier form of familial control (or type): positional. Weak framing reduces the emphasis and marking of boundaries, especially explicit marking of hierarchy, and so is a reformulation of the earlier form of familial control (or type): personal. In this way later concepts build upon and generalise the relations created by earlier concepts.[3]

PEDAGOGIC CODES AND RESEARCH

The classification and framing analysis enabled the integration of the apparently disparate parts of the thesis, the sociolinguistic family-centred and the transmission-centred study of the school. It was now possible to determine the pedagogic codes of families in terms of their classification and framing values, to relate these codes to the pedagogic codes of the school and to examine the implications for the children's experience of school. Research carried out by Isabel Neve did precisely this. Neve carried out an intensive study of a small number of selected families, together with a study of a larger number of families, in which she constructed the pedagogic codes of the families and the pedagogic codes of the school class of the children. Neve shows that detailed descriptions could be derived from the concepts of classification and framing (Morais, Neve et al., 1995). The latter enabled the identification and description of modalities of elaborated code in schools and evaluation of their different outcomes. Further, in the light of hypotheses referring to the relation between modalities of elaborated codes and their acquisition by children of different social backgrounds, more effective pedagogic codes could be specifically designed. Thus by varying the classification and framing values over different elements of the pedagogic practice we could evaluate the effects of the children's attainments. In other words we could *design* pedagogic practices on a rational basis and evaluate their outcomes. Ana Marie Morais et al. did exactly this (1995). She designed three pedagogic practices in terms of variations in their $\pm C^{ie}/F^{ie}$ values. Each practice gave rise to a very explicit and detailed teaching protocol (over 20 pages in length). *One* teacher was trained to teach her subject (Science) to four paralleled classes using a different modality of pedagogic practice for each school class for a period of two years. Over 100 observations of the teacher were carried out in order to check the extent to which each protocol (and deviation from it) occurred. The pupils aged 11–13 in each class came from different social backgrounds and race groups. The pupils were also given Piagetian-type tests of scientific reasoning. Neve, in the work referred to earlier, studies the pedagogic codes of the families of the children. It was now possible to evaluate the complex relations between the pedagogic code of the family, the social background of the family, the level of 'development' of the pupil, modality of the elaborated code realised in the pedagogic practice of the school and different pupils' educational achievement and classroom conduct. Morais's remarkable study shows uniquely the intimate relations between the theory, principles of description and the research (Morais *et al.*, 1994).

We have discussed the codes of pedagogic practice in terms of family and school, but the conceptual language is not limited to these agencies. It can be applied to any pedagogic relation, or more generally to any transmission relation of control, e.g. between doctor and patient, social worker and client, psychiatrist and patient, prison staff and prisoners and, of course, to industrial relations.

DEVELOPMENT OF CLASSIFICATION AND FRAMING

Despite the greater power of this development of the conceptual language there were a number of problems. The first was that in the original formulation of classification and framing the essential focus was upon the transmission/acquisition of a competence (e.g. a curriculum subject). However, the original definition of framing was in terms of the locus of control over the selection, sequencing, pacing and criteria of the discourse to be acquired. Thus hierarchical relations and the concept of order were confounded with the more specific rules for transmission of particular subject competences. Originally, in earlier papers on the school (Bernstein, 1966, 1967; Bernstein et al., 1966) I had separated the transmission of skills (instrumental order) from the transmission of conduct, character and manner (the expressive order). These features were not separated in the earlier formulation of framing. As a consequence it was not really possible to describe *within the conceptual language* the moral order regulating interaction in the classroom or the moral order of the agency, *or* the relation between the moral order and the instructional order *or* between the moral order of the agency and the external constraining moral order. The ideological positioning inherent in the moral regulation of the pedagogic practice, although implicit in the concepts, was not explicit. Because it was only implicit there were no rules for the description of the type of moral regulation. Clearly such rules were available in the earlier work (especially 1967), but these were not integrated in the classification and framing concepts.

This integration arose out of the research project of Emilia Pedro who was studying forms of pedagogic practice in three primary schools drawing upon children from, respectively, lower working-class backgrounds, mixed-class backgrounds and middle-class backgrounds. Pedro carried out systematic classroom observations of the pupils in two subjects, mathematics and language, in primary schools in Lisbon. Tape recordings were made of the lessons and these were to be described. I then revised the concept of framing to make explicit modes of moral regulation as follows. Framing now referred to the controls on two embedded discourses: an *instructional discourse* transmitting specific skills *and* their relation to each other, and a *regulative discourse* transmitting the rules of social order. Framing could be examined in respect of each discourse, separately. As a consequence, it was possible, in principle, for the framing of the instructional discourse to be different from the framing of the regulative discourse. Further, it was now possible to examine classification and framing at the level of the school, as given in documents, rules, rituals, assemblies, etc., for the regulative discourse and curricular programmes for the instructional discourse. Comparison could be made for both discourses between the level of the school, and the level of the classroom and the level of pupils. The regulative discourse of the school could be related to external regulative discourses. All this was now possible in the same conceptual language.

Figure 6.3 shows the model which guided Pedro's research (1981). I should point out that Morais and Neve, referred to earlier, used this formulation of framing. Coming out of these formulations was a definition of any *pedagogic practice* as:

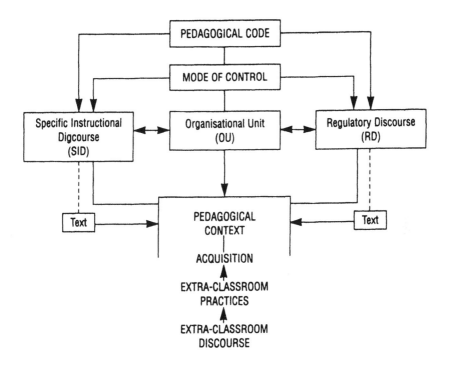

Figure 6.3: Model for pedagogic discourse

$$\frac{ID \quad \text{instructional discourse}}{RD \quad \text{regulative discourse}}$$

which had important, if not crucial, implications.

Before turning to the development of the macro level of the theory and research I want to show how the same language can be used to analyse principles of the *acquisition* of codes.

MODELLING CODE ACQUISITION

Up to this point most of the focus of the overall thesis, whether it referred to sociolinguistic codes acquired in the family, or modalities of elaborated codes acquired in the school, was upon the forms of transmission and principles of recognition, that is, identification of specific codes. The first hint of how codes were acquired was given in an appendix to the revised edition of *Class, Codes and Control,* Vol. I (1974), where the notion of ground rules was proposed. These were rules by means of which the legitimate requirements of a context were read and so appropriate behaviour prepared and executed. Thus different ground rules, different readings, different behaviour. Social class acted selectively on the distribution of ground rules. However, it was all very vague. How ground rules were acquired was a mystery. The notion of ground rules was supplemented by an accompanying notion of performance rule. This appeared in the *Introduction to Code in Context* (Adlam et al., 1977). The performance rule produced the text, but again how was it acquired? Precisely what it was and its acquisition were both a mystery.

Inasmuch as there is no explication of the process whereby codes are acquired then it is not possible to understand how codes bias consciousness. In the same way, in the case of Bourdieu, it is not possible to understand the specific process whereby a particular habitas is shaped nor to understand the generating rules which construct its specific practices and strategies. Unless we can show the rules of acquisition of codes we cannot show how ideology is relayed by the use of codes. In the theory, ideology is conceived as the mode of making relations.

By 1980 I saw the way of integrating rules for creating specific practices/texts on the part of the acquirer with the rules regulating the principle of their transmission. In other words, I saw how specific classification and framing values acted selectively on the rules of the acquirer so that the acquirer could produce the required practice/text.

I started with classification because classification, strong or weak, marks the distinguishing features of a context. It orientates the speaker to what is expected and what is legitimate in that context. For example, some children when they first go to school are unaware or unsure of what is expected of them. They fail to recognise the distinguishing features which provide the school/classroom with its unique features and so particular identity. Such a failure in recognition will necessarily lead to inappropriate behaviour. On the other hand, some children are extensively prepared and are aware of the difference between the family context and the school context. In this case they are able to recognise the distinguishing features of the school, or class, even if they are not always able to produce the range of behaviour the school expects. Inasmuch as some children recognise the distinguishing features of the school, relative to the children who do not, those that do are in a more powerful position with respect to the school. It is likely that those who do recognise the distinguishing features of the school are more likely to be middle-class children than lower working-class children. The basis of such recognition is a strong classification between the context of the family and the context of the school. In our example the strong classification between family and school is a product of the symbolic power of the middle-class family. This power is translated into the child's power of recognition with its advantageous outcomes. Of course if the school context was identical or near to the working-class family context (weakly classified) then the middle-class child would be at a disadvantage, assuming he/she lacked this recognition rule of similarity. We can therefore set up a relationship between the principle of the classification and the *recognition rules* for identifying the specificity *or* similarity of contexts. As the classification principle is established by power relations and relays power relations, then recognition rules confer power relative to those who lack them.

However, although recognition rules are a necessary condition for producing a legitimate context-specific text or practice these rules are not sufficient. It is still necessary to know how to construct the specific text or practice. For example, one may be able to recognise that one is in a sociology class but not be able to produce the texts and context-specific practices. In order to produce the legitimate text it is necessary to acquire the realisation rule. Whereas the recognition rule arises out of distinguishing *between* contexts, the realisation rule arises out of the specific requirements *within* a context. We know that the principle of the classification governs relations between contexts, and that the principle of the framing regulates the transmission of appropriate practice *within* a context. In our examples, framing regulates the pedagogic practice which relays a category of discourse. In this way framing regulates specific *realisation rules* for producing contextually specific texts/practices. Thus principles of control are relayed by variations in the strength of framing (over selection, sequencing, pace and criteria) which at the level of the individual translate into realisation rules. Figure 6.4 models the relation we have just discussed.

We have now, as far as this account is concerned, completed the development of the theory with regard to understanding how the distribution of power and principles of control translate into classification and framing principles, which in turn regulate the recognition and realisation rules which organise meanings and

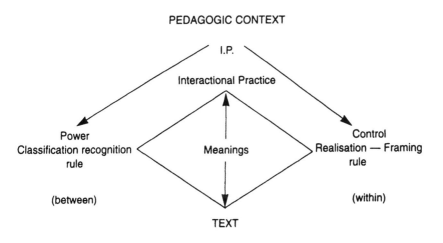

Figure 6.4: **Pedagogic context**

their expression at the level of the individual in specific contexts. Later we shall
see that we are not simply passive in the codes we use.

I shall now review some research bearing upon the relations between modalities of classification and framing and their regulation of recognition and realisation rules.

PEDAGOGIC CODES, RECOGNITION, REALISATION RULES AND RESEARCH

I used this formulation of recognition and realisation rules, and their expected relation to classification and framing values, to set out the different rules used by middle- and working-class children in the various texts they offered in a formal interview context. These listed situations requiring instructional and regulative speech (see 'Codes, Modalities and the Process of Cultural Reproduction: a model'; Bernstein, 1981). I was able in a similar way to write the different rules used by middle- and working-class children at the age of seven, which gave rise to the different classifications produced by these children when they were asked to group pictures of various food items (Bernstein, op cit., 1981). I regarded this as a great step forward: not simply the postulation of text-producing rules, but the ability to be able to write the rules and check empirically their accuracy in accounting for the texts. Conceptually, it meant that specific codes of transmission *at the level of the acquirer* consisted of contextually specific recognition and realisation rules. However, I had not carried out specific research designed to elicit recognition and realisation rules. I had applied the theory to data which were not specifically constructed to elicit these rules.

Finally I want to turn to research which explains the relation between the Cie/F^{ie} values of a pedagogic practice and the recognition and realisation rules which children tacitly acquire. This research shows the relation between the form of the pedagogic practice and what is acquired.

Daniels was concerned to investigate the expected relation between classification and framing and recognition and realisation rules. He selected four schools varying in their $\pm C^{ie}/\pm F^{ie}$ values. This was done through observation of the schools, study of curricular programmes and their theories of instruction. The heads of each school were presented with their descriptions and asked whether these were accurate descriptions. Observations of the school class allowed Daniels to identify the pedagogic code of transmission. The four schools and classrooms represented a continuum from $+C^{ie}/+F^{ie}$ to $-C^{ie}/-F^{ie}$ pedagogic codes. The children were asked to talk about a series of pictures in an Art class and also in a Science class *when they were actually taking these lessons.* These interviews took place at different times. The responses of each class for each lesson, Art and Science, were offered to the teachers to classify. In this way we could determine whether children produced statements which the teachers could classify as either art or science. Thus the production of the statements would indicate realisation rules.

Daniels then selected a group of children, four in each of the four schools on the basis of their teacher's classification of degrees of the children's competence in distinguishing between science and art statements. Teachers' judgements were highly correlated. Paired statements of one child who was very good (10 correct), one who was intermediate (seven correct), and one who was poor (three correct out of 10) were presented to each of the above 16 children. All but one child was able to say which was the science statement and which was the art statement.

We could relate possession of recognition rules, or possession of realisation rules, or possession of both, to the codes of the pedagogic practice of each class, that is to their classification of framing values. We also studied the art work produced by the children in each school in terms of the classification and framing of the images the children produced (Daniels, 1988, 1989, 1995). In general we found that *all* children had the recognition rules for discriminating between science and art statements. This was taken to mean that these recognition rules were probably acquired outside the schools. We came to this conclusion because the realisation rules for the production of a text, which the teachers could recognise as science or art, *depended upon the classification and framing of the pedagogic practice*. Thus children in the mostly weakly classified and framed classroom (emphasis on highly personal control, integration of disciplines, project methods) created texts which teachers could not distinguish as art or science, whereas children in the most strongly classified and framed pedagogic practice produced texts which the teachers could recognise as either art or science. These results are of some interest because there is no specific instruction in any of the schools in either recognising the difference between these types of sentences or producing them. No teacher in the art lesson teaches how to produce a spoken text which is an art text. Nor do the science teachers teach how to construct a science text. Yet the children, at least those in specific pedagogic modalities, are able to so construct.

Daniels's research raises basic questions of what is it about statements which enables children to classify them as art or science statements. What is the origin of this process of recognition? As the process was not linked to any of the pedagogic codes, not even to the most strongly classified, it seems recognition is acquired outside the school. But where and how? The recognition and realisation of these statements refers to fundamental ways of organising our experience of the world. The social origins are of great interest and, perhaps, concern. Daniels's research (1988, 1989, 1994) shows the value of theory in creating new empirical problems of some importance.

In the previous research we showed how variations in classification and framing effected the realisation rules of pupils in the preparation of a text which they had not formally been taught. Now I want to refer to research which is concerned to study the presence and absence of recognition and realisation rules where pupils had been formally taught by differing pedagogic practices. Morais (1993), in the research referred to earlier, carried out a specific study of the conditions leading to the acquisition of recognition and realisation rules for solving scientific problems involving the application of knowledge to new situations. It will be remembered that in her research pupils were taught by the same teacher in classes varying in their classificatory and framing values, although the content of the subject, science, was the same in all modalities of pedagogic practice. Thirty children with similar attributes, 10 from each modality, were selected for interview of their understanding of the recognition and realisation rules necessary for applying knowledge to new situations. In Portugal, science knowledge in schools is divided into two classes: knowledge of definitions, formulae, etc., referred to as 'A' and knowledge of application, referred to as 'U'. Initially all the children (80) were given a set of questions and simply asked to tick the 'U' questions and 'A' questions, or rather the questions the children thought were 'A' and those the children thought were 'U'. The 30 selected children drawn equally from each of the pedagogic modalities were interviewed individually. They were given a set of five problems and were asked a series of questions about each problem. Some questions called for an oral response, others involved choosing between statements which gave alternative answers to the problem, whilst other choices were between statements illustrating different ways of thinking about the problem. On the basis of the classroom text of 'A'/'U' discrimination and the interviews, it was possible to identify children who had both recognition and realisation rules for applying knowledge to new situations and those who possessed only one rule or neither. The results showed that social class background of the pupil was highly correlated (0.51) with possession of recognition rules, the necessary condition for producing the appropriate text; pedagogic practice was also related to the possession of recognition and realisation rule (0.30). That is, the pedagogic practices in which the framing of the instructional discourse was relatively strong were correlated with acquisition of recognition and realisation rules. I must point out that these are only some of the results of this remarkable piece of research (Morais et al., 1994).

The research of Daniels and Morais shows the relation between modalities of pedagogic practice, in terms of their classification and framing values, and the distribution of recognition and realisation rules for the construction of an appropriate text. Thus at the level of the school class we have evidence of the relation between the modality of the pedagogic code and the acquisition of realisation rules in one study and the acquisition of both rules in the other.

BASIC CONCEPTS

It may be useful to pause here and to show how the basic concept of code generates the language we have outlined. We will then go on to discuss the development of the theory and research towards macro-level processes regulating symbolic control through pedagogic discourse. The fundamental definition of code was formulated in 1981. Code is a regulative principle, tacitly acquired, which selects and integrates *relevant meanings,* the *form of their realisation* and *evoking contexts* (see Table 6.2).

This table shows how the basic definition generates the conceptual language and shows the translation of a distribution of power and principles of control into specialised modalities of pedagogic communication.

FIELDS OF PRODUCTION AND SYMBOLIC CONTROL

We shall now turn to the sponsors and shapers of pedagogic discourse before finally looking at the construction, rather than the transmission/acquisition, of pedagogic discourse.

On four occasions (Bernstein, 1973, 1975, 1977, 1991), I developed a set of closely related papers whose primary concern was to distinguish forms of pedagogic practice, their sponsors, their social class location, function and ideology. I returned to the definition of framing and distinguished between pedagogic practices in terms of whether their hierarchical rules and discursive rules were implicit. On this basis it was possible to generate two basic principles of pedagogic practice: *visible* and *invisible*. Each principle could give rise to *a range of modalities.* I called the practice *visible* when the hierarchical relations between teacher and pupils, the rules of organisation (sequence pace) and the criteria were explicit and so known to the pupils. In the case of *invisible* pedagogic practice the hierarchical rules, the rules of organisation and criteria were implicit and so not known to the pupils, for the rules of this practice were derived from complex theories of child development, linguistics, gestalten theories and sometimes deriva-

Table 6.2: Micro to macro

Practices	Interactional	Institutional	Code modalities
	Relevant meanings (Recognition rules)	Discourses	Classification principles (Power)
	Forms of realisation (Realisation rules)	Transmission	Framing principles (Control)
	Evoking contexts	Organisational	Classification and framing

tions from psycho-analytic theories. In the case of invisible pedagogic practice it is as if the pupil is the author of the practice and even the authority, whereas in the case of visible practices it clearly is the teacher who is author and authority. Further classification would be strong in the case of visible forms but weak in the case of invisible forms. Visible forms are regarded as conservative and invisible forms are regarded as progressive. The papers analysed the social class assumptions of both forms, and showed that acquisition depended upon certain economic conditions and symbolic practices in the family. Here I am not concerned with the process of transmission and selective acquisition, its social context and assumptions. I want to focus upon the thrust of those papers in analysing the sponsors of these pedagogic forms, particularly the invisible forms. Briefly I argued that the conflict between visible and invisible forms was an ideological conflict between different fractions of the middle class about the forms of control. One fraction, located in the field of production, carried out functions directly related *to the economic base* of production, circulation and exchange. The other fraction was located in what I called the field of symbolic control. Members of this fraction related directly to *specialised forms of communication,* institutionalised in religious, legal agencies (regulators), social services, child guidance, counselling agencies (*repairers*), education (*reproducers*), universities, research centres, research councils, private foundations (*shapers*), civil service, central and local government (*executors*).

Agents of symbolic control could be said to control discursive codes, whereas agents of production (circulation and exchange) dominate production codes. It also follows that agents of symbolic control could function in specialised agencies of symbolic control or in the economic field. Similarly agents of production could function in the economy or in specialised agencies of symbolic control (e.g. accountants, managers). I proposed that location, hierarchical position in the field of symbolic control or in the economic field would regulate distinct forms of consciousness and ideology *within* the middle class. In essence I was distinguishing between a complex division of labour of symbolic control and a complex division of labour in the economic field. Both divisions and their complexities were the products of new technologies of the twentieth century relayed by the educational system. This is very much a condensation of a more complicated and detailed analysis. Figure 6.5 illustrates the location of agents in fields and sectors.

FIELDS AND RESEARCH

I now want to turn to empirical research using the concepts of the fields of production, symbolic control, their agents, ideologies and their respective forms of consciousness and socialisation. Jenkins (1990) was concerned to investigate the social class basis of progressive education in Britain. She focused upon the New Education Fellowship which, during the inter-war years (1918–39), was a pow-

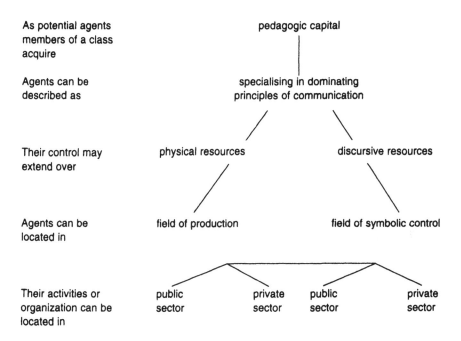

Figure 6.5: The location of agents in fields and sectors

erful, numerically large movement of crucial significance for the construction and dissemination of progressive education. At some of the conferences of the Fellowship, attendances reached over 2,000, drawn from a national and international membership. Unfortunately the membership list of the Fellowship was destroyed during the Second World War, but Jenkins was able to carry out a detailed analysis of *all* issues of the journal of the New Fellowship, *New Era*, for the period between 1920 and 1950. The contents of the journal covered curriculum theory, curriculum reports, psychological theories, applications to school, families, delinquency control and world education. It was also possible to identify authors and their occupations. Jenkins was able to show that the pedagogic practice advocated conformed to the model of an invisible pedagogy; that it was put forward in opposition to a visible pedagogy; that the crucial concern was in no way political in the sense of producing change in the class structure, but was concerned to produce an emancipation from authoritarian modes of socialisation and to encourage internationalism. The occupations of the authors were analysed and were shown to cover almost the whole field of symbolic control in agencies specialising in symbolic control. Thus expected relations were found between ideology, field, agents, and the construction and sponsoring of invisible pedagogies.

The second piece of empirical research focused upon differences in the socialising practices of parents located in the field of symbolic control or in the economic field. Holland (1986) carried out a study of adolescents' perceptions of the domestic and industrial divisions of labour. The subjects were 950 boys and girls aged 12+ and 15+ from a range of schools which drew on middle- and working-class areas. The large sample enabled a fine breakdown of both mothers' *and* fathers' occupations within the middle, and upper middle class, into locations, in either the economic field or field of symbolic control or employed in agencies specialised to either field. The adolescents answered, in written form, a pre-piloted open-ended questionnaire seeking to elicit how adolescents of different ages, social class and class fraction modelled gender divisions in domestic and economic, political and educational contexts. These inferred models were analysed in terms of their strength of classification with respect to gender positioning, hierarchy and social movement (mobility). The data consist, then, of adolescent *reports* and their parents' occupations. We have no direct measure of their parents' socialising practices, only the views of the children. However, Holland was able to re-analyse data collected by Wells (1985) in the course of his study of language development and parents' socialisation practices. Wells (1985) used the instrument developed in the Sociological Research Unit for distinguishing between positional and personal modes of control. When the mothers' mode of control was related to occupational position, Holland found that mothers located in the field of symbolic control were more personal in their mode of control than mothers in families located in the field of production who were more positional. Further, 'white collar' mothers within the working class tended to have personal modes of control. Thus there was indirect evidence from Wells's study, re-analysed by Holland, that socialisation practices vary in their classification and framing according to field location of parents. Holland's analysis of her own data suggested, in general, that adolescents of parents located in the field of symbolic control employed *weaker classification* in their modelling of the domestic and economic divisions of labour. Specifically the most *radical* girls, that is those who held the weakest classification of gender relations, were of parents in the field of symbolic control, whereas those who held the strongest classification of gender relations (boys) were of parents located in the field of production. Perhaps one of the most interesting and unexpected findings was that the greatest difference between boys' and girls' classifactory principles occurred between boys and girls of parents located in the economic field. Here the boys held strong classificatory principles whereas the girls' were relatively weak. It is interesting to speculate (assuming these results are reliable and valid) on the consequences of these girls' classificatory principles upon their own future socialisation principles, and so on the reproduction of their children.

I should also mention briefly a remarkable sociolinguistic study by Isobel Faria (1984). Faria's research interest was in studying how different social groups used language for purposes of self-reference. How do different social groups project their concept of self in the language they use? Faria chose a sample drawn from the field of symbolic control and the economic field where the subjects held different hierarchical positions within the respective fields. The sample drew upon social class membership *within* fields. Samples were drawn from workers within the university, both academics and manual workers, and from a large brewery (managers and manual workers). Faria conducted interviews in which questions were directed to elicit self-referencing. Although the numbers in each cell of the design were small, because of the requirements of the detailed nature of the linguistic description, important differences were found in self-referencing with respect to field location and class position.

We have indicated the development of the theory towards a greater articulation of social class. This entailed a division of labour of symbolic control, a specification of its specialised agencies and agents, distinguished from an economic division of labour with its own specialised agents and agencies. We also proposed differences (opposing differences) in ideology, pedagogic sponsoring and forms of socialisation between those located in the different fields and agencies. We have reported three pieces of empirical research investigating this macro development of the theory.

MODELLING THE CONSTRUCTION OF PEDAGOGIC DISCOURSE

So far the discussion of both theory and research has been concerned with pedagogic codes and their modalities of transmission and acquisition. This discussion was finally placed in a wider context of symbolic control, its field and specialised agents. The theory also deals with the relation between codes and the economy, but as there has been little research here this relation will not be discussed. We will now turn to the structuring of pedagogic discourse which regulates specific contexts. We have hinted at this move in our definition of framing as the controls on selection, sequence, pace and criteria.

In 1981 ('Code, Modalities and the Process of Cultural Reproduction: a study') I sketched in outline a model (using the language of an earlier model, *Class, Codes and Control*, vol. III, 1975, p. 31) for understanding the construction of pedagogic discourse. The basic idea was to view this discourse as arising out of the action of a group of specialised agents operating in a specialised setting in terms of the interests, often competing interests, of this setting. Originally I distinguished between three fields, each with their own rules of access, regulation, privilege and specialised interests: a field of *production* where new knowledge was constructed; a field of *reproduction* where pedagogic practice in schools occurred; a field, in between, called the *recontextualising field*. Activity in this field consisted of appropriating discourses from the field of production and transforming them into pedagogic discourse. This process of recontextualising entailed principles of *de-location*, that is, selective appropriation of a discourse or part of a discourse from the field of production, and a principle of *re-location* of that discourse as a discourse within the recontextualising field. In this process of de- and re-location the original discourse underwent an ideological transformation according to the play of specialised interests among the various positions in the recontextualising field. Over the last 25 years there has been increasing state regulation of all three fields, production, recontextualising and reproduction, and an increase in state control over both pedagogic discourse and the range of its practices and their contexts.

These ideas were developed and systematised in a paper 'On Pedagogic Discourse' (Bernstein, 1986). They appeared in an earlier form in Diaz's PhD (1984). Diaz was studying the institutionalising of primary education in Colombia. He systematised the conceptual language given in seminars and tutorials which formed the theoretical section of the thesis. This section was published as Bernstein and Diaz (1984).

Basically and very briefly, I proposed a crucial distinction between what I called the pedagogic device and the various realisations of the device, pedagogic discourses and their practices. This distinction is a distinction between a relay and what is relayed. I argued that previous research took for granted the structure which carried pedagogic discourse, and so focused on pedagogic discourse as a message, assuming the grammar which made that message possible. The grammar of the pedagogic device consisted of three interrelated, hierarchically organised rules. Briefly:

1. *Distributive rules:* These rules distributed different forms of knowledge to different social groups. In this way distributed rules distributed different forms of consciousness to different groups. Distributive rules distributed access to the 'unthinkable', that is, to the possibility of new knowledge, and access to the 'thinkable', that is, to official knowledge.
2. *Recontextualising rules:* These rules constructed the 'thinkable', official knowledge. They constructed pedagogic discourse: the 'what' and the 'how' of that discourse.
3. *Evaluative rules:* These rules constructed pedagogic practice by providing the criteria to be transmitted and acquired.

Essentially the pedagogic device is a symbolic ruler, ruling consciousness, in the sense of having power over it, and ruling, in the sense of measuring the legitimacy of the realisations of consciousness. The questions become whose ruler, what consciousness? In this way there is always a struggle between social groups for ownership of the device. Those who own the device own the means of perpetuating their power through discursive means and establishing, or attempting to establish, their own ideological representations.

These rules underlie the contexts for the production and reproduction of pedagogic discourse. We shall now go back to our first formulation of fields.

1. *Distributive rules:* These rules specialise access to *fields* where the production of new knowledge may legitimately take place, whether this knowledge

be intellectual (academic) or expressive (arts) or crafts. This does not mean that individuals not in specialised fields of production (usually higher agencies of education) cannot or do not create new knowledge. Only that the history, career and positioning of that knowledge will be different. However, after individuals *outside the field of production* create new knowledge, the field's principles will operate as to whether such knowledge is incorporated into the field.

2. *Recontextualising rules:* These rules regulate the work of specialists in the recontextualising field who construct the 'what' and 'how' of pedagogic discourse. Pedagogic discourse, then, is less a discourse and more a principle for appropriating discourses from the field of production, and subordinating them to a different principle of organisation and relation. In this process the original discourse passes through ideological screens as it becomes its new form, pedagogic discourse. As we know from our previous discussion pedagogic discourse is an instructional discourse embedded in a dominating regulative discourse (ID/RD).

The recontextualising field always consists of an *Official Recontextualising Field,* created and dominated by the state for the construction and surveillance of state pedagogic discourse. There is usually (but not always) a *Pedagogic Recontextualising Field* consisting of trainers of teachers, writers of textbooks, curricular guides, etc., specialised media and their authors. Both fields may well have a range of ideological pedagogic positions which struggle for the control of the field. And these positions in the Official and Pedagogic Recontextualising Fields may well be opposed to each other. Thus the relative independence of the latter from the former is a matter of some importance.

3. *Evaluative rules:* These rules regulate pedagogic practice at the classroom level, for they define the standards which must be reached. Inasmuch as they do this, then evaluative rules act selectively on contents, the form of transmission and their distribution to different groups of pupils in different contexts. At the most abstract level evaluative rules bring *time* (age), *content* (text) and *space* (transmission) into a specialised relation.

The above is a very condensed account of the development of the theory to include the construction of pedagogic discourse as a grammar underlying the fields of production, recontextualising and pedagogic practice. Figure 6.6 shows the key relations of the model.

PEDAGOGIC DISCOURSE: RESEARCH

We shall now turn to empirical research exploring the models outlined earlier. Diaz produced extensive expositions and commentaries on the theory which ap-

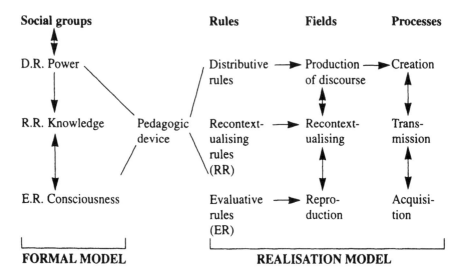

Figure 6.6: The key relations of the model

peared in a number of journals and books which he edited (see 'Bibliography'). I have to choose here between discussing his research into the institutionalising of primary education as a pedagogic discourse and institutional setting, and the research of Cox Donoso (who now publishes as Cox). I have chosen Cox because this was the first use of the model and, of more importance, it drew together the model of pedagogic discourse and its relation to the field of production and the field of symbolic control and so was more pertinent to the purpose of this section of the paper.

The first use of this model, and a stimulus to the integration of the theory, was by a postgraduate PhD student Christian Cox, whose doctorate was a study of continuity, conflict and change in state education in Chile. The research focused upon the pedagogic projects of the Christian Democratic Party (CD) and the Popular Unity Party of Allende. The doctorate was published in 1985 under the name of Cox Donoso. Cox required a means of comparing the policies, organising structures, curricula, pedagogic practices and forms of evaluation of the two political parties. It was also necessary to compare the relation of the educational system to the fields of production and symbolic control: concretely, to show how the party's ideological principles were institutionalised and relayed by the educational system and to show the output relation between the educational system and the economy. Cox was also concerned with understanding the struggle for control over the educational system as a struggle between different class fractions with differing interests in education arising out of their class habitus. This broad and deep study required a model from which could be derived hypotheses, principles of description necessary for the construction of appropriate data and principles of interpretation of the data to establish linkage to the hypotheses.

Cox carried out a comparison of the official construction of pedagogic discourse at different periods in which he showed continuity and change in the relevant discourses of the field of production of discourse; continuity and change in the discourses constructed in the Official Recontextualising Field of the state and in the Pedagogic Recontextualising Field *and* in the relation between these two fields; and continuity and change in the field of reproduction, that is, pedagogic practice. Cox was able to establish, through detailed analysis of documents and interviews of key personnel, the codes institutionalised by the two political parties in terms of their classification and framing values. He analysed the occupational composition of the CD, the Socialist Party and the Communist Party (CP), which made up the short-lived Popular Unity Party headed by Allende. The CD drew upon professional and white-collar groups fundamentally linked to the field of symbolic control. These groups were linked to the University and the Church. The CD also had an important base in the popular class. The party was reformist, both facilitating equal opportunity and attempting to improve equal acquisition *within* an unchanged organisational structure. The Popular Unity Party consisted of the Communist and the Socialist Parties who drew their support from different fields, the latter from the field of symbolic control and the former from the field of production. The Socialist Party drew on the class extremes of the intellectual middle class *and* the most impoverished members of the popular class.

The leaders of the Socialist Party had *no roots in production, only in discourse.* They were influenced by Cuba and the concept of the New Man (*sic*). They saw the educational system not so much as a relay for specialised knowledge and skills but as a means of institutionalising and relaying a new ideological collective consciousness. Thus they were concerned to de-classify the educational system and weaken *all* classification and framing, in particular between education and production (similar to the Chinese model). The CP were opposed (as were the CD) to this programme. The CP's strong base in production, rather than in the discourses of symbolic control, produced an educational programme which retained the classification of pedagogic discourses, CD framing, and the indispensability of education to production in the context of empowering the working class. The opposition between the Socialist Party's programme (*which brought the Church into fundamental opposition*) and the programme of the CP produced a crisis which played an independent role in the tragic end of Allende.

This is necessarily a very condensed summary which does scant justice to the complexity and subtlety of Cox's analysis. Yet in this context it is given much space. This is because Cox's study of the construction of modalities of official pedagogic discourse and their dependencies on sponsorship by agents drawn from different fields, production and symbolic control, having their social origins in different social class fractions, is a major exploration of the models outlined earlier. It is a matter of some interest that Cox's PhD was awarded in 1984 before, in fact, the model was published. Cox and Diaz's research are together good examples of the close relation between research needs and the integration and systematisation of the theory. The complex requirements of their research, involving an examination of different levels of the educational system, their relation to the state, the field dependencies and social class sponsorship, called for a unified theory for generating hypotheses, principles of descriptions and interpretations.

A major test of the theory arose out of the research of Swope (1992). His research was not, as all others reported in this paper, into official pedagogic discourse in state-regulated school education, but into informal pedagogic practices carried out *outside* the educational system and in no way connected to that system. Further, all previous research was on samples of students. Swope's research was on samples of adults with few or no educational qualifications. Finally the context of the pedagogic practices was essentially religious, concerned with the integration of religion and everyday life.

In Chile the Catholic Church was concerned to revivify and confirm the faith as a daily practice offering the means of coping with the problems and dilemmas of everyday life of the poor. To this end informal, voluntary groups of adults, members of local chapels, met regularly in small groups, led by an animator who was either elected by the group or appointed by the Church hierarchy. The animator lived in the same community as the members. These groups were known as Base Christian Communities (BCC). Swope was a fluent Spanish speaker, an American Jesuit, who knew Santiago well. He followed the model, analysing the field for the production of discourse, here the theological field, which contained two fundamental positions, Orthodox Conciliar, and two forms of Liberation Theology. Swope interviewed representatives of these positions and analysed the major texts. He assigned classificatory values in terms of the extent to which the theologies drew upon the social sciences, liberation theologies ($-C$), or only upon orthodox theological sources ($+C$). He attempted an examination of the recontextualising field in which he expected the pedagogic texts would be produced for use in the BCCs. *However, such a field did not exist.* The regulative agencies of the Catholic Church produced policy for the BCCs which implied a pedagogic practice and criteria for that practice but no specific pedagogic texts to guide BCC practice were produced. A very small number of liberation theology pedagogic texts were produced. The Catholic Church relied upon institutional control by the local Chapel over the BCC to ensure the legitimacy of its practice. Here was the first modification of the model: a pedagogic discourse without an explicit official recontextualising field. Swope studied the informal pedagogic practices in eight BCCs selected in terms of the degree of marginality of the members and their previous form of religious socialisation. He observed over 100 of the meetings of these BCCs and interviewed the members. The first problem here was identifying the discourse.

Pedagogic discourse in the model is given as ID/RD (instructional discourse embedded in a dominating regulation discourse). However, in Swope's study the instructional discourse was itself a religious discourse, concerned with showing the relationship between itself and the practical problems experienced by the marginal class members of the BCC. The informal pedagogic practice took the form of members bringing forward problems to be discussed in the light of religion under the guidance of the animator. The regulative discourse here was the *way in which* everyday problems were linked with religion and *what* problems were so linked. And this was a matter of the theological code of the BCC, Orthodox Conciliar, Liberation Theology in either of its modalities, political or cultural. These theological codes were identified by the extent to which secular discourses were embedded in the religious discourse. Thus Orthodox Conciliar is a strongly classified code which only refers to itself and thus produced in BCC talk little reference to secular discourses, e.g. politics, economics, domestic, whereas Liberation Theological codes are weakly classified and drew upon both the social sciences and community discourses. BCC talk here produced an interrelation between theological code and secular discourses (political, economic). The pedagogic practice of each BCC was classified according to the classification and framing values of the animator. It was then possible to see the relation between theological code, transmission code (pedagogic practice), degree of marginality of BCC members and previous forms of religious socialisation.

Swope's research (1992) shows that the theory can be applied to nonofficial pedagogic discourse, where the pedagogic context is informal, where no specially constructed texts are used and where members construct their own contents. Swope's research also shows the modifications required to meet the new demands of such a context.

Finally, we can mention a third piece of research carried out by Parlo Singh, who used the model to examine the institutionalising of computing as a specialised discourse in primary schools. Singh carried out an ethnographic study of the interactions of students with the computer in four primary schools in an Australian city, chosen because they were considered to be exemplary schools for teaching computing. Students were also interviewed in groups of three as were their teachers, software designers, computer consultants and local government administrators and inspectors. It was an exceptionally systematic study of the production of computing as a pedagogic discourse, together with its institutionalisation as a pedagogic practice. Singh was especially interested in the differential positioning, either by the teachers or by the boys, of the girls with respect to the computer, interactions with it and related competences. Singh's research is an imaginative application of the rules of the pedagogic device, production, recontextualising and evaluation, to the discursive interactions within the classroom over power to dominate the computer. She shows how the discourse realised a form of masculine discourse (technocratic masculinity) which served to relay and maintain privileging power for the boys whilst a form of domestic discourse was relayed to the girls. Positioning within this discourse of domesticity further removed the girls from gaining access to elaborated forms of computer-based problem skills. The boys were able to control production, recontextualising and evaluation, and so project an image of technocratic masculinity. Of considerable interest was that Singh showed the inadequacy of the theory to describe and interpret the process of production, fixing and canalising of desire and as a consequence the theory was unable to show how girls internalised voices to construct their own representation of the feminine (Singh, 1993).

Singh's research was the first to study how institutions (both of education and industry) constructed computing as a pedagogic discourse and how this discourse became a classroom practice. In this respect her study integrated macro and micro levels of analysis, and showed how both levels and their relation could be described by the theory.

OVERVIEW

Research

I have tried to show the close relation between the development of the theory and the research, from the first formulation of the analysis of the school, pupils' involvement and the shaping of these involvements by their family according to social background. This formulation showed the power of the school to change the pupil's involvements irrespective of family background. The concepts instrumental (transmission of skills) and expressive (conduct, character and manner) appear nearly 20 years later as the elements of pedagogic discourse; instructional discourse embedded in a dominating regulative discourse. In this way earlier concepts are reworked, made more general and so with stronger powers of description. The decisive change in the conceptual language came with the introduction of the concepts of classification and framing which replaced earlier formulations, and permitted a definition of code showing how power and control relations were transformed into modalities of communication.

At the beginning of this account I set out the conditions the theory must meet in terms of explicit rules for:

1. writing these principles of communication, their social construction and institutional bases;
2. their modalities of transmission and acquisition as pedagogic discourse and their institutional bases;
3. identifying the various realisations of members, groups/classes/agencies as cultural displays of a specialised consciousness.

To my mind there is a stronger basis for (1) and (2) than for (3). Here the major theoretical work and research has focused upon agents (their ideology, sponsorings and socialisation practices) who function in the fields of symbolic control or production (economy). Pupils' response to various modalities of pedagogic practice in the light of their family background also refers to (3).

The research reported here is almost entirely the published research of PhD students whom I have supervised; Maria Domingos's (now Morais; an ex-PhD student) research project is the exception. This complex and detailed project gave rise to a study of the local pedagogic practices and codes of families, and the achievements of the children in three pedagogic modalities. The project included not only a study of the achievement of the pupils across the three pedagogic practices but also an examination of the recognition and realisation rules of the pupils for *both* the instructional and regulative discourses. Domingos's (Morais) research is the most exhaustive and detailed study of the process of transmission/acquisition with respect to class, gender and race that I know. It is also a fundamental exploration of the usefulness of the theory.

I must make it quite clear how much I am indebted to this group of erstwhile postgraduates, now all colleagues. Not only were their particular researches exciting adventures within themselves but they made demands on the theory which led to developments and refinements. In particular, it is unlikely that strong principles of description would have been possible without their research. Their research created further theoretical issues. For example Daniels's research showed that whereas realisation rules were broadly related to the modality of pedagogic practice, recognition rules were unrelated. Faria's research hinted strongly that the forms of self-reference in the field of symbolic control (members of the university) were metaphoric, whereas the forms of self-reference in the field of production (managers of a large brewery) were metonymic. Cook-Gumperz showed that the transmission of personal control by mothers to their children was more effective than the transmission of positional control by mothers to their children. Holland's research showed that the greatest difference between boys' and girls' classification of gender relations occurred in the case of boys and girls whose parents functioned in the field of production (economy). Here the boys held the strongest classification, whereas the girls were relatively weak. Swope's research showed the modifications necessary when the theory was applied to informal pedagogic religious practice involving adults. Singh's research showed the need to extend the theory to include the conceptualising of gendered desire.

An account of the development, over a number of years, of a theory always takes on a rationality not obviously observable at the time. In my case sections of the theory (usually without strong principles of description) always preceded the research. Postgraduates saw the relevance for their particular research concerns. In this way what bits of the theory were developed was up to a point and, perhaps, very much the point, depended upon who knocked on the door with what problem. In general, it seemed that who came depended on the last paper which had been written.

It may be considered a little strange that the only research I have reported is research with which I have been closely connected. This is not because other research does not exist. For example Tyler (1984) carried out a fascinating application of classification and framing to industrial organisations. However, the research reported here is, of its nature, more systematic, detailed and extensive. It is, perhaps, difficult for other researchers because the papers are usually (but not always) highly formal, concerned to outline models, rather than to provide explicit guides for specific pieces of empirical research. As can be seen here this takes place in the context of specific research. It would therefore be necessary to read the publications reported here to get the nuts and bolts of the application of the models. And this, unfortunately, is never or rarely done by commentators or recontextualisers as evidenced by the following as an example:

> To reproduce in scholarly discourse the fetishizing of the legitimate language which actually takes place in society, one only has to follow the example of Basil Bernstein, who describes the properties of the 'elaborated code' without relating this social product to the social condition of its production and reproduction, or even, as one might expect from the sociology of education, to its academic conditions. (Bourdieu, 1991, p. 53)

Perhaps the above quotation should be compared with apparently Bourdieu's own views on language and education.

> Language, however, is not simply a vehicle for thought. Besides a vocabulary more or less rich, it provides a syntax—in other words, a system of categories, more or less complex. The ability to decode and to manipulate complex structures logical or aesthetic would appear to depend directly on the complexity of the language first spoken in the family environment, which always passes on some of its features to the language acquired at school. (Bourdieu, Passeron and de St. Martin, 1994, p. 40)

Although originally published much earlier in 1965 the authors state, 'But the main finding and central arguments of the study, concerning above all, the role of language and linguistic misunderstanding in the educational process—retain their significance to-day' (preface).

There also seems to be something of a hiatus between the theory as it appears in textbooks and commentaries and the theory itself, and perhaps even more of a hiatus between what appears in textbooks and commentaries and the range of research to which the theory has given rise. In part this arises from the problem of publication inasmuch as it is difficult to publish books composed of empirical research organised in relation to an informing theory. This creates even greater difficulty for a theory where the empirical research crosses disciplines and thus publication outlets.

Finally the research called for by the models is far more extensive than has been carried out and more repetition of existing research is required. The theory, and the contributions of my colleagues with whom I have worked, show its relevance to a sociology of education and perhaps to the broader issue of symbolic control as both a cultural relay and a means of its change.

Methodology

It might be useful finally to try to examine the methodology which underlies the research projects I have outlined. I must point out that this is my view of this methodology and may not in all cases be the views of those who carried out the research. Neither may it be the case that initial work within this methodology was followed later by its further acceptance. I therefore take responsibility for this methodology and for the analysis of the research projects discussed here in its light.

Basically the theory addresses forms of symbolic control as regulators of cultural reproduction and of its change. In particular it addresses those forms of symbolic control institutionalised formally or informally as pedagogic practices. It seeks to understand how such practices, directly or indirectly, relay power and control and, more specifically, relay the distribution of power and principles of control which are a function of class relations. Thus there are two elements: one modelling agencies, agents, practices and specialised forms of communication, so as to reveal varieties or modalities of regulation and their organising principles as cultural relays; the second showing how such principles are themselves, directly or indirectly, media for the reproduction of class relations. It is important to separate these two elements because it is possible for the theory to be more successful in one case than the other. Of the two elements, clearly the first, the organising principle regulating the form, contents and practices of forms of symbolic control, is logically prior even though in any one analysis the two elements are intertwined. Perhaps as the theory developed I became more interested in the more general question of symbolic controls than in their class specifics.

It is often said that the theory works by producing opposing dichotomies in which each side functions as an ideal type: elaborated/restricted, positional/personal, stratified/differentiated, open/closed, visible/invisible, collection or serial/integrated. That these are opposing forms (models) I certainly agree. That they are ideal types I certainly disagree. Classically the ideal type is constructed by assembling in a model *a number of features* abstracted from a phenomenon in such a way as to provide a means of identifying the presence or absence of the phenomenon, and a means of analysing the 'workings' of the phenomenon from an analysis of the assembly of its features. Ideal types constructed in this way cannot *generate* other than themselves. They are not constructed by a principle which generates sets of relations of which any one form may be only *one of the forms* the principle may regulate. Thus if we take the *early* dichotomies positional/personal, stratified/differentiated, open/closed, then these dichotomies all can be generated on the basis of *boundary rules: things must be kept apart: things must be put together.* How things are kept apart, how things are put together depends upon the formulation of the organising principle to generate a range of forms. We can ask further questions: In whose interests is the apartness of things? In whose interests is the putting together of things? These questions immediately raise the issue of the relation of power relations to boundaries. Whose power is maintained and relayed by whose boundaries?

I would certainly agree that the organising principles underlying the early opposing dichotomous forms were limited in their generating power, but the forms are not ideal types. Their generating grammar is very weak. However, I would argue that the powers of this grammar increased somewhat, by their replacement by the more general concepts of classification and framing, together with a stronger specification of their concepts.

This leads, naturally, on to the tradition to which the theory belongs. I myself have always referred to, even emphasised, its Durkheimian roots. First because this is clearly true, and second because in Britain, and particularly in the United States, Durkheim is seen as a conservative, functionalist positivist. This view I believe had its origins in the U.S.A. where 'Suicide' was recontextualised, together with the 'Rules', as the legitimator of American empiricism and of subcultural theory. Parsons' patterned variables were no more than a reworking of the concepts of mechanical and organic solidarity. I, and this is obvious, drew upon the works of Durkheim. However, perhaps a little perversely, I unashamedly waved the Durkheim banner. But it is the linking of Durkheim with structuralism, particularly forms of structuralism originating in linguistics, which had, I believe, the strongest influence upon the *form* the theorising took. Atkinson (1985) identified the theoretical form as structuralist. This view has been taken up by others, more recently by Sadovnik (1991). Certainly I have the greatest respect for Atkinson's extensive commentary, and particularly for his insights, which have on occasion anticipated the development of the theory. But I am not sure whether this identification as structuralist is not a little too excluding of other influences.

It is the case that there is a strong drive 'to discover the system of rules which govern our conceptual space', 'to make explicit the conventions which govern the production of meaning' (Lyons, 1973, pp. 28, 35). This appears to presuppose that there is a system (as a linguistic system of finite choices): that this system is external to us with a life of its own, regulating us, rather than us regulating it; that the conventions by means of which we read the signs of others, they of us and us of ourselves, trap us as we tacitly use them. Such readings of this theory are entirely erroneous and arise because of the too ready, perhaps overwhelming, definition of the theory as structuralist. Change, in the theory, arises out of two origins. One is intrinsic to the acquisition of codes and the other is extrinsic to this acquisition. As codes are acquired which establish, or rather attempt to establish, a particular modality of order and perhaps exclude others in so doing, at the same time *the potential of disordering* is also acquired. Further, extrinsic to individual acquisition is the context. The institutional structure, relations between social groups, the play of power relations which position and place in opposition social groups (be these classes, race, gender, region, religion) create the struggle to dominate and change codes.

This side of the thesis points away from *determining* systems and towards other influences. At the micro level it is made explicit, although sometimes missed by some commentators, that 'message' can change 'voice'. That is, that the outcome of framing in interaction has the potential for changing classification. Finally, it is worth pointing out that the theory of ideology I have found the most congenial, in the sense of resonating with the problems addressed, is that of Althusser: the imaginary subject.

Perhaps the work on pedagogic discourse makes the structuralist identifications even less exhaustive as a defining category. The modelling of the construction and relaying of this discourse through processes of recontextualising points to *both* the openness of discourse and the attempts to close it by regulating its legitimate shaping and reading. There is an excellent discussion of the relations between this theory and the grand theorising of Foucault in Tyler's (1988) book.

In a sense the label given is a function of the time in which it is given. Even more it is a function of some commentators who regard the last paper they have read as either the only paper or more usually the terminating paper. They seem to ignore that a paper is part of a development leading to a new development. It has always seemed to me that one's allegiance is less to an approach and more to exploring a problematic.

I would like to narrow this general discussion of methodology to the more specific issues of the relation between theory and research. It seems to me that when I analyse this relation in terms of the account given here there is a formal model underlying the activity.

1. The theory produces models. These models generate modalities of control on the basis of a set of rules which specialise agencies, agents, practices, communication, their interrelations, external relations and consequences. The consequences then function as hypotheses about the possible performances to which the model can give rise.

2. When the model is referred to something other than itself, then it should be able to provide the principles which will identify that something as falling within the specification of the model and identifying explicitly what does not so fall. Such principles we can call the *recognition rules* for identifying an external relevant something. However, this something will always generate, or have the capacity to generate, greater ranges of information than the model calls for. The *realisation rules* of the model regulate the descriptions of the something. They transform the information the something does, or can put out, into data *relevant* to the model. However, if the realisation rules produce descriptions which are limited to transforming only that in-

formation into data *which at that time* appears consonant with the model, then the model can never change and the whole process is circular. Nothing therefore exists outside the model.

3. Thus the interface between the realisation rules of the model and the information the something does, or can produce, is vital. There then must be a discursive gap between the rules specified by the model *and* the realisation rules for transforming the information produced by the something. This gap enables the integrity of the something to exist in its own right, it enables the something, so to speak, to announce itself, it enables the something to re-describe the descriptions of the model's own realisation rules and so change.

4. Thus the principles of descriptions of the something external to the model must go beyond the realisation rules *internal* to the model.

5. Clearly such principles of description can never exhaust the information the something can produce. First, because what it *can* produce may not even be known to the something, let alone to anyone else, and second, because principles of description of the something become part of the information whereby another has access to the something. However, there are methods of creating descriptions which close off or open up a dialogue between the model and something external to it.

6. Theory encompasses, in the end, everything from (1) to (4). The question is not that it so encompasses it but *how* it does so.

Finally it is relevant to point out that we all have models—some are more explicit than others; we all use principles of descriptions—again some are more explicit than others; we all set up criteria to enable us both to produce for ourselves, and to read the descriptions of others—again these criteria may vary in their explicitness. Some of our principles may be quantitative whilst others are qualitative. But the problem is fundamentally the same. In the end whose voice is speaking? My preference is to be as explicit as possible. Then at least my voice may be deconstructed.

NOTES

1. See Gee (1990): 'Bernstein states his distinction somewhat poorly and his work has been badly misused. Nevertheless, his work on the sociology of education (though not on dialects) is essential reading for educators.' I might add here that I have explicitly stated since 1959 that sociolinguistic codes are independent of dialect!

2. This was essentially the view of Dittmar (1976 English translation, 1973 German edition) who believed the theory was a product of what he called bourgeois sociology celebrating the middle class and constituting the working class as a homogeneous deficit group. It was then very perplexing to receive a letter (10 December 1984) in which Dittmar wrote, 'As you know linguists often ask for an adequate sociological model of explana-

tion. Yours seems to me a crucial contribution to this issue'. Even more perplexing is that
he adds 'I do not hope that my book of 1973 [original German edition] will be a reason for
you not to come. At that time I wrote it from the point of view of the student movement.
Since then my opinions have changed and are now more differentiated'. It is unusual to
have evidence of a self-conscious willful recontextualising. I might add that more recent
editions and translations of Dittmar's work are unaffected by his apparently revised evaluations.

   3. Perhaps the most extraordinary criticisms are those made in a textbook *Sociological Interpretations of Education* (1985). The authors, Blackledge and Hunt, state: 'However it is only by rigorous critical examination that some of the fundamentally important
ideas of Bernstein can be clarified and made useful' (p. 61). Here it is claimed that the theory is unworkable without the rigorous therapy of recontextualisers. It is worthwhile looking at their criticism. Blackledge and Hunt, whose evaluation is wholly confined to *Class,
Codes and Control*, vol. III (Bernstein, 1977), complain about the original definition of
classification (1971) in terms of relations between contents, and propose that the concept
should be redefined in terms of relations between categories (p. 58). But I had already introduced the change on p. 176 of the book they cite: 'Now we can use the concept of classification to refer to the relations between categories whether these categories are agencies
(schools of various kinds), agents (teachers) or acquirers'. Another of their 'clarifications'
is to suggest that classification strength may vary between areas: 'Unfortunately Bernstein
does not go into these possibilities' (p. 58). Yet on p. 180 I wrote, 'In contemporary
schools, particularly comprehensive schools, as we have indicated in chapter 5, we are
likely to find a range of codes (Bernstein, 1977). Further, Blackledge and Hunt state that
I failed to note that weakening of classification and framing would be likely to occur with
younger students and the 'less able'. But the expectation is explicit on pp. 215 and 229 of
Class, Codes and Control, vol. III. Blackledge and Hunt also recycle errors from other
textbooks. A good example is their view that what they call 'positional socialisation' is
linked to a restricted code, whereas 'personal socialisation' is linked to an elaborated code
(p. 45). This is despite the text and diagram given on pp. 160 and 164 of *Class, Codes and
Control*, vol. III, which show clearly that specific codes and family structures can vary independently. Perhaps most perplexing is Blackledge and Hunt's comment that I did not see
an implication of what these authors call 'the erosion of specialist groups' which might indicate a trend to mechanical solidarity (p. 49), yet on p. 52 of their book, they note that this
trend is adumbrated in the formulation of the paradox of codes (*Class, Codes and Control*,
vol. III, p. 110). Unfortunately textbooks serve more and more as the substitute for reading original texts and this does not only hold for students. There are so many examples of
recontextualising strategies of textbook writers that it is difficult to select without appearing to be unappreciative of the many absences. The particular illustration which follows
should not therefore be given any superior significance. Demaine's textbook is entitled
Contemporary Theories in the Sociology of Education (1981) and pp. 35–40 are devoted
to a discussion of my work. However, the 'exposition' of the theory is contained within
one paragraph and the rest is essentially a discussion of the deficit position with respect to
a paper published in *New Society* in 1969, 'Education cannot compensate for society'. Demaine argues that my thesis involves no 'elaborated conception of 'class' ' (p. 39), and that
'The working-class, like the middle-class has no internal differentiation in Bernstein's conception' (p. 39). Yet in the references cited by Demaine there is a discussion of the differentiation within the middle class in terms of the oppositions between the old and the new

middle class, and a differentiation within the new middle class which gives rise to ideological conflicts (Bernstein, 1975, p. 128). Equally, in the case of the working class, differentiation was discussed in terms of family types and modes of communication (Bernstein, 1971, p. 161; Bernstein and Brandis, 1974). Nowhere in Demaine's exposition is there any account of the development of the code theory to show the class regulation of official pedagogic practices. Indeed, according to Demaine, 'Bernstein's comments on provision cannot be deduced from his theory on codes' (p. 40). Clearly not, if this theory is absent from the discussion.

APPENDIX

It is relevant to mention briefly the research undertaken by Hasan and her colleagues on class differences in ongoing talk between mothers and children and class differences in joint book reading with children.

Williams (1995) analysed ongoing talk during interaction in joint book reading between mothers and children. The sample consisted of two groups classified in terms of the degree of autonomy of their occupations, i.e. a low-autonomy and a high-autonomy group. These groups closely correspond to a manual group and a group of major and minor professions. Williams used a delicate theory of description derived from Halliday's systematic functional grammar and Hasan's theory of semantic variation. Williams (1995, p. 289) concludes:

> The family linguistic interaction does appear to vary as a function of location of participants within social class locations. Though there are many similarities in the practices of the two groups—in extent of reading, the enthusiasm with which both mothers and children talk about object texts and in the general sense that children are 'apprenticed' to literate practice within their families—what they are apprenticed to is from another perspective, quite different.

Williams interprets this difference according to the theory presented in *Class, Codes and Control*, vol. IV (Bernstein, 1990).

Over the past decade Hasan has developed a theory of semantic variation which looks back to the sociolinguistic code theory of the 1960s and 1970s and forward to a much more integrated, systematic and perhaps more general theory. Hasan followed up my early research with a vastly superior empirical study producing a corpus of 20,000 messages of spontaneous conversations between mothers and their children at home. Over 100 hours of naturally occurring dialogue between 24 mothers and their children were recorded. This sample consisted of 12 upper professionals (termed high-autonomy professionals or HAP) and 12 lower professionals (termed lower-autonomy professionals or LAP, e.g. truck driver, factory worker). Hasan created context-specific networks based on Halliday's systemic functional grammar to describe the speech (Halliday, 1985).

On the basis of the questions and answers arising out of spontaneous mother-child interaction Hasan states:

> The mothers (LAP) who do not score high on PCI [an index of the differentiation of the two social class groups] are mothers who find the primary source of reflexive relation in the shared experience of practical living: for them the basis for assuming knowledge of the other lies not in the verbally revealed selves but in the shared patterns of practical existence; what creates and maintains reflexivity for these mothers is not talk as such it is the experience of living and sharing contexts as members of a collectivity. If the former group of mothers (HAP) subscribe to the principle of individuation, acting as if hardly anything can be taken for granted between persons then the latter group (those who do not score high on PCI) subscribe to the principle of naturalised reflexivity acting as if most things can be taken for granted. . . . These are two different orientations to what is relevant. (Hasan, 1991, pp. 103–4)

Hasan also examined her data to see whether there were differences in the way mothers controlled their children. She constructed a specific network of choices to examine what she calls sociosemantic variations in maternal control. The total corpus of all the speech yields over 20,000 messages, which were sampled for control messages. Hasan summarises her conclusions as follows:

> The HAP child is thus sociosemiotically produced as an individual with his (*sic*) own unique subjectivity the sharing of which is in his (*sic*) personal discretion. This granting of unique individuality, the masking of maternal power and the granting of discretion combine to produce a sense of the world under one's own control, where the external control on the child's actions is rendered invisible, its motivation being presented as either above human manipulation (reasons are logical, guided by 'unavoidable rational principles') or as self-regulated, the child has discretion and own judgement. The LAP child is sociosemantically produced as someone whose experience of the collectivity is an aspect of his (*sic*) subjectivity the sharing of which does not depend on his personal discretion: the control on the child's actions is quite visibly external. The power that controls his (*sic*) actions is derived from the speaker's social position *vis-à-vis* the addressee. But this position is not unique to the speaker: it is the condition of being a mother—a status recognised by the community—which gives the speaker greater discretion than the child. (Hasan, 1993, p. 99; see also Hasan, 1992)

The findings and conclusions of Hasan's empirical research based on spontaneous talk between mothers and children, realising an unusually large speech sample, are wholly derivable from the model of control presented in Bernstein (1971, 1975). The findings on the study of both questions and answers, and maternal control are similar to the research carried out under my direction (Cook-Gumperz, 1973; Robinson, 1973). However, these studies were not of spontaneous, naturally occurring talk but were based on interviews of mothers in which they *reported* how they interacted with their children. Hasan and her colleagues have taken great care to avoid their research being recontextualised a supporting a deficit position. Whilst her general theory of semantic variation ought to defeat such a positioning of her work, it is very probable that this will not be the case, despite:

> If the views presented here are accepted, it would seem a tension exists in our society: middle-class practices are geared to maintaining hierarchy by making subjugation invisible: working-class practices are geared to challenge subjugation. And it is here that we can highlight the function of unquestioned belief in the superiority of middle-class practices. (Hasan, 1993, p. 101)

Chapter 7

Research and Languages of Description

INTRODUCTION

In the conclusion of the last chapter I discussed very briefly the methodology underlying the research. Since writing that chapter, some two years ago, I have developed the concept of 'languages of description' and generalised the earlier position. What follows here is, I hope, a less dense and fuller exposition. There is some repetition of the illustration of network analysis given in the previous chapter, but the network, or rather a subsystem, is given in much greater detail. It also gives me an opportunity to show empirically how a discursive gap may be introduced between the descriptions generated by a model and the potential enactments of the described. In this way the described can change its own positioning, or in the appropriate language of today, enter into a reflexive relation. I have set this discussion in the contemporary context of the new research economy.

THE RESEARCH ECONOMY

Before coming to a discussion of the title for this chapter, 'Research and Languages of Description', I do not think it would be untoward, it is perhaps even necessary, to place research into the new contemporary context. I would like, then, to look at the new official research economy and its relation to methods of research. Research Methods have been foregrounded since the late 1980s under the influence of the Economic and Social Research Committee (ESRC). Studentships have been tied to what has been dogmatically defined as effective research training. HEFCE (Higher Education Funding Council Executive) has also been a strong influence in buttressing the demands of the ESRC. It is also likely that the new funding economy contributes to the positioning of methods of inquiry, which in turn influences research training. The new funding economy puts competitive pressure on applicants, to promise more with fewer resources. Under such a regime, time is at a premium and this affects how data are collected, and especially the mode of analysis and so the report. Government developmental contract research may circumscribe the research by a tight sample or design frame. The redesigning of the PhD as a driving license rather than a license to explore has incalculable consequences for methods as the student and staff struggle to complete within the specified period.

This is not a culture which encourages either theoretical innovation or methodological disturbances. The field of empirical research is less likely to be a springboard for developing theory, languages of description, but more likely a field of routinised procedures and quick fixes. In this context the move to qualitative procedures does not bode well for their appropriate developments. Qualitative procedures usually generate complex, multi-layered and extensive texts, for which there are rarely ready-made quick fix descriptors. It is rare to find much thought about the description prior to the data collection. Textbooks are replete with how one approaches either the field or informants, the responsibility of the researcher to the researched but are sometimes vague about the problem of description. It is sometimes more a moral position than data positioning. But respect for the informants requires something more than introspection, on the one hand, or telling quotations on the other. Yet the exigencies of the official research economy facilitate, if not encourage, such practices. This in turn leads some to question the very approach. Perhaps we should view research procedures from a wider perspective than the specific particularities of the research.

If one looks at research method courses, research students are introduced to what could be called a botanical garden (nicely domesticated and epistemologically labelled) or perhaps such courses resemble a menu. But the menu is abstracted from the kitchen, the menu is abstracted from the imagination responsible for the concept of the dish. The research menu renders this concept invisible and offers instead a set of technological choices. The determinant of the choice of procedure may lie less in the necessity of the research, but more in the economic context in which the research is positioned.

LANGUAGES OF DESCRIPTION

I now want to turn to the question of languages of description. Briefly, a language of description is a translation device whereby one language is transformed into another. We can distinguish between internal and external languages of description. The internal language of description refers to the syntax whereby a conceptual language is created. The external language of description refers to the syntax whereby the internal language can describe something other than itself. Sociological internal languages of description may have an apparently strong syntax but usually have a weak external language of description. Research students soon find this out. For example, if we take a popular concept, *habitus,* whilst it may solve certain epistemological problems of agency and structure, it is only known or recognised by its apparent outcomes. Habitus is described in terms of what it gives rise to, and brings, or does not bring about. It is described in terms of the external underlying analogies it regulates. But it is not described with reference to the particular ordering principles or strategies, which give rise to the formation of a particular habitus. The formation of the internal structure of the particular habitus, the mode of its specific acquisition, which gives it its specificity, is not described. How it comes to be is not part of the description, only what it does. There is no description of its specific formation. We cannot therefore replace habitus by X, that is by the description of its internal relation. Habitus is known by its output, not by its input. Putting it crudely, there is no necessity between the concept or what counts as a realisation. This means that once an illustration is challenged or a correlation, or an alternative interpretation given, there are problems.

This does not mean that we abandon such a conceptual syntax but we should recognise it for what it is, something good to think with, or about. It may alert us to new possibilities, new assemblies, new ways of seeing relationships. In a sense, such a conceptual array functions as a metaphor and their manifestation could be considered metonyms. Perhaps we have here what we could call M-M (Metaphor/Metonym) conceptual languages of description.

So far I have referred to internal syntaxes as languages of description (L^1). I now want to spend more time on external languages of description (L^2) and then finally on the relation between the two. Internal languages are the condition for constructing invisibles, external languages are the means of making those invisibles visible, in a non-circular way.

Sometimes languages of description are confused with content analysis. But content analysis seems to suggest that something bounded is taken apart, searched and inspected rather than subject to a process of translation. I think from this point of view it is misleading to confound content analysis with a language of description. Often content analysis is concerned with apparently self-announcing contents. I would rather say that principles of description construct what is to count as empirical relations and translate those relations into conceptual relations. A language of description constructs what is to count as an empirical referent, how such referents relate to each other to produce a specific text and translate these referential relations into theoretical objects or potential theoretical objects. In other words, the external language of description (L^2) is the means by which the internal language (L^1) is activated as a reading device or vice versa. A language of description, from this point of view, consists of rules for the unambiguous recognition of what is to count as a relevant empirical relation, and rules (realisation rules) for reading the manifest contingent enactments of those empirical relations. Principles of description, then, consist of recognition and realisation rules. Let us leave on one side where those rules come from for the moment. The rules may be derived from a strong internal language of description. In this case, the rules are the means whereby this model can interact with something other than itself. However, often the researcher does not have a strong internal language of description (L^1) but rather, orientations, condensed intimations, metaphors which point to relevancies.

MODES OF ENQUIRY

I want now to give some examples of opposing modes of enquiry to illustrate what I have been saying. In the first example I shall give there does not appear to be a language of description or rather the language appears to be entirely un-problematic. This is so because what is to be described is less a performance, but more a *context* which releases the performance. The identification of what counts as a performance is unambiguous, or should be, for the recognition of the performance is a function of the design of the context, that is, a problem of its description. This is the classical experimental context. Variables are tightly controlled, the performance usually leads to statistical description. The imagination lies in the design of the context. Here we can say that the language of description (L^2) is embedded in the context it created. The text produced by the 'subject' is less the response but more the created context. We can abstract the following from this example: from the point of view of the researcher, it is the realisation rule which is the problem, for it is the realisation rule which is responsible for the design of the context. The trick here is to design a context that removes ambiguity from the response to it, that is to design a context which creates an unambiguous recognition of the response to it. The realisation rule here minimises issues of the description for the performance. However, from the point of view of the performer, it is crucial for that performer to read the context correctly. The performer must possess the recognition rule for, without it, the unambiguous response will not occur. In this mode of enquiry the researcher has the realisation rule that generates the context and the recognition rule is embedded in the realisation rule.

Now the extreme opposite is where performers have the recognition and realisation rules *and* an implicit, tacit model from which these rules are derived. The game here is for the researcher to find the rules and the model. This we could call the ethnographic position. In the classical ethnographic position, the researcher has first to learn the language of the group or society and know the rules of its contextual use. From here on, the researcher is developing reading rules (of recognition and realisation) to grasp how members construct their various texts or manage their contexts. The researcher here is modelling the members' recognition and realisation rules, or the strategies of practice those rules constrain. We could call this description II. The problem is to construct the tacit model. If the researcher fails to construct the model s/he is marooned in the specific contexts and their enactments, and is in no position to appreciate the potential of the meanings of that particular culture, and thus its possible enactments. Without a model, the researcher can never know what could have been and was not. Without a model, the researcher only knows what his/her informants have enacted. S/he is fixed in their temporal and spatial frames. But the model the ethnographer constructs to grasp the potential semantic of the culture will not be only the tacit models of the members. Such models enable members to work the culture but not to know its workings. Cultures are not transparent in this respect. The models that attempt to show the transparency of the culture are constructed by the internal language of description (L^1). This language must meet at least two requirements. The external language of description (L^2) must be derived from the internal language, otherwise it will not be possible for this internal language to describe anything except itself. Secondly the descriptions of the internal language should be capable of going beyond the descriptions created by members.

However, the real problem is that the two processes of constructing description are not discrete in time. They are going on together, perhaps one more explicit than the other. Description II (the external) is rarely free of description I (the internal), but I believe we must struggle to keep L^2 as free as possible. This struggle is for pragmatic and ethical reasons. It is pragmatic, because unless there is some freedom, description I (the internal) will never change. It is ethical, for without some freedom the researched can never re-describe the descriptions made of them.

From this point of view L^2, the external description, irrespective of the translation demands of L^1 (the model), must as far as possible, be permeable to the potential enactments of those being described. Otherwise their voice will be silenced. From this point of view, L^2, the external description, becomes an interpretative interface, or the means of dialogue between the agency of enactments and the generating of the internal language of the model.

AN ILLUSTRATION

I now would like to turn to an empirical illustration of the previous discussion of languages of description. During the extensive research undertaken by the Sociological Research Unit, the earlier stages required a conceptualising of forms of familial control of children to show variations in the specialisation of communication and in their contexts. A somewhat primitive distinction was made between positional and personal focused family structures and their implications for the division of labour, and the differential specialisation of communication and contexts were made explicit (Bernstein, 1971a). In the language of the theory today, modalities of control would be described in terms of variations in the values of classification and framing, but these concepts were not available then. The basic difference between positional and personal family types lay in the way boundaries were constructed, maintained and relayed. From the 'theory' of family types, an abstract model of control relations between mothers and children was derived. The model had two independent axes. One axis referred to the focus of the controller on the controlled. The second axis referred to the discretion accorded by the controller to the controlled in the context of control (and the discretion the controlled was able to achieve). The focus of the controller could be on very general attributes of the controlled, attributes the controlled shared with all those holding a common status of age, gender, race, child, pupil, peer group member or common age relation parent–child, teacher–pupil, older–younger. The focus of control need not fall upon general attributes of the controlled but upon particular attributes. Where the focus was upon general attributes, the control was of the positional type and where the focus was upon particular attributes, the control was of the personal type. Here the controller would be sensitive to the particular history of the controlled, to their particular motivations, intentions, aspirations and to the consequences for the controlled which were particular to them. With respect to the second axis, the discretion accorded to the child or which the child gained, could be low or high. Where discretion was low, the child was accorded little discursive space by the controller's communication. Where

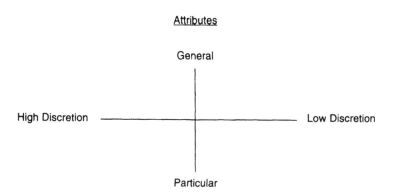

Figure 7.1

discretion was high, the child was accorded a much greater discursive space for communication by the controller.

The axis yielded the above highly abstract modes of control and differential specialisation of communication and expected consequences. The theory and derived model could be seen as language I (or L^1). What of language II (or L^2), the device for transforming information about control provided by mothers (or *observed*) into theoretically relevant data? This language must be capable of enabling the researched to redescribe the descriptions expected by the theory. The data available were reports of mothers as to how they would control their own child in six hypothetical contexts. However, from the point of view of Figure 7.1, the nature of the data is irrelevant. It could just as well have arisen out of observations of ongoing interactions between mother and child, in which case, the redescription of the speech would have to be supplemented by description of the context and paralinguistic.

The first step was to ignore the theory and model, and concentrate on the semantics of the control relation; that is to consider the *potential* semantic such a context would generate. Thus, if this potential could be articulated as a space of specialised semantic possibility, then it would be possible to see how different mother/child dyads realised different possibilities of this space, i.e. their repertoires. This raises the issue of 'how does one know when one has successfully modelled the specialised possibilities of control semantics?' The answer is that one can never know. But one of the outcomes of research should be that the potential of this space is better known. In our case we conceived of the control semantic as a set of independent subsystems. Each subsystem realised a set of

Table 7.1: The subsystems displayed in no order of importance

Rationale Subsystem	contains choices which realise types of justification for the control or its absence.
Avoidance Subsystem	contains choices which realise different strategies of the controller to avoid the necessity of applying control.
Concessional Subsystem	contains choices which pre-suppose according to the control powers of negotiation or powers the control has gained.
Evaluation Subsystem	contains choices of different types of punishment and direction of responsibility.
Appeal Subsystem	contains choices offering different grounds for a change in conduct of the controlled.
Motivational Subsystem	contains choices realising different dispositional states of the controller and controlled.
Reparative Subsystem	contains choices realising different strategies for restoring the relation damaged or potentially damaged by the conduct of the controlled or the form of control. (See Appendix for example.)

binary choices. It would be possible to see which controllers preferred which subsystems, and, within subsystems, which choices were preferred, in what contexts of control. At a greater level of delicacy, it would be possible to determine the order in which different subsystems were entered in different contexts. Of course the claim is not made that these subsystems exhaust the potential semantic of control. They merely illustrate a procedure. Crucial to the procedure is that it is constructed independently of the L^1, that is, independent of the theory and the derived model. The question is how does this L^2 relate to L^1, or, alternatively, how can L^1 read L^2?

DISCUSSION

Now, clearly, the theory is more general in its scope than the specific control context, although specific realisations of that context most certainly are relevant to the theory. The formal model derived from the theory regulates the *initial* conceptualisation of the choice points within relevant subsystems and so the formulation of the expected sentences/observations. The theory may be strong with respect to expected variations within one subsystem, but only able to specify whether one subsystem is entered or not with respect to other subsystems. In the latter case, the theory gives no purchase on the choices that will be made within this subsystem. In the *process* of the interaction between the initial L^2 and the information it is translating/transforming, choices within a subsystem may lead to extension of that subsystem, depending on how exhaustive the translation is to be of the original information. Thus a fully developed L^2 will:

1. Specify the potential semantic of the structuring of a specific discursive space (subsystem specification).
2. Enable entry or otherwise to particular subsystems. Choices within a particular subsystem can be 'read' by L^1, mediated by the model.
3. Create interaction with the information (sentences, observations) and may generate extensions of the network within a subsystem or lead to the development of a new subsystem. Subsystem here refers to an extension of the subsystems defining the discursive space. Such addition should only occur when it is not possible to raise the generality of an existing subsystem.

Thus the limits of L^1 may be revealed or alternatively the restriction of its assumptions. L^2 is both independent of L^1 and yet relates to it.

There is a question of the reliability of this translation/transformation process. L^2 is the process whereby translation/transformation occurs. But how reliable is the translator? How reliable is the person operating L^2? Clearly, as with any language which, after all, is a contrastive system, the contrasts should be as unambiguous and explicit as possible, otherwise choice points will not be recognised, in which case the language cannot be acquired. Thus in the case of L^2 the paradigmatic features (the set of subsystems) and the syntagmatic features (networks within a subsystem) must be unambiguous and explicitly defined. However, although this is a necessary condition, it is not a sufficient condition to achieve reliability of the translator.

The translator is faced with a problem of second language acquisition, and effective acquisition cannot be acquired solely on the basis of knowledge of the contrastive rules. The translator must be able to recognise and formulate acceptable sentences in L^2. This can be achieved by extensive opportunities for both *encoding* and decoding with a competent speaker of L^2. In this way the translator will get a 'feel' of the language and develop that intuitive grasp without which acquisition is not possible. For knowledge of the rules is not enough.

The translator's competence can be examined, as in the case of any language. Checks can be carried out to see how well formed her/his sentences are, within and across subsystems, on request for examples. In this way it is possible to see whether the translator can make up, imaging acceptable sentences which may not occur in the actual translation. Checks can be carried out to see whether competent decoding has been achieved. The advantage of such checks is that they will reveal both the strengths and weaknesses of the translator's competence with respect to any subsystem and choices within a subsystem.

Perhaps the most elaborate, systematic and exhaustive networks (L^2) have been constructed by Hasan on the basis of sociolinguistic models. Dowling (following Bernstein, 1981, 1986, 1995) constructed a language of description for the translation of maths textbook into sociological discourse. Whereas Hasan's research dealt with open texts, ongoing talk between mothers and children, teachers and children. Dowling was concerned with closed texts. Bliss, Monk and Ogborn (1988) edited a book containing papers illustrating network analysis influenced by Halliday, yet very few of the papers show the relation between L^1 and L^2 as given here.

CONCLUSION

In conclusion, I have tried to sketch an approach which places, in the centre of research, the role of description, especially in the case of ongoing 'open' contexts, an approach which accords to the researched power of redescription. The illustration of this approach shows how a language of description, L^2, goes beyond a theory and its derived model, L^1, and opens the possibility of showing both the strengths and limits of a theory.

Finally to return to the opening remarks on the new research economy, the approach outlined here probably falls well outside its budget. It is very time consuming. However, respect for the researched and the enterprise does not come cheap.

APPENDIX ON SUBSYSTEM NETWORKS

I will give here an example of the network we constructed (Bernstein and Cook-Gumperz, 1973) to code choices within the Rationale Subsystems arising out of information given by 120 working-class mothers and 116 middle-class mothers when answering six questions about how they would act towards their five-year-old boy or girl where they thought the conduct of the child required some response on their part. To be coded in this subsystem the mother, spontaneously, must offer a rationale for her response.

We give the network below:

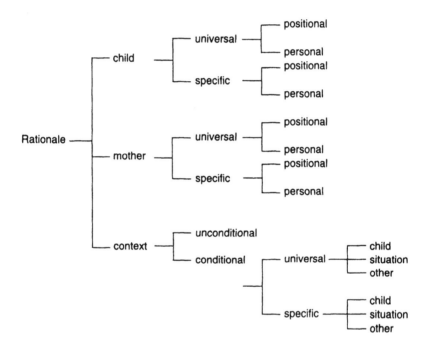

Universal ('general' in our diagram) refers to only statements in which the subject is a member of a general class, e.g. children, mothers, fathers, boys, girls; generalised pronouns one, they.

Specific ('particular' in our diagram) refers to any statement in which the subject is a member of a particular class, e.g. personal pronouns: he, she, we; possessive pronouns: our, my; proper nouns: Jane, John.

Positional refers to behaviour seen in terms of development, disposition or special attributes.

The positional-personal dimension refers to the way an individual is perceived in terms of his/her attributes: the universal–specific dimension refers to the way in which the mother expresses this perception, as a general norm (universal) or as a particular case (specific) referring to her child or herself as distinct and separate.

The rationale could focus on the child, mother or context, and this is the first choice in the network. I shall give examples simply for brevity only for the rationale focusing on the child.

Rationale: *Child*
  Universal Statements
    Positional (age, gender, age relation, other)
    Age: 'They're always like that at five.'
    Gender: 'Boys should be able to . . . .'
    Age Relation: 'Children are often like that with their father.'
    Other: 'All children should . . .'
    Personal (feelings, intention, abilities)
                  'They always get tired easily.'
                  'Children are upset by things like that.'
  Specific Statements
    Positional
    Age: 'He's only five so we . . . .'
                  'Now she's six . . .'
    Gender: 'Johnny's a real little boy.'
                  'Most girls are tidy, so is Jane.'
    Age Relation: 'Peter behaves better with his father so . . .'
    Other: 'She's got to learn not to do this so . . .'
    Personal
                  'Mary is a generous child so . . .'
                  'He's always nervous about going to school so . . .'

We found that the network coded nearly all the rationales offered. It is of course possible to extend the network further to the right if more idiosyncratic choices are relevant. Analysis of the choices in the network can create a very differentiated picture and in this way the description respects the responses.

Part III

Critique and Response

Chapter 8

Sociolinguistics: A Personal View

I think that my contributions, if any, to the origins and development of sociolinguistics is at best tangential or even negative. I refer here to the trajectory taken by most sociolinguistic studies. My interest in language was not a primary interest. It arose out of a thoroughgoing dissatisfaction with sociological theories of socialisation which were, in the 1950s, very much influenced by functionalist role theory and, of course, by the theoretical studies of Talcott Parsons. Parsons viewed language in culture as analogous to money in the economy. The key concept in functionalist approaches to socialisation was the concept of 'internalisation' and, although it had resonances with psychoanalysis, these were rarely explored. The concept seemed to be a term pointing to the need for its own description. In those days of the late 1950s (and still today) I was preoccupied theoretically with what was then conceptualised as the outside → inside → outside → problematic and empirically, with problems of the class specialisation of the cultures of schools and families which gave rise to differential access and acquisition.

I came to the study of language by a diverse set of routes driven by the inadequacy of sociology to provide an orientation. How different today, where, perhaps, there is an abstracting of discourse from social structure. I drew on work in U.S. cultural anthropology, Russian work on speech as an orientating and regulative system (Luria and Vygotsky), within sociology on Durkheim and Mead, and, especially, Cassirer's *Philosophy of Symbolic Forms*. The discourse was somewhat distant from my work as a teacher of post-office messenger boys in the East End of London. I had previously been a resident settlement worker in the area for three years. The difference between the expected pedagogic displays and those offered became the source of transformations which took me beyond sociolinguistics. I was a passenger, who both joined and departed (or was deported) early. As a consequence it would not be appropriate for me to attempt to give an opinion on the many questions requested by our editors. Certainly my intellectual background, and orientation, contributed, to say the least, to a sense of marginality to the developments, conceptualisations and orientations of most, but not all, of the early sociolinguists, and probably to those of today. Even when we appeared to share a common empirical problem it was clear that conceptualisations drew on different traditions and produced languages of descriptions separated by levels of analysis.

My first introduction to linguistics was not auspicious. I had collected speech from discussion groups of lower working-class and upper middle-class male adolescents and was worried about the issue of their description. I decided to apply to University College London to read for a higher degree in linguistics. By amazing good fortune I was sent to see the Professor of Phonetics, Dennis Fry, to whom I explained my background, research problem and occupation (schoolteacher). He said 'Don't bother about linguistics, go and talk to Freida Goldman-Eisler'. Perhaps these were the most crucial meetings of my career. Professor Fry encouraged me to apply for a research grant to analyse my tapes and not, as he put it, bother about linguistics. At that point he was absolutely right.

My next encounter with linguistics was equally, but differently, crucial. I was invited to give a seminar in the early 1960s to the Department of Linguistics at the University of Edinburgh, where I met Michael Halliday, who at that time was a lecturer in linguistics. I would say without hesitation that that meeting, and the relationship which followed when Halliday came to London as Professor at University College London was, and is, crucial to my understanding of the workings of language in society. When Halliday came to London I was already involved in extensive research, but without any systematic theory of description which would enable the data I had collected to be viewed from a semantic, linguistic and sociological perspective. I had already developed a semantic network of choices entered through a series of related subsystems forming what we called, after Halliday, the regulative context, later regulative discourse. However, what was required was a linguistic theory whose basis, assumptions and conceptual language was driven by meanings, social meanings. This theory would describe the specialisation of *patterns of meanings* across levels of the grammar, where the unit of the analysis was above the level of the sentence. A theory where mutual translation between the languages of sociology and linguistics was possible, effective and creative for both languages. I certainly found this in what in those days was called Scale and Category grammar. Ruqaiya Hasan joined the Sociology Research Unit in 1964 and provided an exciting, theoretically driven, expansion of the research beyond cohesion analysis. We have kept up a correspondence since, and her theory of semantic variation opens up new vistas in our understanding of the role of language in the construction of consciousness and its power positioning. 'My claim is that as Saussure limited the domain of linguistics, so also Labov limits the domain of sociolinguistics, which is reduced to social diagnostics, ignoring deeper issues in the role of language in the creation, maintenance, and change of social institutions' (Hasan, 1992, p. 8). Thus the Halliday/Hasan contribution to my development is incalculable.

At the time of my initial relations with Halladay and Hasan my concerns were not consciously sociolinguistic. They were driven by the theoretical and empirical necessities of the research, and it was these necessities, not those arising from a new intellectual field which, then and now, were and are primary concerns. I found I had little in common with the theoretical orientations of sociolinguistics in the 1960s and onwards. This was entirely related to differences in the traditions we drew on and the level of the analysis. This difference was transparently revealed at a seminar organised by John Gumperz at Berkeley in 1968. However, Dell Hymes, for me, stood apart from the micro-level preoccupations of interactive communicative/conversational analysis or correlational diagnostics. Dell Hymes's work seemed to me to be distinguished by a breadth of scholarship, vision and generosity (rare in those days as today). Language, culture and society were held together, and the forms of their embeddedness traced across different levels of manifestations. The direction he offered and manner of analysis were unfortunately, to my mind, not always followed.

To my recollection, sociolinguistics in the 1960s and 1970s had a very selective, narrowly focused sociological base. John Gumperz apart, sociolinguistics attracted ethnomethodologists and as a consequence it was preoccupied with intra-contextual speech displays, essentially concerned with the construction and negotiations of order as members' practical accomplishments. At that time ethnomethodology was in a rampant, radical, messianic stage, antagonistic to mainstream sociology, and sociolinguistics may well have been seen as an attractive temporary resource. The emphasis upon members' competence, communicative competence, ensured a welcome. Competence became the focus of convergence across the social sciences embracing the study of culture (Lévi-Strauss), ethnography of communication (Dell Hymes), child development (Piaget), linguistics (Chomsky), conversational analysis (Garfinkle et al.). Thus we have cultural competences, communicative competences, linguistic competences, cognitive competences and, finally, the competence of members' practical accomplishments. We have an extraordinary convergence across the social sciences, in this period, and across disciplines with different assumptions, some structuralist, others radically opposed to structuralism.

Competence was conceptualised in the social, not the cultural sense, in that competence is not the product of any one particular culture. Cultures are always specialised but competences are not specialised to any one culture. Thus competences are beyond the reach and restraints of power relations and their differential unequal positionings. Competences are intrinsically creative, informally, tacitly acquired, in non-formal interactions. They are practical accomplishments. Not necessarily intrinsic to the concept but empirically often collocating with it, is an antagonism to communication specialised for formal, explicit procedures and institutions. Thus we have Labov's 'lames' and Willis's 'earholes'.

The social logic of the concept competence may reveal:

1. an announcement of a universal democracy of acquisition. All are inherently competent. There is no deficit;
2. the individual as *active* and *creative* in the construction of a *valid* world of meaning and practice. There can only be *differences* between such worlds, meanings and practices;
3. a celebration of everyday, oral language use and suspicion of specialised languages;
4. official socialisers are suspect, for acquisition is a tacit, invisible act, not subject to public regulation or, perhaps, not primarily acquired through such regulation;
5. a critique of hierarchical relations, where domination is replaced by facilitation and imposition by accommodation.

Perhaps we can now glimpse how the concept of competence resonated with, was legitimised by, the liberal progressive and radical ideologies of the heady 1960s, especially those which dominated education in that period and later.

However, the idealism of competence, a celebration of what we are, in contrast with how we have been positioned, is bought at a price: the abstracting of the individual from the analysis of the distribution of power and principles of control which selectively specialise modes of realisation and their acquisition. Thus the announcement of competence points away from such a specialisation, away from the macro blot on the micro context, and points, instead, to 'difference' as the key to understanding the selective specialisings of the exploration of meanings and the forms of their realisation. Some differences are legitimised as superior by dominant groups, others are judged as inferior, but, *as all are competent,* inadequate communication displays on the part of those judged inferior are a function of the contexts, interaction, meanings, criteria and the values in which these are embedded, created by the dominant group.

It was in this area that the code theory was contextualised, or rather selectively recontextualised. Chomsky provided one legitimisation with the judgement that the thesis 'was below rationality' whilst Labov provided an apparent empirical dismissal. Indeed the theory became a means of bestowing ideological purity on those who denounced it. I was, at the time, essential to this intellectual field, for I had created almost single-handed a focus for the field's ritual cleansing. In this respect Labov's paper, 'The Logic of Nonstandard English', achieved canonical status (see Appendix). This is not the place to give another view. There are other places where it can be found.

There is no doubt in my mind that the difference/deficit debate which preoccupied much of sociolinguistics in the 1960s and early 1970s was of little theoretical significance and, indeed, obscured more than it revealed. However, from another point of view it was undoubtedly powerful and influential. It sucked in a steady flow of research funds and opened up new academic positions in universities. It brought together linguists, anthropologists, sociologists, psychologists and educationists with a common focus, and so facilitated a new inter-disciplinary effervescence. It led, on the one hand, to educationists and teachers having to re-examine their value assumptions, expectations and methods, and on the other hand, the deficit/difference debate served to legitimise what might be called pedagogic populism.

As I said in the beginning, I know I do not have the warrant to respond to some of the important issues raised by the editors, as I virtually ceased any relation to the field after the early 1970s, although I clearly maintained relations with individuals. What I found particularly exciting about the take-off period was the opportunity to share and follow the work of Susan Ervin-Tripp, Dan Slobin and especially Courtney Cazden. Cazden seemed to me to play a crucial dual role, informing sociolinguists through her own classroom research and exposing education (especially child development) to the new approaches and findings developing in sociolinguistics. Alan Grimshaw played a similar analogous and crucial function for sociology. It may well be that all involved in the take-off period performed dual roles, facing inward to the original discipline and outward to the new field. Perhaps with specialisation of the field as an autonomous discourse, issuing its own licences for access, study and practice, in short with professionalisation, the inter-disciplinary effervescence may well have been weakened, and with that weakening more puzzle solving than producing new paradigms.

From another point of view I am reminded of Dell Hymes's judgement that sociolinguistics has extended the horizon of linguistics but has done little for the other social sciences. I wonder about this; certainly, in my narrow experience, this seems to be the case. The 'socio' of sociolinguistics seems to be very narrowly focused, selected more by the requirements of linguistics than developed by the requirements of sociology (for example).

Very complex questions are raised by the relation of the socio to the linguistic. What linguistic theories of description are available for what socio issues? And how do the former limit the latter? What determines the dynamics of linguistic theory, and how do these dynamics relate, if at all, to the dynamics of change in those disciplines which do and could contribute to the socio. If 'socio' and linguistics are to illuminate language as a truly social construct, then there must be mutually translatable principles of descriptions which enable the dynamics of the social to enter these translatable principles. These principles should facilitate descriptions of the relations between micro encounters and their macro contexts, where appropriate. Thus the linguistic and sociological theories (for example) should be so formulated that their level of analysis in the local instance of their application should function horizontally *and* vertically. Both theories, then, should be capable of describing on-going, context-specific encounters, in a language which can transpose the intra-contextual into the inter-contextual. Central to such a linguistic theory must be the status accorded to meaning. For it is meaning which is central to a truly social theory of language. With meaning as central we can ask: What meaning and where? Whose meaning? Why this meaning and no other? And so on. From this point of view language becomes the interface of interrelated systems. Language as a social construct requires mutually translatable principles of description among the interface disciplines concerned with the formulations, maintenance and change of that social construct (Hasan, 1992).

Perhaps an example would be relevant here. If we take a micro context of control (parent/child, teacher/student, social worker/client, doctor/patient, prison warden/inmate), what is subject to control (i.e. selection) is the embedding of an instructional discourse in a regulative discourse. It seems to me that in order to understand the ongoing interaction and describe it, a sociological model of the *potential semantic* (even better, semiotic) is required. Such a model might take the form of a series of subsystems, each opening to a set of choices sensitive to the particularities of a context of control. Different modalities of control would act selectively on interactional realisations, and this would lead to specific emphasis on some subsystems and upon their grammar, lexes and paralinguistics. In this way the linguistics and paralinguistic realisations would be signifiers of modalities of control and their outcomes. Different modalities of control in turn would be signifiers of different forms of symbolic control. And these different forms of symbolic control might well be the expected relays of certain distributions of power: some less effective than others, some challenged more by some groups than others.

Finally, in conclusion, looking back over this contribution. I am conscious, acutely conscious, that most of it refers to my own relation to sociolinguistics, rather than to the field itself. But that may be because I am not really a field person. Perhaps, even so, such a perspective may not be entirely irrelevant.

APPENDIX

It might be valuable from a historical point of view to take seriously Labov's (1972) paper 'The Logic of Non-standard English' which seems to me to have lacked such attention. It has been enthusiastically reprinted but rarely analysed on its own terms. Perhaps this exercise might shed some light on the ideological assumptions of the early period of the field of sociolinguistics.[1]

The opposition deficit/difference received much of its power from Labov's paper, in which he contrasts the arguments of two black speakers, one middle class and the other working class. He shows that the working-class youth's argument is succinct, pithy and logical, whereas the middle-class black is verbose, redundant, hesitant. This is an unwarranted conclusion. Both arguments are logical, as judged by rules of inference, but the modalities of the argument are different. They follow different paradigmatic forms and in consequence they should not be judged by antitheses such as verbose–succinct, redundant–pithy, economic–uneconomic and hesitant–fluent. Larry's argument is essentially a matter of denial: some say if you are good you go to heaven and if you are bad you go to hell, but there is no god and so no heaven. The middle-class black is not redundant, verbose; he is producing an argument based on a different paradigmatic form entailing rules of evidence, falsification, abstraction, generalisation. The crucial difference lies not in the content but in the *form* of the argument offered by the two speakers (pp. 193–4, 1972).

It is of interest that in the endlessly recycled account of Larry's discussion of black and white gods it is rarely noted that Larry is given five probes to assist in the structuring of his argument (pp. 193–4): 'What?', 'What happens to your spirit?', 'And where does your spirit go?', 'On what [does it depend]?', 'Why?'. Further, in another exchange (p. 217), which appears later in the paper but may have preceded the interchange referred to above (p. 186), Larry is specifically asked what colour God is, white or black, and is given three probes to focus the answer. In contrast, the question to the black middle-class speaker is, 'Do you know of anything that someone can do to have someone who has passed on visit him in a dream?' (p. 197). Not the clearest question to answer. The respondent is given no probes to assist in the structuring of his reply. The first half of the reply is concerned with the relation between dreams and reality and the second half is concerned with whether it is possible to induce a dreamer to dream of something specific. In light of the question, perhaps not a bad effort. However, this is not Labov's view, nor of those who recycle the quotations and interpretations unmediated by an analysis. The 'liberal' ideology of white sociolinguistics paradoxically here transforms difference into deficit.

Nothing is shown by this comparison because no comparison using Labov's criteria should be applied. The issue which is raised refers to the social origins of the forms of argument and the rules of their selective, contextual realisation and interactional practices. It may well be the case on this analysis that the middle-class black adult has access to two argumental forms whereas the working-class black man well have access to only one. This would require further investigation.

Earlier in the same paper Labov presents spoken texts of a black child who in a formal experimental context was virtually silent, but when placed in a context with a friendly black adult interviewer who sat on the floor, and where the child was accompanied by his friend sharing a Coca Cola, spoke freely and managed the interaction effectively. The example is used to illustrate the effect of context upon speech and the management of interaction, and this it undoubtedly does, but it also raises more fundamental questions. How was it necessary for the context to be changed so drastically and what was the relation between the distinguishing features of the changed context and the management of interaction, and this it undoubtedly does, but it also raises more fundamental questions. How was it necessary for the context to be changed so drastically and what was the relation between the distinguishing features of the changed context and the management of interaction and communication? In terms of my theory an analysis of the child's speech shows that it is a restricted variant, which is precisely what it should be, given the distinguishing social features of the context. In both cases offered in the paper the sociological level of analysis is bypassed in order to demonstrate an underlying competence, and this is not unusual where a 'difference' position is to be favoured, but I would submit that the fundamental issue is not an illustration of a communicative competence but the question of the *controls on the distribution of sociolinguistic rules of contextualised performance.*

We shall consider in more detail Labov's second major example, taken from the speech of a black boy under different contextual constraints. It is worth spending time over these examples, as they have been received enthusiastically and repeated, usually without comment. In the first situation the boy is expected to make comments in response to the elicitation 'Tell me all you can about this'. The reference is a block or fire engine. Even with six probes offered by the white interviewer the boy rarely replies in more than one nominal group (p. 185). In another context the white interviewer is replaced by a black one (Clarence Robins), who interviews Leon (aged 8) (p. 186). The latter again gives minimal responses to the following question accompanied by 11 probes: 'What if you saw somebody kickin' somebody else on the ground or was using a stick, what would you do if you saw that?' No other description of the contexts is given in Labov (1972). Labov's explanations are that here Leon is defending himself against possible accusations, and that, in the first example, it is the asymmetry of the relationship, not the ineptness of the interviewer, which responsible for the silence.

Further, Leon is interviewed by a skilled black interviewer raised in Harlem and offered: 'You watch—you like to watch television?' (Leon nods.) 'What's your favourite programme?' Despite eight probes Leon's replies are minimal (p. 182). Labov comments that, despite the skills, sensitivities, and experience of the black interviewer, Clarence Robins, Leon is not communicative and Robins is unable to break down what Labov calls the 'prevailing social constraints'. For Labov it is because the social relationship is asymmetrical, not because of the race of the interviewer. But is it? Is it the asymmetry, a property of the form of the social relationship, or is it the form of the discourse?

In all the contexts so far described the child is positioned in an interrogative, instructional discourse, whether official within the school or informal in the case of interrogation on a moral issue or a favourite television programme. This discourse is specialised, first, with respect to the child's social relation to the discourse and, second, as an interrogative of an open form. The child is positioned within a request for unique information, that is, information which only he can give. In this sense the social basis of the child's relation to the discourse is egocentric. He is differentiated from his social base and its competences, as a figure differentiated from its ground. The fact that the interrogative is of an open form intensifies the egocentric social base.

In the other contexts which follow the asymmetry is no less explicit but, on the argument offered here, the child's relation to the discourse is *sociocentric* and, in consequence, he can drawn upon competences which make that position possible (p. 188). Thus when Clarence Robins sits on the floor, introduces taboo words, topics, when Leon is with his best friend, then a lively interaction takes place. Yet in this interaction the lead is taken by Leon's friend Greg. Labov argues that Greg and Leon talk as much to each other as they do to Robins, the black interviewer. In fact this is not the case. Robins makes 11 interventions, all of them *interrogative*. In other words the asymmetry holds in the context despite its apparent informality. The interchange is lively between boys because they both draw on common rules and shared knowledge.

In the next section, which consists of 18 interchanges, Clarence makes six interventions, most of them explicit or implicit interrogatives, while the Greg and Leon exchanges consist almost entirely of affirmation or negations, and this pattern continues in the final sequence of exchanges. It is a little difficult to accept Labov's interpretation that 'we have two boys who have so much to say that they keep interrupting each other and who seem to have no difficulty in using the English language to express themselves'. The conclusions are based on criteria which are inappropriate to the context and in an important respect are patronising. Further, Labov's local interpretation of the exchanges seems on analysis to be unwarranted. Yet these examples of interchange (or rather the interpretations) are repeatedly quoted and virtually sacrosanct.

The view here is that we have neither expressive speech nor a rich (*sic*) array of grammar in one context and that we have severely reduced speech in another. What we have are interchanges which are embedded in difference social bases and thus founded upon different rules and competences. It has little to do with asymmetry. Robins maintains an interrogative mode in all contexts, and his questions press from the *outside,* whereas Greg's and Leon's affirmations, negations and interrogations are generated from *within* the age and gender rules they both share. I agree only with Labov's conclusion: 'We see no connection between verbal skill in the speech events characteristic of the street culture and success in the school'. However, what is required is less *ad hoc* ideology and interpretation and a more systematic, general understanding of the social basis of modalities of communication and their distributive principles and differential outcomes.

The meeting of such a requirement invites an analysis of the distribution of power and principles of control which regulate and distribute, unequally, communicative performance principles which differentially position speakers with respect to interactional power and context management. This is the focus of study of the code thesis (Bernstein, 1990).

NOTE

1. The page numbers refer to the reprint of 'The Logic of Non-standard English' published in Giglioni P.P. (Ed.) (1972) *Language and Social Context*, Penguin Modern Sociology Readings, Harmondsworth: Penguin, pp. 179–215.

Chapter 9

Vertical and Horizontal Discourse: An Essay

INTRODUCTION

It might be useful to recall the development of the work that leads up to the present analysis. Up to the 1980s the work was directed to an understanding of different principles of pedagogic transmission/acquisition, their generating contexts and change. These principles were conceptualised as code modalities. However, what was transmitted was not in itself analysed apart from the classification and framing of the categories of the curriculum. In the middle 1980s what was transmitted became the focus of the analysis (Bernstein, 1986). A theory of the construction of pedagogic discourse, its distributive, recontextualising and evaluative rules and their social basis, was developed: the pedagogic device. However the *forms* of the discourses, that is the internal principles of their construction and their social base, were taken for granted and not analysed. Thus there was an analysis of modalities of elaborated codes and their generating social contexts, an analysis of the construction of pedagogic discourse which the modalities of elaborated codes pre-supposed, but no analysis of the discourses subject to pedagogic transformation.

This analysis will proceed by distinguishing between two fundamental forms of discourse which have been subject to much comparison and contrast. The two forms are generally seen as oppositional rather than complementary. Indeed one form is often seen as the destruction of the other. Sometimes one form is seen as essentially a written form and the other is essentially an oral form. Bourdieu refers to these forms in terms of the function to which they give rise, one form creating symbolic, the other practical mastery. Habermas sees one form as constructing what he calls the "life world" of the individual and the other as the source of instrumental rationality. Giddens following Habermas sees one discursive form as the basis for constructing what he calls 'expert systems'. These 'expert systems' lead to a disembedding of individuals from the local experiential world which is constructed by a different form. Underlying these contrasts or oppositions is a complex multi-layered structure of pairs operating at different levels of individual and social experience[1].

Evaluative	spontaneous	contrived
Epistemological	subjective	objective
Cognitive	operations	principles
Social	intimacy	distance
Contextual	inside	outside
Voice	dominated	dominant
Mode	linear	non-linear
Institutional	gemeinschaft	gessellschaft

Although any one author may single out one pair of contrasts from the above (not exhaustive) set, the remainder of the set like the nine tenths of an iceberg lurk invisible below the surface of the text.

In the educational field one form is sometimes referred to as school(ed) knowledge and the other as everyday common sense knowledge, or 'official' & 'local' knowledge. These contrasts are often ideologically positioned and receive different evaluations. One form becomes the means whereby a dominant group is said to impose itself upon a dominated group and functions to silence and exclude the voice of this group. The excluded voice is then transformed into a latent pedagogic voice of unrecognised potential.

To my mind much of the work generating these oppositions, homogenises these discursive forms so that they take on stereotypical forms where their differences or similarities are emphasised. It is not unusual for one form to be romanticised as a medium celebrating what the other form has lost.

What I shall attempt here is to produce a language of description which produces greater differentiation within and between these forms and explores the social basis of this differentiation. This will involve using yet another set of descriptors with internal subdivisions. The justification for yet another language can only be whether, on the one hand, its use enables a more productive, a more general perspective, and on the other hand, whether it leads to new research possibilities and interpretations.

VERTICAL AND HORIZONTAL DISCOURSES

To begin with I shall distinguish between a *Vertical discourse* and a *Horizontal discourse*, and give brief definitions which will be developed later. These definitions will take as criteria *forms of knowledge*. Different forms of knowledge will be realised in the two discourses.

Horizontal Discourse

We are all aware and use a form of knowledge usually typified as everyday or 'common sense' knowledge. Common because all potentially or actually have access to it, common because it applies to all, and common because it has a common history in the sense of arising out of common problems of living and dying. This form has a group of well known features: it is likely to be oral, local, context dependent and specific, tacit, multi-layered and contradictory across but not within contexts. However, from the point of view to be taken here, the crucial feature is that is it segmentally organised. By segmental I am referring to the sites of realisation of this discourse. The realisation of this discourse varies with the way the culture segments and specialises activities and practices. The knowledge is segmentally differentiated. Because the discourse is *Horizontal* it does not mean that all segments have equal importance, clearly some will be more important than others. I shall contrast this *Horizontal discourse* with what I shall call a *Vertical discourse*.

Vertical Discourse

Briefly a *Vertical discourse* takes the form of a coherent, explicit and systematically principled structure, hierarchically organised as in the sciences, or it takes the form of a series of specialised languages with specialised modes of interrogation and specialised criteria for the production and circulation of texts as in the social sciences and humanities. I want first of all to raise the question of how knowledge circulates in these two discourses. In the case of *Vertical discourse* there are strong distributive rules regulating access, regulating transmission and regulating evaluation. Circulation is accomplished usually through explicit forms of recontextualising affecting distribution in terms of time, space and actors. I am not here concerned with the arenas and agents involved in these regulations. Basically, circulation is accomplished through explicit recontextualisation and evaluation, motivated by strong distributive procedures. But how does knowledge circulate in the case of *Horizontal discourse* where there is little systematic organising principles and therefore only tacit recontextualising? Of course in *Horizontal discourse* there are distributive rules regulating the circulation of knowledge, behaviour and expectations according to status/position. Such distributive rules structure and specialise social relations, practices and their context and local agents of its enactment and begin to circulate? In order to answer this question I want to sharpen and delimit the definition of *Horizontal discourse*:

> A *Horizontal discourse* entails a set of strategies which are local, segmentally organised, context specific and dependent, for maximising encounters with persons and habitats.

With this definition in mind I want to consider a fictitious community operating only with *Horizontal discourse*. Here a distinction can be made between the set of strategies any one individual possesses and their analogic potential for contextual transfer, and the total sets of strategies possessed by all members of this community. I shall use the term *repertoire* to refer to the set of strategies and their analogic potential possessed by any one individual and the term *reservoir* to refer to the total of sets and its potential of the community as a whole. Thus the *repertoire* of each member of the community will have both a common nucleus but there will be differences between the *repertoires*. There will be differences between the *repertoires* because of differences between the members arising out of differences in members contexts and activities and their associated issues. Now it is possible to ask about the relation between *reservoir* and *repertoire*. What is the regulation on the relation between *reservoir* and *repertoire*? Or what is the relation between the potential and the actual practice of a member? How do new strategies circulate?

Clearly the more members are isolated or excluded from each other, then the weaker the social base for the development of either *repertoire* or *reservoir*. If there is to be a development of either *repertoire* or *reservoir* then this development will depend upon how social relationships are structured. The greater the reduction of isolation and exclusion then the greater the social potential for the circulation of strategies, of procedures and their *exchange*. Under these conditions there can be an expansion of both *repertoire* and *reservoir*. The exchange of strategies will affect the analogical potential of any one *repertoire*. Under these conditions the relation between a member's actual and potential practice becomes dynamic. Consider a situation where a small holder meets another and complains that what he/she had done every year with great success, this year failed completely. The other says that when this has happened he/she finds that this 'works'. He/she then outlines the successful strategy. Now any restriction to circulation and exchange reduces effectiveness. Any restriction specialises, classifies and privatises knowledge. Stratification procedures produce distributive rules which control the flow of procedures from *reservoir* to *repertoire*. Thus both *Vertical* and *Horizontal discourses* are likely to operate with distributive rules which set up position of defence and challenge.

From the idealisation constructed it is possible to see the inter-relations between *Horizontal discourse* and the structuring of social relations. The structuring of the social relationships generate the forms of discourse but the discourse in turn is structuring a form of consciousness, its contextual mode of orientation and realisation, and motivates forms of social solidarity. *Horizontal discourse* in its acquisition becomes the major cultural relay. I shall now consider briefly the mode of acquisition. I shall propose that the mode of acquisition is created by the form taken by the pedagogy. And the pedagogic interventions, in turn, are a function of the different 'knowledges' required to be acquired. These 'knowledges' are related not by integration of their meanings by some coordinating principle, but the 'knowledges' are related through the functional relations of segments or contexts to the everyday life. It follows then that what is acquired in one segment or context, and how it is acquired, may bear no relation to what is acquired or how it is acquired in another segment or context. Learning how to tie up one's shoes bears no relation to how to use the lavatory correctly. These competences are segmentally related. They are not related by any principle integrating their specific acquisitional 'knowledge'. I have called the form of this pedagogy *segmental*. Later I will distinguish this segmental pedagogy and the segmental 'knowledges' or literacies[2] to which it gives rise, from the institutional pedagogy of *Vertical discourse*.

The segmental organisation of the "knowledges" of *Horizontal discourse* leads to segmentally structured acquisitions. There is no necessary relations between what is learned in the different segments. Further, as acquisition arises from discrete segments pedagogic practice may well vary with the segment. Thus similar segments across social groups/classes may differ in the code modality regulating acquisition. Or to put it another way *Vertical discourse* may regulate more segments of acquisition in one social group/class than another, and this entails a different mode of learning and context management[3]. I am here contrasting a segmental pedagogic control with an institutional or official pedagogic control.

Segmental pedagogy is usually carried out in face to face relations with a strong affective loading as in the family, peer group or local community. The pedagogy may be tacitly transmitted by modelling, by showing or by explicit modes. Unlike official or institutional pedagogy the pedagogic process may be no longer than the context or segment in which it is enacted. The pedagogy is exhausted in the context of its enactment, or is repeated until the particular competence is acquired: learning to dress, running errands, counting change, addressing different individuals, using a telephone, selecting a video. The segmental pedagogies of the peer group may well depend strongly on modelling/showing. In general the emphasis of the segmental pedagogy of *Horizontal discourse* is directed towards acquiring a common competence rather than a graded performance[4]. Clearly competitive relations may well develop, as in the peer group, on the basis of these common competences.

Thus in the case of *Horizontal discourse*, its 'knowledges', competences and literacies are segmental. They are contextually specific and *context dependent*, embedded in on-going practices, usually with strong affective loading, and directed towards specific, immediate goals, highly relevant to the acquirer in the context of his/her life. The activation of the learning strategies may require the features of the original segment. Where these features are absent the learning strategies may not be demonstrated. Segmental competences/literacies are culturally localised, evoked by *contexts whose reading is unproblematic*. Although the competences, literacies are localised they do not necessarily give rise to highly coded inflexible practices. Indeed any one individual may build up an extensive *repertoire* of strategies which can be varied according to the contingencies of the context or segment. (As I have proposed earlier, any individual *repertoire* may depend on its relation to the *reservoir* of the group.) From the point of view of any one individual operating within *Horizontal discourse*, there is not necessarily one and only one correct strategy relevant to a particular context. *Horizontal discourse* relayed through a segmental pedagogy facilitates the development of a *repertoire* of strategies of operational 'knowledges' activated in contexts whose reading is unproblematic.

I now want to turn to *Vertical discourse* which it will be remembered has two forms: one a is coherent, explicit and systematically principled structure, hierarchically organised; and the second takes the form of a series of specialised languages with specialised modes of interrogation, specialised criteria for the production and circulation of texts, e.g. the Natural Sciences and the Humanities and Social Sciences. In the case of any *Vertical discourse*, this, unlike *Horizontal discourse*, is not a segmentally organised discourse. The integration of a *Vertical discourse* is not integration at the level of the relation between segments/contexts as in *Horizontal discourse*, but integration at the level of meanings. *Vertical discourse* consists not of culturally specialised segments but of specialised symbolic structures of explicit knowledge. The procedures of *Vertical discourse* are then linked, not by contexts, horizontally, but the procedures are linked to other procedures hierarchically. The institutional or official pedagogy of *Vertical discourse* is not consumed at the point of its contextual delivery but is an on-going process in extended time.

The social units of acquisition of this pedagogy (that of a *Vertical discourse*) have a different arbitrary base than the arbitrary base of the social units of the pedagogy of *Horizontal discourse*. The social units of the pedagogy of *Vertical discourse* are constructed, evaluated and distributed to different groups and individuals, structured in time and space by *principles* of recontextualising. We have context specificity through *segmentation* in *Horizontal discourse* but context specificity through recontextualisation in *Vertical discourse*. Both discourses, *Vertical* and *Horizontal*, have an arbitrary pedagogic base. The arbitrary of both discourses is constructed by distributive rules regulating the circulation of the discourses.

Summarising the pedagogy so far in the contemporary context:

	Vertical discourse	*Horizontal discourse*
Practice	Official/Institutional	Local
Distributive Principle	Recontextualisation	Segmentation
Social Relation	Individual	Communalised
Acquisition	Graded Performance	Competence

DISCOURSE AND KNOWLEDGE STRUCTURES

The language of description I have developed has examined the oppositions that began this paper and has illuminated their internal structures, and in the case of *Horizontal discourse*, its social base, mode acquisition and form of knowledge. However, if this language I have developed was limited only to such a context then it would only produce the homogenising which I argued underpinned the oppositions. I want now to examine in more detail *Vertical discourse*. The way forward has already been adumbrated by the distinction between the different modalities of knowledge of *Vertical discourse*. These modalities will be conceptualised as *Hierarchical Knowledge Structures* and *Horizontal Knowledge Structures*.

Briefly a *Hierarchical Knowledge Structure* looks like the following:

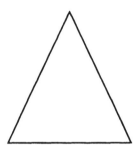

This form of knowledge attempts to create very general propositions and theories, which integrate knowledge at lower levels, and in this way shows underlying uniformities across an expanding range of apparently different phenomena[5]. *Hierarchical Knowledge Structures* appear by their users to be motivated towards greater and greater integrating propositions, operating at more and more abstract levels. Thus it could be said that *Hierarchical Knowledge Structures* are produced by an *integrating* code.

In contrast *Horizontal Knowledge Structures* consist of a series of specialised languages with specialised modes of interrogation and criteria for the construction and circulation of texts. Thus any one of the specialised disciplines within the form of a *Horizontal Knowledge Structure* found within the Humanities and Social Sciences can be visually portrayed as below:

$$L^1\ L^2\ L^3\ L^4\ L^5\ L^6\ L^7\ \ldots\ldots L^n$$

Thus in the case of English Literature, the languages would be the specialised languages of criticism, in Philosophy the various languages of this mode of inquiry, and in Sociology, on which we shall focus, the languages refer for exam-

ple to functionalism, post-structuralism, post-modernism, Marxism, etc. The latter are the broad linguistic categories and within them are the idiolects (theories)
of particular favoured or originating speakers. *Horizontal Knowledge Structures*,
unlike *Hierarchical Knowledge Structures* which are based on integrating codes,
are based upon collection or serial codes; integration *of* language in one case and
accumulation of *languages* in the other.

It is interesting to inquire what counts as a development of *Hierarchical
Knowledge Structures* and of *Horizontal Knowledge Structures*. In the case of *Hierarchical Knowledge Structures* development is seen as the development of theory which is more general, more integrating, than previous theory. In the case of
Horizontal Knowledge Structures, this criterion, as we will see, cannot apply. It
cannot apply because the set of languages which constitute any one *Horizontal
Knowledge Structure* are not translatable, since they make different and often opposing assumptions, with each language having its own criteria for legitimate
texts, what counts as evidence and what counts as legitimate questions or a legitimate problematic. Indeed the speakers of each language become as specialised
and as excluding as the language. Their capital is bound up with the language and
therefore defence of and challenge of other languages is intrinsic to a *Horizontal
Knowledge Structure*. A particular field is constructed by the internal characteristics of a *Horizontal Knowledge Structure*. Thus the internal characteristics and
external field amplify the serial character of a *Horizontal Knowledge Structure*.[6]

Development in the case of a *Horizontal Knowledge Structure* cannot be a
function of the greater generality and integrating property of the knowledge because as has been shown such developments simply are not possible in the case
of a *Horizontal Knowledge Structure*. So what counts as development? I suggest
that what counts as development is the introduction of a new language. A new
language offers the possibility of a fresh perspective, a new set of questions, a
new set of connections, and an apparently new problematic, and most importantly
a new set of speakers. This new language is likely to be taken up by the younger
speakers of the particular *Horizontal Knowledge Structure*.[7] This new language
can then be used to challenge the hegemony and legitimacy of more senior speakers. The latter may be cut off from acquiring the new language because of trained
incapacity arising out of previous language acquisition, and a reduced incentive,
arising out of the loss of their own position.

Now let us turn to *Hierarchical Knowledge Structures*. In a way the opposition
between theories in *Hierarchical Knowledge Structures* is analogous to the oppositions between languages in a *Horizontal Knowledge Structure* but it would be
a mistake to view this similarity as indicating no difference between these knowledge structures. Opposition between theories in *Hierarchical Knowledge Structure* is played out in attempts to refute positions where possible, or to incorporate
them in more general propositions, At some point, sometimes later than sooner,
because of special investments, a choice is possible provided the issue can be settled by empirical procedures. However, in the contrasting case of a *Horizontal*

Knowledge Structure within the Social Sciences (for example Sociology which I have in mind here and above) then neither of these possibilities are possible because the discreteness of the languages defy incorporations into a more general language. Indeed built into the construction of the language here is the protection of its discreteness, its strategies of apparent uniqueness, its non-translatability and its essential narcissism. Motivations under this discursive regime are oriented to speaking/acquiring/developing the hegemonic language or its challenge or marketing a new language.

HORIZONTAL KNOWLEDGE STRUCTURES: STRONG AND WEAK GRAMMARS

I want now to turn attention to issues arising out of acquisition and I have in mind, as before, Sociology. One of the problems of acquiring a *Horizontal Knowledge Structure* is the range of languages which have to be managed, each having its own procedures. It might be useful here to make a distinction within *Horizontal Knowledge Structures*, distinguishing those whose languages have an explicit conceptual syntax capable of *relatively* precise empirical descriptions and/or of generating formal modelling of empirical relations, from those languages where these powers are much weaker. The former I will call strong grammars and the latter weak grammars. It is important to add here that "strong" and "weak" must be understood as relative within *Horizontal Knowledge Structures*. From this point of view Economics, Linguistics and parts of Psychology would be examples of strong grammar. Mathematics would also be considered a *Horizontal Knowledge Structure* as it consists of a set of discrete languages for particular problems. Thus Mathematics and Logic would be regarded as possessing the strongest grammars, although these languages *for the most part* do not have empirical referents nor are they designed to satisfy empirical criteria. Examples of weak grammars would be Sociology, Social Anthropology, and Cultural Studies.

The strong grammars of *Horizontal Knowledge Structures* (excluding Mathematics and Logic) often achieve their power by rigourous restrictions on the empirical phenomena they address. For example the formal precision of transformation grammar arises out of the exclusion of meaning from its concerns; whereas Halliday's systemic functional grammar addresses meanings as the fundamental focus of the grammar and is a much less tidy system.

Following these distinctions within *Horizontal Knowledge Structures*, I can return to issues of acquisition. In the case of *Hierarchical Knowledge Structures* the acquirer does not have the problem of knowing whether she/he is speaking Physics or writing Physics, only the problem of correct usage. The strong grammar visibly announces what it is. For the acquirer the passage from one theory to another does not signal a break in the language. It is simply an extension of its explanatory/descriptive powers. However, if the Social Sciences are considered, then problems of acquisition arise particularly where the grammar is weak. The acquirer may well be anxious whether he/she is really speaking or writing Sociology. In these conditions it is likely that canonical names will be a useful resource. Later the names will be associated with languages or in some cases the language will come before the exemplars. Thus managing names and languages together with their criticisms, becomes both the manner of transmission and acquisition. There is, however, a prior issue. Because a *Horizontal Knowledge Structure* consists of an array of languages any one transmission necessarily entails some selection, and some privileging within the set recontextualised for the transmission of the *Horizontal Knowledge Structure*. The social basis of the principle of this recontextualising indicates whose 'social' is speaking. The social basis of the principle of the recontextualising constructs the perspective of the *Horizontal Knowledge Structure*. Whose perspective is it? How is it generated and legitimated? I say that this principle is social to indicate that choice here is not rational in the sense that it is based on the 'truth' of one of the specialised languages. For each language reveals some 'truth', although to a great extent this partial 'truth' is incommensurate and language specific. The dominant perspective within any transmission may be a function of the power relations among the teachers, or of pressure from groups of acquirers, or, particularly today, a function of indirect and direct external pressures of the market or the state itself. Thus a perspective becomes the principle of the recontextualisation which constructs the *Horizontal Knowledge Structure* to be acquired. And behind the perspective is a position in a relevant intellectual field/arena.

At the level of the acquirer this invisible perspective, the principle of recontextualisation structuring the transmission is expected to become how the acquirer reads, evaluates and creates tests. A 'gaze' has to be acquired, that is a particular mode of recognising and realising what counts as an 'authentic' sociological reality.[8]

Perhaps this is why the acquirer has such difficulty in recognising what he/she is speaking or writing, for to know is to 'gaze'. And this is I suspect a tacit transmission. To be inside the specialised language probably requires oral transmission; the experience of a social interactional relationship with those who possess the 'gaze'. I am not suggesting for one moment that this component does not facilitate acquisition of a *Hierarchical Knowledge Structure*, only that 'gaze' is not crucial to the acquisition. Here what it important is mastering the procedures of investigation and instruments of observation and understanding the theory; developing the imaginative potential of the language comes much later if at all. However, work in a laboratory does not proceed only by a mechanical regulation of the procedures. Measurement is the result of something prior to measurement. And a component of that something is a developed sense of the potential of a phenomenon arising out of practice.

Basically in the case of *Hierarchical Knowledge Structure*, in the end, it is the theory that counts and it counts both for its imaginative conceptual projection and the empirical power of the projection. Clearly acquisition of a *Hierarchical Knowledge Structure* also may involve acquisition of a perspective; a perspective that a *Hierarchical Knowledge Structure* is the only and sole pathway to 'truth'. Its procedures the only valid way to 'truth'. Where choice of theory is possible such choice may well have a social base. Indeed in areas of Biology, as in the case of the nature/nurture issue, the social base of choice is often revealed. Nor does my position deny that any one *Hierarchical Knowledge Structure* may entail a principle of recontextualisation for its transmission which is influenced by interests which may well relate to advancing social, economic and cultural capital or simply survival. But the recognition and construction of legitimate texts in a *Hierarchical Knowledge Structure* is much less problematic, much less a tacit process than is the case of a *Horizontal Knowledge Structure*, particularly those with weak grammars. In the latter case what counts in the end is the specialised language, its position, its perspective, the acquirer's 'gaze', rather than any one exemplary theory (although the exemplary theory may be the originator of the linguistic position). In the case of the *Horizontal Knowledge Structures*, especially those with weak grammars, 'truth' is a matter of acquired 'gaze'; no one can be eyeless in this Gaza.

There is a resemblance, at a fairly abstract level, between *Horizontal Knowledge Structures*, particularly and especially of the weak grammar modality, and the *Horizontal discourse* I discussed at the beginning of this essay. These two forms share some common features. Both are horizontally organised, both are serial, both are segmented. In both the contents are volatile. In the case of *Horizontal discourse* volatility refers to the referents of this discourse and in the case of *Horizontal Knowledge Structures*, especially of the weak grammar modality, volatility refers to additions and omissions of the specialised language of a particular *Horizontal Knowledge Structure*. Perhaps there is a deeper resemblance. Acquisition of *Horizontal discourse* is a tacit acquisition of a particular view of cultural realities, or rather of a way of realising these realities. The 'way' itself is embedded in the unity latent in the contextual segmentation of this discourse. The 'way' may be likened to the 'gaze' as it becomes active in the experience and ongoing practices of the speakers. This is similar to the 'gaze' embedded in the acquisition of the specialised languages of a *Horizontal Knowledge Structure* with a weak grammar.

To recoup, the contrast between *Hierarchical Knowledge Structures* and *Horizontal Knowledge Structures* lies in the fight for *linguistic hegemony* and its acquired 'gaze' within a *Horizontal Knowledge Structure* and the competition for *integration of principles* or for furthering, or for challenging, such integration in the case of *Hierarchical Knowledge Structures*. The fight for linguistic hegemony and the competition for, or to further integration, may well share common field strategies but the issues are different.[9] It is therefore important to relate the external condition of the context of the field/arena to the internal conditions of the discourse. Separation of field from discourse may well distort analysis. Indeed, from the point of view taken here, field and discourse are inter-related and inter-dependent.

HORIZONTAL KNOWLEDGE STRUCTURES, CHANGES AND ORIENTATIONS

The seriality of *Horizontal Knowledge Structures* may vary as between those with a strong grammar and those with a weak grammar. The number of languages internal to any *Horizontal Knowledge Structure* may be fewer in the case of a strong grammar than the number internal to a *Horizontal Knowledge Structure* with a weak grammar. This raises the question as to whether the serial organisation and its variations are internal to the phenomena studied. Broadly speaking all the specialised knowledges of *Horizontal Knowledge Structures* from the Social Sciences to the Humanities address human behaviour, conduct or practice in one form or another. What is of interest is that those knowledges produced by particular methodological procedures (the Social Sciences) share a similar linguistic organisation to the Humanities, the disciplines of which operate quite differently as a group and differ within that group. It seems then that what, on the contrary has to be accounted for, is the shape of *Hierarchical Knowledge Structures*. Clearly this is not a function of its methods as the Social Sciences claim that in the most part they operate with similar methods. Popper insisted that there were no differences between the Social and Natural Sciences, and that differences in the phenomena studied were irrelevant to the question of the status of the knowledge. The status is a function of methods. But I have shown that for the most part there is a common method for the most part in the Social Sciences; a common method but an organisation of knowledge similar to that of the Humanities.

As a first approach to this similarity it might be useful to look at changes in the development of specialised languages across time. It might be useful to plot the increase in the number of languages for example in Sociology across time to see whether the rate of increase is linked to a particular period of societal development or change. Certainly the number of practitioners engaged in the Social Sciences has increased enormously over the past 40 years. It is also the period of the greatest economic, cultural and technological change, possibly since industrialisation. Certainly in Sociology, and I suspect in other Social Sciences and the Humanities, there has been an increase in the number of languages and procedures of inquiry. It has been noted that the ritual of the generations provides a dynamic of intellectual change. Bourdieu (1984, 1993) sees this as a function of new class habituses entering a particular field. But the increase in numbers, the rituals of the generations, the new habituses are the resources, perhaps the necessary conditions but not the sufficient conditions to explain *changes in languages*. It is possible that the languages of *Horizontal Knowledge Structures* especially those of the Social Sciences have an inbuilt redundancy. They could be called retrospective languages. They point to the past and the hegenomic conceptual relations they generate have that past embedded in them. Thus their descriptions presuppose what has been. But under conditions of rapid social change what is to be described is not describable or is only inadequately describable in a retrospective language. This fuels the fight for linguistic hegemony within a *Horizontal Knowledge Structure*.[10]

But why are the languages within *Horizontal Knowledge Structures* retrospective? Why is the past projected on to continuous becoming? I think it is necessary here to return to *Horizontal discourse*. As others have also noted, the contributors to *Horizontal Knowledge Structures* have no means of insulating their constructions from their experience constructed by *Horizontal discourse*. The contributors cannot think beyond the sensibility which initially formed them, a sensibility embedded in a knowledge structure and on an experiential base, local in time and space. The specialised languages the speakers therefore construct are embedded in projections from the past. What of the future? Language again limits such projections, but language, here, as a formal set of combinatory rules. This finite set of rules is potentially capable of generating 'n' number of other rule systems, consequently language is an open system and opens the way to a universe of potential futures. At the level of speakers, language creates reflective feedback from on-going experience and practices. This introduces constraint on the determination of the future. Such determination weakens with the period of time entailed. Thus in the case of the Social Sciences their knowledge structures are likely to be retrospective with respect to intellectual orientation and sensibility, and restricted with reference to the time period of their future projections. There is then built into *Horizontal Knowledge Structures* an internal obsolescence of the languages.

This has two potential consequences. There is an expectation of change which facilitates and legitimates attempts to add to the existing set of languages. It also encourages, at a lower level of description, idiosyncratic terms; all have the power of naming and re-naming. Further, the more contemporary the specialised language the less retrospective it appears to be and the more its terms and syntax, to some, appear to create more relevant descriptions. Such consequences are more probable in the case of a *Horizontal Knowledge Structure* with a weak grammar than in the case of a *Horizontal Knowledge Structure* with a strong grammar. I would expect then that *Horizontal Knowledge Structures* with weak grammars, as a consequence of their acquisition, would generate speakers obsessed with issues of language which in turn would serve to construct, destruct, affirm and so reproduce the positional structure of a particular intellectual field.

This obsession with language is transferred through initiation into a particular *Horizontal Knowledge Structure*. The obsessive orientation is particularly pronounced where derivations from the specialised language yield very weak powers of specific unambiguous, empirical descriptions. This disguises any mismatch between the description and that which prompts it. Weak powers of empirical descriptions removes a crucial resource for either development or rejection of a particular language and so contribute to its stability as a frozen form. Textbooks, particularly in the case of Sociology, devote little space to reports of empirical research in comparison to the space devoted to the specialised languages, their epistemologies and their methodologies (rather than methods).

Summarising, *Horizontal Knowledge Structures*, especially and particularly those with weak grammars as in some of the Social Sciences, give rise to speakers obsessed with languages characterised by inherent obsolescence, weak powers of empirical descriptions and temporarily retrospective.

Discourse

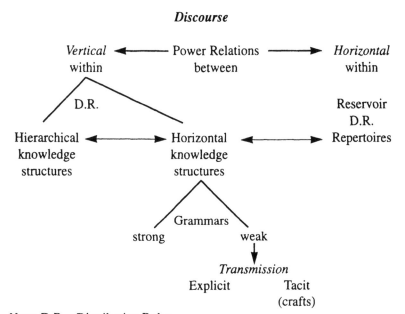

Note: D.R.= Distributive Rules

The above is, of course, an implied contrast with *Hierarchical Knowledge Structures*, where it will be recalled that the orientation is towards the experimental potential of a generalising theory. Whilst the field strategies typical of *Horizontal Knowledge Structures* may well be common to any *Hierarchical Knowledge Structure*, ultimately survival of a theory in the latter case, depends on its power to deliver the empirical expectations. The obsolescence of theory in this discourse is not because of inbuilt obsolescence but because of a failure to meet empirical expectations or its absorption into a more general theory. Although there may well be field strategies to delay failure. There are contexts within *Hierarchical Knowledge Structures*, with characteristics and consequences possibly similar to the 'natural' state of *Horizontal Knowledge Structures*, especially those with weak grammars. This is the case where theories compete in a context where experimental procedures are not available or inadequate. Such theories are usually at the edge or over the edge of 'established' knowledges. The plausibility of these theories, however, will draw on their relation to existing more established theory in the particular field.

Before turning to the relationships between *Vertical discourses* and *Horizontal discourses* as these arise in education, it might be useful to produce a map of the discourses and knowledge structures I have discussed (see page 168).

In the map a level has been added. Within weak grammars of *Horizontal Knowledge Structures* a distinction has been made in terms of the manner of their transmission and acquisition. Explicit transmission refers to a pedagogy which makes explicit (or attempts ro make explicit) the principles, procedures and texts to be acquired. This is usually the case with the Social Sciences and perhaps less so for the Humanities where the transmission tends to be more implicit. A 'tacit' transmission is one where showing or modelling precedes 'doing'. This is likely to occur with the transmission of crafts. From this point of view a craft is a modality of *Vertical discourse* and is characterised as a *Horizontal Knowledge Structure* weak grammar, tacit transmission. This knowledge structure is the nearest to *Horizontal discourse* emerging as a specialised practice to satisfy the material requirements of its segments.

VERTICAL AND HORIZONTAL DISCOURSES IN EDUCATION

As part of the move to make specialised knowledges more accessible to the young, segments of *Horizontal discourse* are recontextualised and inserted in the contents of school subjects. However, such recontextualisation does not necessarily lead to more effective acquisition for the reasons given earlier. A segmental competence, or segmental literacy acquired through *Horizontal discourse*, may not be activated in its official recontextualising as part of a *Vertical discourse* for space, time, disposition, social relation and relevance have all changed[11]. When segments of *Horizontal discourse* become resources to facilitate access to *Vertical discourse*, such appropriations are likely to be mediated through the distributive rules of the school. Recontextualising of segments is confined to particular social groups, usually the 'less able'. This move to use segments of *Horizontal discourse* as resources to facilitate access, usually limited to the procedural or operational level of a subject, may also be linked to 'improving' the student's ability to deal with issues arising (or likely to arise) in the students' everyday world: issues of health, work, parenting, domestic skills, etc. Here, access and recontextualised relevance meet, restricted to the level of strategy or operations derived from *Vertical discourse*. *Vertical discourses* are reduced to a set of strategies to become resources for allegedly improving the effectiveness of the repertoires made available in *Horizontal discourse*.

However, there may be another motive. *Horizontal discourse* may be seen as a crucial resource for pedagogic populism in the name of empowering or unsilencing voices to combat the élitism and alleged authoritarianism of *Vertical discourse*. Here students are offered an official context in which to speak as they are thought to be: Spon-Tex (the sound bite of 'spontaneous text')[12]. This move at the level of the school is parallelled by the confessional narratives of a variety of Feminist and Black Studies in higher education. The 'new' ethnography celebrates *Horizontal discourse* through extensive use of quotations which serve as experiential 'evidence'[13]. The 'ethno' is the 'unconstructed' voiced informant; what is missing is the 'graphy' (Moore & Muller, 1998).

From various points of views, some diametrically opposed, segments of *Horizontal discourse* are being inserted in *Vertical discourse*. However, these insertions are subject to distributive rules, which allocates these insertions to marginal knowledges and/or social groups. This movement has been described and analysed by Marton 1998 as a discursive shift in legitimation from knowledge to knower.

The shift in equity from equality ('of opportunity') to recognition of diversity[14] (of voice) may well be responsible for the colonisation of *Vertical discourse* or the appropriation by *Vertical discourse* of *Horizontal discourse*. This, in turn, raises an interesting question of the implications for equality by the recognition and institutionalisation of diversity. There may be more at stake here than is revealed by attacks on the so-called elitism, authoritarianism, alienations of *Vertical discourse*.

CONCLUSION

In this somewhat wide-ranging essay I began with a complaint that the contrasts and oppositions between specialist knowledges and everyday local knowledges (as if the latter were not specialised) produced limiting, often homogenising descriptions in which the social basis of these forms was inadequately conceptualised. I have tried to show how by developing a more systematic and general language of description, albeit at the cost of introducing a new conceptual vocabulary (an irony of this analysis), a more general and delicate perspective may be gained. Further, the language of description contains within the analysis it generates, new research issues and re-positions some present research. The analysis which takes as it point of departure the internal properties of forms of disclosure, reveals the inter-dependence between properties internal to the discourse and the social context, field/arena in which they are enacted and constituted. Briefly 'relations within' and 'relations to' should be integrated in the analysis. Contrasts, variations and relationships in the form taken by different knowledges is related to the social contexts of their production, transmission, acquisition and change.

There are other implications of the analysis. I have referred to the tacitly acquired 'gaze' of a *Horizontal Knowledge Structure* by means of which the acquirer learns how to recognise, regard, realise and evaluate legitimately the phenomena of concern. This 'gaze' is a consequence of the perspective created by the recontectualising principle constructing and positioning the set of languages of a particular *Horizontal Knowledge Structure*, or privileging a particular language in the set. This is a conscious process giving rise to a tacit acquisition, but there is I suggest an unintended consequence of acquiring the set of languages of a *Horizontal Knowledge Structure*. I can illustrate this with my own discipline of Sociology. The array of specialised languages which fragment the experience of the acquirer, and shatter any sense of an underlying unity, yet may reveal the various ways the social is imaged by the complex, projections arising out of the relationship between individuals and groups. This diverse imaging shows the potential of the social in its different modes of realisation.

Looking through the set of languages and their fractured realities, forever facing yesterday rather than a distanced tomorrow, is rather like visiting a gallery where paintings are in continuous motion, some being taken down, others replacing and all in an unfinished state. The invisible energy activating this movement is changes in the landscapes already taken place or taking place, some disfiguring, some eroding, some opening new prospects.

Yet I suppose that the view would be markedly improved if the discursive centre of gravity shifted from the specialised languages to issues of empirical description: a shift from commitment to a language to dedication to a problem and its vicissitudes. Latour makes a distinction (see note 9) between science and research. Science refers to established canons, research refers to a dynamic interactional process. In the case of Sociology and many of its 'ofs' the specialised languages are the equivalent of science. What is being advocated here is linguistic challenge by the dynamic interactional process of research; not a displacement but a re-positioning of the role of specialised languages.

NOTES

1. In Dowling (1993, 1998) he gives the following list of authors who contrast abstract thought with concrete thought; Bernstein, Bourdieu, Foucault, Freud, Levi-Strauss, Levi-Bruhl, Lotman, Lumà, Piaget, John-Rethel, Vygotsky, Walkerdine, to which he adds his own contrast, high discursive saturation, low discursive saturation. Dowling (1998) a development of Dowling (1993) analyses what he describes as the Public Domain (the everyday world) contrasted with the Esoteric Domain (specialised knowledge structures). His analysis of the Public Domain draws on Bernstein (1996, pp. 169–181). Dowling's major contribution is the construction of a language of description of great power, rigour and potential generality, which he applies to mathematical textbooks written for students of different assumed ability levels. He shows successfully how the texts constructed for these 'ability levels' incorporate, differentially, fictional contexts and activities drawn from the Public Domain in the classification and framing of mathematical problems; in-

serted in such a way that the 'low ability' textbooks orient the student to a world of manual practice and activity to be managed by restricted mathematical operations.

2. It may be interesting to compare this discussion with that of Lave, Murtaugh and de la Rocha (1984), and also Lave (1988). Gemma Moss's research (1991, 1993, 1996, 1998) on informal literacies and their relation to formal schooled literacies is of particular interest as she has developed an original language for their description and interpretation.

3. For such differences see Bernstein (1990) chapters 2 and 3. See also Heath (1984) who I understand is now about to publish a new edition with an added epilogue.

4. Bernstein (1996) gives a detailed analysis of differences within and between 'performance' and 'competence' modes of pedagogic transmission in chapter 3.

5. There is likely to be more than one triangle in a *Hierarchical Knowledge Structure*. The motivation is towards triangles with the broadest base and the most powerful apex.

6. As languages are based on different, usually opposing, epistemological/ideological/social assumptions then the relations between them cannot be settled by empirical research. The relations can only be those of critique. Each specialised language, or rather their sponsors and authors, may accuse the other of failures of omission and/or epistemological/ideological/social inadequacies of the assumptions.

7. Bourdieu makes a similar point with reference to both the intellectual field (1984) and the cultural field (1993) where he sees change arising out of new opposing class habituses entering a field. Examples can be found in Sociology (Garfinkle and Parsons) and in Linguistics (Chomsky and Bloomfield), but I doubt whether this explanation of change holds across *Hierarchical* and *Horizontal Knowledge Structures* or necessarily within all *Horizontal Knowledge Structures*. However, it is possible, in the case of a *Horizontal Knowledge Structure* where there is an expansion of access to Higher Education under conditions of rapid social change (access and change appear to go together) new authors and their sponsors of new languages appear, arising out of their own history of such change.

8. I believe 'gaze' was first introduced by Foucault in 'The Birth of the Clinic' (1973) where it referred to the 'medical gaze' which transformed the body into a positivist object. That specialised knowledge selected and constructed a particular object, on the basis of recognition and realisation procedures internal to the specialisation of that knowledge. Dowling (1998) puts his own spin on Foucault's 'gaze' with a twist of Bernstein (1986, 1996).

'The gaze lights upon external practices which are recontextualised by it. Recontextualising entails the subordination or partial subordination of the form of expression and/or contents of practices of one activity to the regulatory principle of another' p. 136. 'We can say that the gaze of school maths recontextualises shopping practices. In so doing shopping is constituted as a set of virtual practices, it is mythologised.'

Gaze it seems is the motivator and shaper of the recontextualising process. So what is it?

'Gaze refers to a mechanism which delocates and relocates, that is which recontextualises ideological expression and content. The result of such recontextualising is to subordinate the recontextualising ideology to the regulatory principles of the recontextualising ideology' p. 136. . . . Clear?

More concrete perhaps? . . .

'That mathematics can be exchanged for shopping is contingent upon mathematics incorporating recognition and realisation principles that facilitate that exchange: the mathematics string for that retail transaction and so forth. That is what I mean by "gaze" '.

But surely what is meant here is that a specialised discourse must contain features which make 'gaze' possible. However, the conditions for 'gaze' is not what 'gaze' is. It seems to me that 'gaze' is the *result* of the recontextualising principle, 'a principle which removes (de-locates) a discourse from its substantive practice and context and relocates that discourse according to its principles of selective reordering and focusing. In this process of the de-location and the re-location of the original discourse the social basis of its practice including its powers relation is removed. In the process of the de- and re-location the original discourse is subject to a transformation which transforms it from an actual practice to a virtual or imaginary subject'. From this point of view 'gaze' is not a mechanism but is entailed in the *outcome* of the recontextualising principle. The 'mechanism' is more likely to be the principle of selection of a theory of instruction. This theory (implicit or explicit) is the means whereby a specialised discourse is pedagogised. The theory of instruction selects both the 'what' of the specialised discourse and the modality of its realisation. It guides the recontextualising process. If the matter is to be pressed further to ask what regulates this process then the answers in Bernstein's terms would be a modality of classification and framing ($\pm C^{ic}/\pm F^{ic}$). The recontextualising process translates the theory of instruction into a specific pedagogic form.

This rather lengthy comment is necessary to disentangle the use of 'gaze' in this paper. It is used to refer to the acquirer *not* to the discourse to be acquired. The pedagogic discourse to be acquired is constructed by the recontextualising process of the transmitter(s) which creates a specific modality of the specialised knowledge to be transmitted and acquired. The acquirer rarely has access to the transmitter(s) recontextualising principle but this principle is tacitly transmitted and is invisibly active in the acquirer as his/her 'gaze' which enables the acquirer metaphorically to look at (recognise) and regard, and evaluate (realise) the phenomena of legitimate concern.

9. See Latour (1979, 1987) and Serres (1995). Latour makes a crucial distinction between science and research and produces a complex description of the invisible mediations of the social process in which research is embedded. He argues that 'truth' emerges out of the relative weight of mediations of opposers and affirmers. However, Latour considers that the 'Modern Constitution' has attempted explicit work of purification by separating nature from society whilst invisibly colluding with society through processes of mediation. Truth is essentially a hybrid. From this point of view it does not make sense to ask any more where nature leaves off and society begins. Clearly there are outcomes where the dialectic of mediation is suspended and the battle lines drawn elsewhere. But the outcome must *work* discursively, that is it has to bear not simply the weight of successful mediations, but also work retrospectively with respect to the past and prospectively as a springboard to further explorations. See also Nader (1996). For different views see Wolpert (1992).

10. Indeed the issue of the relevance of the descriptions of a particular specialised language raises the even more controversial question about social change and its nature. What changes, where, extent, and with what consequences are the cause of the alleged descriptive inadequacy? In this way the demise or rise of a language may be bound up with a theory of social change which unfortunately again exists only in the pluralities of specialised languages.

11. Cooper and Dunne (1998) analysed national curriculum Mathematics texts and showed social class differences on those texts which incorporated segments from horizontal discourse in the framing of the question. Middle-class students tended to read these

questions as calling for mathematical principles, that is, they identified these questions as elements of the school's Vertical discourse. Whitty, Rowe and Aggleton (1994) showed that when a school subject drew extensively on segments of Horizontal discourse as in the theme, Personal and Social Education, the students did not regard this subject as 'academic', that is, as a realisation of Vertical discourse. Lave, Murtaugh and de la Rocha (1984) in their classic study gave an example of the lack of transfer of arithmetic competence from a shopping context to a school context. Thus the incorporation of segments of Horizontal discourse by the school may lead to such contents being defined as non-pedagogic. On the other hand, transfers of apparent competences from Horizontal discourse to the Vertical discourse of the school may not occur.

12. Interesting work remains to be done examining the recontextualising of social anthropology, linguistics, history, literature/English to provide a legitimation for what is called here pedagogic populism. A favoured position in the 70s of the school subject English. Now a position strongly held in some quarters in the U.S.A. with respect to marginalised social groups.

I should make it quite clear that it is crucial for students to know and to feel that they, the experiences which have shaped them, and their modes of showing are recognised, respected and valued. But this does not mean that this exhausts the pedagogic encounter. For to see the pedagogic encounter only in terms of a range of potential voices and their relation to each other is to avoid the issue of pedagogy itself; that is the appropriate classification and framing modality. When this is considered then, institutional, structural and interactional features are integrated in the analysis. Necessary resources (material and symbolic) can be assessed to become the site for challenge of what is and demands for what should be.

13. See any issue of the *British Journal of the Sociology of Education* for examples.

14. An important discussion of the relation between equality and diversity is in Solstad (1997).

Chapter 10

Codes and Their Positioning: A Case Study in Misrecognition

INTRODUCTION

Misrecognition takes a few lines but its exposure takes many. In this detailed case study of misrecognition I shall, perforce, have to explicate what Harker and May (1993) have silenced. This will take time and, unfortunately, cannot be done with the internal coherence and development I would wish. To begin with I will comment on the quotation from Bourdieu which Harker and May reproduce without comment, and so I take it with acceptance. I will then briefly deal with their charge that codes limit ambiguity. Here I will refer to texts 20 years old. The main study then commences. This will deal with rules and pedagogic practice, and rules and pedagogic discourse. I will then examine the construction of the concept of code and how structuralist features are integrated into the language of the theory. Finally I will consider the implications of the concept of the 'arbitrary' work in the work of Bourdieu. The appendix considers some general features of the positioning of the theory. I must make it transparently clear that I am not concerned with Bourdieu as such, or with code and habitus. I am concerned only with Harker and May's positioning of the theory and how they legitimise that positioning.

FETISHING

I am not concerned here to discuss the relationship between code and habitus, but only to respond to Harker and May's curious exposition, discussion and interpretation of my thesis, and to respond to their recycling of the accounts of others. It may be useful to start with their use of Bourdieu's comment which they accept, as this sets the scene they wish to play.

> To reproduce in scholarly discourse the fetishing of the legitimate language which actually takes place in society one has only to follow the example of Basil Bernstein who describes the properties of the elaborated code without relating this social product to the social conditions of its production and reproduction or even as one might expect from the sociology of education to its own academic condition. (Bourdieu, 1991, p. 53)

This comment, reproduced with evident approval by Harker and May, is not simply inaccurate, or only slovenly scholarships, but bizarre. If it reveals anything it reveals the activities of the intellectual field, its positioning, position taking and strategies in a somewhat primitive mode.

How does 'fetishing' square with 'The theory in these volumes focuses upon the *principles* underlying the process of interiorisation and exteriorisation, yet the focus must be such that the social relationships which this process rests upon are not abstracted from the wider institutional and cultural situation' (italics in original; Bernstein, 1975, p. 23)?

Thus the form of the social relation acts selectively on the meanings to be verbalized, which in turn affects the syntactic and lexical choices' (Bernstein, 1971, p. 177).

More formally:

> The simpler the social division of labour and the more specific and local the relation between the agent and the material base, the more direct the relation between meanings and a specific material base, and the greater the probability of restricted coding. The more complex the division of labour, the less specific and local the relation between an agent and the material base, the more indirect the relation between meanings and a specific material base and the greater the probability of elaborated coding. (Bernstein, 1981, p. 332)

Whilst the origin of codes *historically* does not lie in the productive system but in kinship systems and religious systems, that is, in the field of symbolic control, the *location* of codes lies in the class regulation of forms of social relationships *and* distribution of activities. Thus codes arise out of different modes of social solidarity, oppositionally positioned in the process of production, and differentially acquired in the process of formal education.

The original Bourdieu quotation confounds the notion of legitimate language with the concept of code. If the 'legitimate language' refers to elaborated codes then such confounding or blurring is not in my language: to understand positioning arising out of 'standard' syntax, lexes and phonology is not the project of the thesis. Indeed I would not have thought such understanding difficult to achieve. But code theory attempts to understand 'how the distribution of power and principles of control generates, distributes, reproduces and legitimates dominant and dominated principles regulating communication within and between social groups' (Bernstein, 1981, p. 327). So much for fetishing.

How about the failure 'to describe the properties of the elaborated code without relating this social product to the social conditions of its production and reproduction or even as one might expect from the sociology of education to its academic conditions'? If the fetishing charge is bizarre then the above can only have issued from a deliberate wilful misrepresentation and/or a 'reading omnipotence'. 'Reading omnipotence' is a clinical condition which renders texts which disturb one's own interpretation unread, even when they are. Omnipotence here is the author of denial.

Consider: 'From another point of view it [the paper] considers different forms of institutionalising of elaborated codes and their consequences' (Bernstein, 1971, p. 202).

Perhaps more specific:

> The realisation of elaborated codes transmitted by the family are *themselves* regulated by the form of their transmission in the school. The class assumptions of elaborated codes are to be found in the classification and framing of educational knowledge and in the ideology they express. (Italics in original; Bernstein, 1975, p. 22)

What is remarkable is that Bourdieu was well aware of Bernstein 1971 because he was responsible for the management of the French translation on *Langage et Classes Sociales,* which appeared in *Le Sens Commun* edited by Bourdieu. Indeed the foreword written by Chamboredom, with the full knowledge and agreement of Bourdieu, contains:

> C'est cette ligne d'analyse qu'ouvre le chapitre 11 ('Classification and Framing of Educational Knowledge') l'analyse des formes de socialisation reconnait deux types d'inculcation dans les formes apparement opposées de la 'restriction' de l'expression ou de l'encouragement à l'expression personnelle critique radical du spontanéisme. Cette vue peut être le point de départ d'une théorie des modes de contrôle et leur trasformation. (p. 23)

One does not have much confidence after such an introduction that my thesis will be presented with any accuracy. And sure enough, despite my own exposition of the origin of my thesis, Harker and May clearly know better. They recycle one of the few misconceptions of Atkinson (1985) that the origin of codes lies in Piagetian genetic structuralism. Harker and May make this move (strategy?) to resonate with Bourdieu's criticism of generative (or genetic) structuralism to close the circle of misrepresentation. I have written 'From Vygotsky and Luria I absorbed the notion of speech as an orienting and regulative system' (Bernstein, 1971a, p. 6). 'Whorf's psychology was influenced by the writings of the *gestalt* school of psychology whereas the thesis to be put forward here rests on the work of Vygotsky and Luria' (Bernstein, 1971c, pp. 122–3). And it so rests because my thesis was opposed to Piaget and rested on Vygotsky because of the latter's opposition to Piaget and the placing of the *social* to displace Piaget's abstracted generative structuralism. So before Harker and May's paper really gets off the ground Bernstein is:

1. a fetisher of language;
2. oblivious of the social;
3. a genetic structuralist.

Phew. What an opening!

CODES AND LIMITERS OF AMBIGUITY

I want now to look rather briefly at Harker and May's notion of code as a limiter of ambiguity, and a normaliser of practices, as I shall be returning to these matters later. The first step is a simple textual refutation. Code modalities as practices may result in attempts to control or silence ambiguities, as in the case of the early formulation of positional modalities, or *provoke* ambiguity as in the case of personal modalities.

> At the basis of meanings of an elaborated code (object) is the notion of an integrated system which generates order. In an odd way it is objective idealist in character. At the basis of meanings of an elaborated code (person) is a pluralism, a range of possibilities. It is subjective idealist or romantic in character. *Another way of seeing this might be to suggest that the major latent function of an elaborate code (object) is to remove ambiguity. Whilst the major latent function of an elaborated code (person) is to create it.* (Italics in original; Bernstein, 1971a, p. 166)

This would not be the language I would use today, as positional and personal would be entailed in the concepts of classification and framing, but the force of the quotation makes nonsense of Harker and May's notion of code even over 20 years ago. Let us be quite clear, as will be shown very explicitly later: I have pointed out on a number of occasions that code meanings are translations of social relations, within and between social groups. They are translations of the specific form taken by these relations. These meanings have arisen out of specialised forms of social interaction and control, which in the case of the modalities referred to in the above quotations are fully explicated in the text.

A little later in time we have:

> The new middle-class, like the proponents of invisible pedagogy, are caught in a contradiction: for their theories are at variance with their objective class position. A deep rooted ambivalence is the ambience of this group. On the one hand, they stand for variety against inflexibility, expression against repression, the

inter-personal against the inter-positional; on the other hand there is the grim obduracy of the division of labour and of the narrow pathways to its positions of power and prestige. (Bernstein, 1975, p. 126)

The contemporary new middle-class is unique, for in the socialisation of its young there is a sharp and penetrating contradiction between a subjective personal identity: between the release of the person and the hierarchy of class. (Bernstein, 1975, p. 136)

The empirical appropriateness of these statements is not the issue here, only the refutation of codes (modalities) as limiters of ambiguity and the constructors of mechanical, automated actors.

RULES AND PEDAGOGIC PRACTICES

Harker and May see the fundamental concept of the thesis as rules, construct the antithesis between code and habitus and reproduce Bourdieu's strictures against structuralism, in particular that of Lévi-Strauss: a nice closed circle. As Harker and May commence with a discussion of what they take to be my analysis of pedagogic practice, I will also begin at that point and spend a little longer than they did on the exposition.

It is the case that any pedagogic practice is considered as a set of rules, hierarchical, selective, sequential/pacing and criterial, but these rules do not *constitute* the code. These rules, in themselves, do not cause anything, they simply direct attention to the controls on the form taken by the temporal features (selective, sequential/pacing), the textual features (criteria) and contextual features (hierarchy) which *specialise pedagogic practice as a form of communication*. 'I shall argue that the inner logic of pedagogic practice as a cultural relay is provided by a set of rules and the nature of these rules acts selectively on the content of any pedagogic practice' (Bernstein, 1990, p. 63). But the inner logic is not the code, although it may appear similar to the distinction between language and speech.[1] *How* these rules position interactions, discourse and contexts reveals the code, the interests the code serves, those whose interests are not so served, the form challenge takes, and by whom. Now if we want to know how an actual practice is played out, if we want to now about the game (in popular academic speak), then according to the theory we must examine the code modality, that is the *classification and framing*.

I shall deal with framing first. Harker and May are a little coy about definitions with respect to my thesis; they are more concerned with epistemological gloss. Framing is conceptualised as the locus of control over pedagogic communication and its context. Framing varies according to whether the locus of control is towards the transmitter or towards the acquirer. From the beginning this has been the case. 'Thus frame refers to the degree of control teacher and pupil possess over the selection, organisation, pacing and timing of the knowledge transmitted and received in the pedagogic relation' (Bernstein, 1971, pp. 205–6). Since 1971 the concept has, of course, undergone further theoretical and empirical analysis, but it is basically as above. Thus framing arises out of the teacher/pupil (or its symbolic equivalent doctor/patient, social worker/client etc.) relationship, according to the locus of control, and creates the pedagogic arena, game (in popular speak) or specific practice. We have now moved from rules which distinguish the practice to the *particular* interactional practice and its *specific locational* and *communicative realisations.*[2] With this move, wherever we are, we are certainly not in the abstracted rules of structuralism of Lévi-Strauss or Saussure.

Now what about strategies, the creative, indeterminate feature of practice, an outcome of the 'feel' of the situation, games played and desire to maximise or optimise position? Strategy resonates between the practical sense and cognition. What a winner of a concept. But rules construct a mechanical world which, watch for it, can become the actual world. Strategies humanise, and arise out of practice. Unfortunately strategies appear to realise a sort of social Hobbesian world, not mechanical, only exploitative. Perhaps a touch of social Darwinism. The strategic, if not the fittest, survive, under the best conditions. But 'strategy' is missing from code theory which is therefore inflexible and rigid.

Let me take here, to illustrate my own position, a somewhat extreme case: the feeding of a baby. To begin with, this seems to be unproblematic, with respect to its recognition as a practice. But a little thought shows this is not the case. Imagine a member from a remote culture, although a breast-feeding culture, confronted by a man with a bottle thrust in a baby's mouth. The member might well consider that she/he is witnessing a barbaric ritual or worse. Consider a case of our remote members beamed down into a park where a woman is breast feeding a baby seated on a long park bench in the company of men. This may not be recognised as a feeding situation, as the context is inappropriate, for in this remote culture, breast feeding is a very strongly classified activity with regard to location and gender. Baby feeding may well presuppose recognition rules provided by the classification values. This does not mean that all baby feeding necessarily meets the condition for its legitimate recognition, otherwise one recourse for changing classification values (strong/weak) would be excluded.

Now let us consider two situations nearer home in space but not, in our first example, in time. In our first example of baby feeding (a primary and fundamental pedagogic practice from the baby's perspective) the locus of control lies with the feeder. The feeder decides when feeding (transmission) takes place, feeding times (sequencing), and feeding duration (criteria). Very strong framing. The baby's strategy to announce hunger, particularly unconsummated, delayed hunger, is to produce a particular cry, which signifies this unpleasant state. But the feeder is impervious to this cry if it threatens the sequencing rules, and is likely to dismiss the cry as irrelevant or, even more likely, as an ineffective strategy. In fact the feeder, by ignoring the strategy (crying), hopes to eradicate the strategy. However the baby is unlikely to relinquish one of the few strategies in the potential repertoire. The baby creatively elaborates the strategy; not only by amazing feats of endurance, but by embellishing the acoustic display with truly frightening visual displays, turning blue or even purple, and perhaps in a last creative effort draining colour completely. Another possibility is to develop, through discipline, an opposing, rather dangerous, strategy: refusal to feed at the imposed time. Simply close lips—withhold the sucking response. Extreme, perhaps, but strong framing calls for extreme measures. This strategy has good chances of success as it threatens the feeding relation, the feeder, and the concept the feeder has of being a feeder. There are, of course, other strategies, which we can call displaced strategies, as their object is not directed to change the locus of control in the context of their exercise, but in another context chosen by the baby.

Now if we take a second situation where the locus of control over transmission, sequence and criteria lie with the baby, we have demand feeding or in my terms very weak framing. Here the baby may easily have the 'illusion' that there is no desire except his own, and no criteria except its own. It apparently has complete control over all of its orifices. Orificial control. It may well be that it can begin to generalise such control to other contexts. Here the baby begins to develop a range of strategies for maximising the submission of others as a means of maximising the possibilities of its position. Its creativity is differently specialised compared with the sibling discussed earlier. Practices are differentially specialised. Both babies are creative in their strategies, both develop situational 'feel', but strategies and 'feel' are selectively elicited and facilitated by variations in framing. I am a little uncertain here about the transposability of strategies across framing modalities.

Perhaps another example of classification and framing, rules, practices, strategies and creativity also drawn from orificial regulation would be useful.

Imagine a lavatory, clinically white, stark and bare, except for functional cleansing equipment, supports and resources and functional removal facilities, separated from the outside by a door with an effective lock. A very strongly classified space and function, associated I would suggest with two rules of usage; one for between-context relationships (classification) and one for within-context practice (framing).

Between Contexts

No noise on the inside should be heard on the outside or, more generally, no leakage between contexts (one flush allowed).

Within Context

Leave the space as you found it and evacuate with reasonable speed (temporal rule). However, as we know, in no sense are these rules casual. But whatever the communicative realisation *within* the context (framing) there will be *selective realisations* (strong framings + F) whether these realisations are supportive or subverting of the rules. Note that framing realisations maintain, disturb or challenge classificatory values *both* within and between contexts.

Let us start with the between-context rule, regulating leakage between contexts. There is a range of strategies available (some gender specific) with respect to *sound* (position, posture and direction, momentum, pacing, etc.) and considerable potential for creative intuitive practice. '

A range of strategies is also available for the within-context rule: leave the space as you found it. A safe strategy may be to avoid altogether the cleansing equipment, supports and resources. Minimal use of cleansing equipment, etc., is another possibility. But both strategies may not be safe to the discerning eye of the next user. On the other hand, the over-compensation of vigorous cleansing may lead to spillage. This has to be removed, leading perhaps to an overly damp and possibly stained towel. This, in turn, requires considerable inventiveness in the rearrangement and placing of the towel. Flapping the towel as a manual dispenser may be a creative transfer strategy from another context (game?). And so on.

It might be queried that these strategies are not maximising strategies with respect to position, position taking and capital, but this would be incorrect. Inasmuch as the between and within-context rules translated by $+C^{ie}/+F^{ie}$, do not give rise to contextually specific appropriate strategies of practice, then cultural, social and possibly economic capital may be reduced. The situation calls for maximising the *prevention* of a diminution of capital.

It may be useful to continue this analysis. Both between-context rules (classification) and within-context (framing) rules do not specify the practice to follow. They do not instruct *how* that practice is to be realised. These rules specify the *criteria* any practice must meet. There is a general pacing, criterial rule (evacuate with reasonable speed). Perhaps some sequencing rule within the activity of removal (flush second), but this is probably a derivation from the criterial rule, 'leave the space as you found it'. However, *how* the practice is realised is not rule governed. Agency is essentially trammelled only by criterial rules, which act selectively on the practice, whether the practice meets the criteria or otherwise. Here we have a situation where the agent (subject?) can produce his or her own style. And this is because it is invisible to others provided the criterial rules are observed.

Now imagine there is a tiny spy-glass whose cover can be removed, hidden in the door. And we have two observers who both produce the same statement about the completed activity: 'Good God, they do it that way!' However, for one observer 'that way!' is located in regulative discourse and is a positional shaming statement. For the second observer 'that way!' is located in instructional discourse, 'Really interesting. I must make a note of that' and in a personal modality. These differences in evaluation flowing from the same statement I would attribute to different code modalities through which the respective habitus has been constructed. In this way we can see how code modalities construct different structuring structures and, if we want to use this language, how specialised habituses can become more transparent with respect to the specific conditions of their formation.

In contrast with the lavatory I have just described and analysed, I remember a rather different one constructed in the home of a new miss-class Hampstead pair I visited. A uniquely personal construction represented by plants, books, journals and one wall on which were pasted a number of postcards. The lock on the door was inoperable and the door itself was not easy to close as it had warped. Without a doubt an apparent $-C^{ie}/-F^{ie}$ modality. I happened to have a postcard myself which I added to the display. I was the only guest and, a little later, one of the pair took me on one side and said, 'Darling, it's a lovely card but don't you think it should go a little higher, perhaps towards the left'.

This response is an aesthetic shaming response in the personal modality of regulative discourse. Quite deadly, as it is an evaluation of my style entailing a considerable reduction in, at least, cultural capital. Agency had been found wanting, the practical sense had failed. I had failed to recognise the principle of the display; a deficit habitus! I failed to produce an appropriate 'text'. The principle was implicit and, perhaps, could not be put into words successfully, but could be demonstrated, The principle is a style realisation. Only a close relation, a possibly enduring relation, with the Hampstead pair would have enabled me to model their style successfully (model *not* imitate). I would be exposed to a range of exemplars. I would be able to watch the construction of displays and note the acceptance of certain positions, colours, textures, movements, etc., and the rejection of others. In this way I might be able to grasp the principle and produce an acceptable practice. Nothing mysterious here. But note the process of acquisition of this style, the pedagogising, is regulated by a restricted code as the modelling principle, the generative principle is shown, demonstrated, experienced, rather than verbally elaborated. However, if this style is acquired via a restricted code the *ultimate display* is part of the discourse of an elaborated code modality.

The analysis of 'style' suggests that there may well be fundamentally different modes of pedagogising, a primary mode where the acquisition process is exclusively local, context dependent, implicit and non-linguistic. Where principles are virtually unrecoverable and the consequences enduring and very difficult to eradicate. A mode of pedagogising where the pedagogue is as unaware of pedagogy as the pedagogised. This is the perfect form of the restricted code: exclusively local, totally context dependent, implicit, non-linguistic. What is specialised by such a code? The acculturation of the body and its relation to other bodies in space (see on habitus Mauss, 1935). The cultural coordination of the muscular system, the specialisation of its release of activity, movement and posture, 'style', is from this point of view acquired through modelling kinship exemplars. However, although this *process* is a tacit outcome of enduring intimacy, the realisations are still monitored, and corrections given if bodily displays fail criteria. 'Don't slouch'. 'We do it like this', etc. 'No, not like them dear'. This suggests that the *monitoring procedure* can be realised through a variety of code modalities. This analysis can be extended to the acquisition of styles of dress; the tacit acquisition of what goes with what, where and how. It does seem that the theory can throw some light on generating practices and their intuitive sense.

Are these analyses examples of Saussurian, Lévi-Straussian, Piagetian structuralism? Where is the fetishing of communication? Is it clear that we can distinguish between classification and framing modalities of different strengths. How a practice is put together may be subject to either explicit or implicit principles. Strong framing may closely restrict how a practice is put together and developed in time, by laying down explicit rules and procedures for the construction of a particular practice (Morais et al., 1993), thus limiting or delaying the appearance of indeterminacy. It should also be clear that classification and framing not only specialise communications, but also specialise the construction of locations—spatial arrangements within context and thus their 'readings'.[3]

Perhaps a final example might not come amiss, although I have given it previously. This example shows the transposability of strategies across classification and framing modalities in *different* contexts. Consider a secondary school with code values $+C^{ie}/+F^{ie}$ in which the pedagogic relations are between a teacher and a class of students who have been disabled by the code. If the code is to be challenged then it cannot be done by the practice of an isolated student. The challenge requires changing the social positioning of acquisition from isolated, privatised, competitive student relationships to communal, collective, non-competitive relations. There must be a chance in students' mode of social integration. Given this change the transformed group can substitute its own norm of production for that of the teacher's norm. The group can now impose its own realisation rules. These may well include sabotaging the means of pedagogic practice, setting up collective challenges, etc. These strategies and practices may well be transferred from education to the work site (depending upon its code modality).

RULES AND PEDAGOGIC DISCOURSE

Let me now turn to the analysis of pedagogic discourse according to Harker and May: 'Bernstein's analysis of pedagogic discourse with its concerns deriving from code theory to explore the principles of selection and combination'. This, as a description, is to say the least entirely misleading. It is best understood as a strategic move to produce a resonance with their apparently Bourdieu-based interpretation of codes. The move here is identical to their positioning of pedagogic practice as *only* a set of combination rules. Rules are abstracted from the process of the structuring of social relations, groupings and contexts through which specific pedagogic practices are constructed, appropriated and legitimised: rules are not codes.

In the case of the formulation of pedagogic practice, rules refer to the set of controls which are considered to give this practice its distinguishable communicative form and context. The rules become resources for appropriation in the construction of specific pedagogic practices/communications and contexts. They also become sources of challenge and defence. How the rules are realised as *resources* is a function of classification and framing produced by the power and control relations of those groups dominating the specific realisations. Here we have the codes, specialised practices, 'feel' of particular contexts, development of practical intuition *and* the arenas to which they give rise.

In the case of the pedagogic discourse paper, that paper is concerned with production, reproduction and change of pedagogic discourse. The paper is concerned with identifying the general conditions which distinguish any pedagogic discourse, and also how specific pedagogic discourses are constructed, maintained and changed. The first formulation is not referred to as a code but as a *device*. The *second* formulation, which shows how specific pedagogic discourses are constructed, maintained and changed through processes of recontextualisation, the fields in which this takes place, and the positions which activate this process, *gives rise to code modalities*. The distributive, recontextualising and criterial rules of the device are referred to as a grammar, in the sense of ordering principles connecting the various levels of activity which are entailed in the production of pedagogic discourse and which give this discourse its distinguishing features. The device is considered as a symbolic ruler of consciousness, giving rise to the question 'Whose ruler, what consciousness?'. Groups attempt to appropriate the device to impose their *rule* by the construction of particular code modalities. Thus the device or apparatus becomes the focus of challenge, resistance and conflict, both within and between social groups. The function of the device is to translate power relations into discourse and discourse into power relations. However, in the process of controlling the discourse, the discourse made available necessarily carries the potential of its own disturbance. The model which shows how specific code modalities are constructed and relayed and changed traces this process from the state to families and local communities.

How this analysis can be written off as 'to explore principles of selection and combination' is beyond my understanding except as a field-positioning strategy. As a matter of interest the analysis of pedagogic discourse was referred to by Shilling (1992) as one of the first *poststructuralist analyses* in the sociology of education. So much for the fetishing and objectifying.

THE CONCEPT OF CODE AND SPECIFIC MODALITIES

At this point I would like to consider the concept of code in more detail. Nowhere in Harker and May is there a definition of code, only repetitive reference to rules. We are offered instead 'Bernstein has employed the notion of code *together* [my italics] with his concept of classification and framing, visible and invisible pedagogies to pursue in a relentless analytic manner the way symbolic control is exerted over the educational system', or '. . . principles of selection and combination'. The first quotation separates, dislocates codes from classification and framing and the latter from visible and invisible pedagogies; indeed from the construction and description of other pedagogic forms. It is as if there is code and a series of *ad hoc* conceptual add-ons.

From the early formulations code has been analysed with regard to the distinction between orientation to meanings *and* realisation of meanings. Thus, for example, it is possible to have similar orientation (elaborated) but different forms, modalities of realisation. In the late 1960s positional and personal modalities were distinguished (see Bernstein, 1971c, pp. 152–163). Briefly, social class distributed orientation to meanings elaborated/restricted, mediated by particular cultural and structural specialisations of families and occupational positions. Modalities of realisations have more complex origins (Bernstein, 1986).

The general definition of code first appeared in Adlam et al. (1977) and is formally explicated in Bernstein (1981) as follows:

A code is a regulative principle, tacitly acquired which selects and integrates
(a) relevant meanings,
(b) forms of their realisation,
(c) evoking contexts.

I have changed here only the spatial lay-out of the definition. From this general definition it is possible to conceptualise specific code modalities by a process of translation of the above three elements.

- *context* translates as interactional practices
- *meanings* translates as orientation to meanings
- *realisation* translates as textual productions.[4]

Different distributions of power and principles of control differentially shape interactional practices according to different classification and framing values and thus give rise to different orientations to meaning, forms of realisations and so 'texts'. The formulation, above, shows visually the possibility of the produced text having consequences for expected meanings and their generating interactional practices. The formulation for specifying specific code modalities then becomes as follows. The horizontal line indicates the embedding of the orientation to meaning in the conditions of its realisation and their contexts:

$$\frac{O^{E/R}}{\pm C^{ie}/\pm F^{ie}}$$

where

$O^{E/R}$ refers to orientation to elaborated/restricted meanings

C　refers to the principle of the classification, that is the relation between categories

F　refers to the principle of framing

$+$　refers to strong–weak values

i　refers to internal control within a context

e　refers to external control/direction of communicative relations between contexts, e.g. family–school, community–school, school–work.

(Bernstein, 1986, p. 350)

In view of the above, and the previous discussion, it is interesting to compare Harker and May's positioning of the concept of code. Throughout their paper Harker and May hide behind Bourdieu who becomes the front for their own position. They take, in their paper, the criticism of Bourdieu against structuralism then state that my theory is structuralist *in the same way* as those of Lévi-Strauss and Saussure.

> The premise underlying Bernstein's conception of language is as we have already suggested *reminiscent* [my italics] of the distinction drawn by Saussure (1974) between language as la langue and la parole and articulated by Lévi-Strauss in similar fashion in structural anthropology through his notions of 'unconscious structures' and rules as separated from generating practices (see Bourdieu, 1990). Bernstein may be a politicised version of such a model but it is still one Bourdieu rejects.

I am not interested in what Bourdieu may happen to accept or reject, although I may share part of his objections to Lévi-Strauss and Saussure. I am more concerned with Harker and May's textual swerves in the above quotation. My conception is 'reminiscent', reminds who and in what way? Not that the code thesis is structuralist *in a particular way*, but that it resonates with a *particular kind* which Bourdieu rejects and which Harker and May reject.

The formulation of code and code modalities is far removed from the disembodied structures and decontextualised rules of Lévi-Strauss's culturalism and of Saussure. Although in the latter case *I do agree with Halliday that language is one system with la langue and la parole in a dialectical relation with each other.* There is a surface/structure distinction in my thesis, of course, but how do we regard theories which reveal that apparently dissimilar 'texts' are analogic products of a common generative structuring structure? Clearly there are structuralist features. Indeed I have referred to these myself. But, and the 'but' is crucial, how are these structuralist features integrated with other features so as to distinguish *the* theory or for that matter any theory? Indeed the integration may be such that it is futile and misleading to abstract one feature from the language of the theory. And it is this act which Harker and May have carried out with such relentless and dedicated misrecognition. How do the rules Harker and May refer to operate?[5]

1. They function to distinguish the set of controls which distinguish the object(s) of the theory.
2. They are *resources* for the construction of code modalities. They are *not* codes.
3. The *specific* practices to which the rules give rise are not contained within the rules, within the devices, but arise out of the classification and framing of practices, communication and contexts.
4. The code modalities translate distributions of power and principles of control into discursive practices, and discursive practices into power and control relations.
5. Arena (fields) arise out of the construction, appropriation defence, resistance and challenge of code modalities by social groups/social classes.

I have given examples of how the theory shows in what way the specialisation of practices, communications and contexts constructed by different code modalities act selectively on the generation of practices, communications, strategies, sense and 'feel'. In this way the theory provides some understanding of the different specialisations of the habitus; a much needed specification.

THE CONCEPT OF 'ARBITRARY'

I would like to change focus at this point and briefly look at Harker and May's view of my views about Bourdieu. I shall not spend too much time here as I am not concerned with Bourdieu as such. First, Harker and May state that my analysis of pedagogic discourse 'starts where Bourdieu and Passeron (*Reproduction in Education, Society and Culture*) left off'. This is nonsense. The basic recontextualising model is set out in the Introduction to *Class, Codes and Control*, Vol. III, 1975, p. 31, developed in Bernstein, 1981, whilst the concepts of instructional and regulative discourse go back much earlier (Bernstein, 1965). From the initial analysis of the school my concern had always focused on how 'relations within' are constituted, before extension to 'relations between'. I clearly have gained much from reading Bourdieu; in particular, the concept of field. But there is a considerable difference which emerges out of my development of the importance of exploring within/between relationships. I would still hold that, certainly with respect to reproduction, and even with respect to features of production, Bourdieu is not interested, for conceptual reasons in 'relations within', despite Harker and May's protestations. Edward Li Puma (1993) in a perceptive, critical essay distinguishes three uses of 'arbitrary' in Bourdieu's project. First, any particular cultural manifestation is arbitrary from a cross-cultural perspective. Second, there is what Li Puma calls a formal arbitrariness *within* a culture, e.g. the high but arbitrary valuation of upper class culture or any one of its distinguishing features (taste). Li Puma maintains there is a third, far more thoroughgoing use, that Bourdieu holds 'an absolute substantive theory of arbitrariness'. Thus '*any* feature, accent, aesthetic judgement or text can have served the same function within the historical evolution of bourgeois distinction'. It is this which is responsible for Bourdieu's disinterest in the constitution of a specific signifier of distinction, that is 'of relations within'. *Homo academicus* is not about the constitution of academic discourses, their systems of transmission, their formations of specialised consciousness, it is about power games and their strategies. What is exposed is the game. This necessarily follows from Bourdieu's relational analysis of fields. There is no need to show how a *specific* should have a determinate content.

CONCLUSION

The primary social unit of the thesis is not an individual but a relationship: a pedagogic relation, formal or informal. The theory is not, and has no pretension of being, a general social theory as designated by Harker and May. It is perhaps a sociological theory of the pedagogising of communication, part of a more general theory of symbolic control. It is general inasmuch as it can be, and has been applied to a range of societies and cultures. It gives'rise to research in which macro and micro levels are integrated (e.g. Cox Donoso, 1986; Jenkins, 1990). It can and has been applied to a range of cultural forms, e.g. architecture, painting, music.

Finally I would like to quote, yet again, the following:

But the transmission/acquisition systems the thesis projects do not create copper etching plates in whose lines we are trapped. Nor are the systems, grids, networks and pathways embedded in either concrete or quicksand. The transmission/ acquisition systems reveal and legitimate the enabling and disabling functions of power relations which they relay and upon which they rest. Attempts to model the internal principles of such transmission do not make them eternal. Such analysis may show the poles of choice for any set of principles and the assemblies possible within these poles. It calls attention to the selective effects of transmission, their social costs and the basis for change (Bernstein, 1990).

Harker and May have transformed the logic of things into a thing of logic, their logic.

NOTES

1. I have referred to the distinction between rules which distinguish the crucial features of a specialised form of communication (practice or discourse) from the various forms of its realisation as similar to the distinction between language and speech. This is to draw attention to what I consider important, the unambiguous recognition of the crucial features which construct a specialised form of communication *and* the way these features become resources for appropriation in the construction of specific practices. This form of conceptualising is not an ideal typical construction. In the case of pedagogic practices, the hierarchical rules, and in the case of pedagogic discourse, the distributive rules (always discussed first), regulate the other rules. This makes the too ready identification with Saussure important for dissimilarities. I have, of course, acknowledged my debt to Saussure via Durkheim, 'It is the linking of Durkheim with structuralism particularly forms of structuralism originating in linguistics (Saussure) which had I believe the strongest influence upon the *form* the theorising took' (italics in the original; chapter 4). Indeed, anyone working in the field of semiotics cannot but acknowledge the influence of Saussure, but to acknowledge this influence does not mean replication of a model. It means to absorb an influence and integrate it with others to produce an evolving language of description.

2. It is important to note that framing refers to the locus of control over:
   1. Interaction . . . the selection, organisation sequencing criteria and pacing of communication (oral, visual and written) together with the position, posture and dress of communicants.
   2. Location . . . physical location and the form of its realisation (i.e. the range of objects, their attributes, their relations to each other and the space in which they are constituted (Bernstein, 1981, p. 343).

It should be clear from the above that the feel of the situation/game varies with the form taken by the interaction and location: that is, with framing and internal classificatory values.

3. On spatial displays and their cultural specialisations see *Class, Codes and Control: Towards a Theory of Educational Transmission* (Bernstein, 1975, pp. 134–135).

4. This formulation is a micro-level formulation but it is possible to translate to macro-institutional levels.

Interaction		Institutional
relevant meaning	→	discursive practices
forms of realisation	→	transmission practices
evoking contexts	→	organisational practices

5. There are rules in the theory to which Harker and May do not refer, and, for completion of this account, I will introduce them here and show their function. Classification and framing values give rise to recognition rules (criteria), by which relevant contexts are distinguished, and realisation rules for assembling legitimate texts and interactions. The

extent to which a realisation rule excludes variation is a function of the strength of classification and framing ($\pm C^{ic}/\pm F^{ic}$). Consider a school where when a new student delivers an
essay as part of a homework assignment. The teacher says, 'This is an excellent essay. Did
you do it by yourself?', to which the student replies, 'No, as a matter of fact, I talked it
over with some friends first. They were really helpful.' The teacher answers firmly, 'OK
this time but next time I want you to do it by yourself!'. Note, it is not entirely clear how
restrictive is 'by yourself'. Our student transfers to another school and an identical situation arises. This teacher says 'I really liked your essay. How did you do it?', to which the
student replies proudly 'I did it by myself!'. The teacher replies gently 'OK, this time but
next time why don't you talk it over with Jane, Dick, Sarah and Bill. You'll find them very
helpful.' (For more restrictive recognition and realisation rules see Morais et al., 1992;
Daniels, 1989; and for other contexts see Bernstein, 1981, Appendix.)

APPENDIX

In general the most puzzling features of the representation of the code thesis are:

1. selective recontextualising;
2. dislocation of the thesis from its development;
3. abstracting one feature of the analysis (structuralism), or one discipline,
   from its integration in the language of the thesis;
4. fracturing the integration of codes with the forms of their institutionalisation;
5. parasitic recycling of 'representations' culminating in the invisibility of the
   original text;
6. the positioning of the thesis in a moral and/or epistemological economy (a
   notable feature of sociological activity often preferred to empirical research
   or to the empirical grasp of a thesis);
7. the absence of reference to the author's own intervention in the closed cir-
   cuit of legitimate field comment.

Clearly these puzzling features must be distinguished from serious, critical
engagement without which there can be no development of a theory or of the intellectual field.

There appear to have been three powerful motivations at work in the positioning of the thesis: religious, moral, discursive and epistemological, although it is
difficult sometimes to separate the three.

Religious/Moral

Critics here are less critics but more priests performing ritual cleansing. Texts
must undergo simplification and reduction, both of their temporal development
and conceptual structure, as a pre-condition for revealing pollution and to activate

a sacred purging of the field. Research apparently influenced by the thesis must render that influence invisible or at least opaque. Referees' comments ensure that the parasitic circle is closed and reproduced as their comments call for the recycling of criticisms which take on a facticity through repetition rather than validity.

Epistemological

The second motivation produces what could usefully be called epistemological botany. Here the assumptions of the theory, or what are taken to be the assumptions of the theory, are classified. Acceptance or rejection follows from this classification of what counts or otherwise as a legitimate knowledge form. Once the theory has been found wanting by the botanist the theory can be dismissed. Such epistemological botany renders great service to both the recontextualising field and to the agents of reproduction and acquisition. It produces an important reading economy for both lecturers and students.

It is interesting to note the recognition criteria used by epistemological botanists to pin and identify a knowledge form. Sometimes a cursory glance at a model expressed in diagrammatic form. Sometimes a cursory glance at a model expressed in diagrammatic form equipped with directional indicators is sufficient for classification. The explanatory text, network of concepts, powers of description are irritating and obscure digressions. Indeed sometimes a visual model itself triggers a classification almost as if the botanist is genetically programmed.

Discursive

A third motivation for positioning can arise from the discursive base of the theory. If a theory's base is not discourse specific, but is a mixed category, there are fascinating possibilities. Any one discourse can be abstracted and disembedded from such a base. The abstracted discourse can then be put to the litmus test of moral, epistemological pollution *and,* as a bonus, discursive violation. The latter refers to what is taken to be a vulgarisation of the discourse. Here we can have a combination of pollution and violation. Pollution refers to categories and violation to interaction. This can be played out, separately, with every discourse which is integrated in the theory. What a winner.

Time Warping

This is not a motivation but an optional field strategy. If the theory can be placed in the temporal plane of its development then time warping is a potential and effective positioning strategy. A theory which can attract this strategy is one which over a relatively long period of research develops greater generality, explicitness, integration of levels and powers of description. Here the time warp strategy can operate. Recontextualisers may decide in which time frame they are going to situate their re-presentation. Once the time frame becomes self-sealing we can say a time warp has been established.

Now if we relate religious, epistemological and discursive positioning possibilities with temporal possibilities (time warping), we have a truly formidable set of combinations for generating and particularising practices. We can render this slightly more formally. Religious, epistemological and discursive positioning are category relations, and so spatial and therefore subject to classificatory principles, whereas time warping is temporal, and so subject to framing. This we can begin to see how classification and framings regulate positioning and how modalities are a realisation of field-constructed motivations.

Oh dear, is this a structuralist analysis?

Postscript

Chapter 11

Bernstein Interviewed

INTRODUCTION

Basil Bernstein's theory of symbolic control and cultural production, reproduction and change, developed since the late 1950s until today, is famous for its complex, formal and generative character and has gained international acknowledgment. It has provided inspiration for theoretical work in a variety of disciplines and the conceptual framework for robust and sensitive sociological empirical research on cultural and particularly pedagogic practices and their effects, in many parts of the world (Bernstein, 1990, pp. 3–6 and 1996, pp. 91–133). This research in turn was used in the continuous development and refinement of the theory.

For a variety of reasons (cf. Atkinson, Delamont and Davies, 1995, p. x) the theory was not always welcome, or well treated, in the Anglo-Saxon intellectual milieu. It has caused strong controversy and has sometimes become the object of crude oversimplification, miscomprehension, as well as of political and ideological misuse. The case of language codes, elaborated and restricted, constitutes a notorious example of all of the above.

The theory is explicitly grounded on selected and inventively 'remolded' elements of modern social theory and critically incorporates features of more recent currents of thought. Bernstein is an author who consistently gives detailed accounts of the theorists and their concepts used, as well as of the way they are used in his own work (e.g. Bernstein, 1973, pp. 17–39, 168, 194–198; 1977, pp. 1–33; 1990, pp. 133–134; 1996, pp. 147–152), and several analysts of his work have engaged in locating and discussing its many and sometimes seamingly disparate theoretical bastions (see Atkinson, 1985; Solomon, 1989; Dickinson and Erben, 1995, etc). Nevertheless, this theory is in many respects original, if not unique. Although generally positioned within the broad category of cultural reproduction theories, it is, to my knowledge and understanding, the only theory which:

1. systematically encompasses and connects in one device different contexts of experience, such as work, family and education, and different levels of regulation: from class relations and the state, through curriculum and pedagogy, down to the level of individual subjects;
2. aims at the creation of a language to provide consistent sociological descriptions of practices of regulation and conceptual tools for research;
3. contains from its outset variation and change, actual or potential, at and between all levels of the device.

What makes the taking and publication of an interview with Basil Bernstein in the late 1990s an interesting enterprise? To start with, there is a set of relatively recent events that mark a change in climate about his work in the English speaking intellectual community which has proved to be rather suspicious of this 'indigenous' complex theoretical discourse; such events are the publication of two collections of texts on or drawing from Bernstein's work, one edited by Atkinson, Davies and Delamont (1995), the other edited by Sadovnik (1995). Another, more recent one of a similar nature is the conference 'Knowledge, Identity, Pedagogy', organised by the University of Southampton and realised in March 1998, which almost exclusively was focused on Bernstein's theory and contribution to research (to be published in *Education and Linguistics*).

The publication in early 1996 of Basil Bernstein's most recent book, *Pedagogy, Symbolic Control and Identity: Theory, Research, Critique* (referred to by many as 'Vol. 5', although it is the only one among his books not titled or subtitled *Class, Codes and Control*) is the other crucial event. In this book Bernstein deals, in a distinctly formalised and more narrative and personal style than usual, with the basic themes and further elaborations and extensions of 'codes theory' and its relations to research (see also *British Journal of the Sociology of Education*, 18, 1, 1997, pp. 115–128 for a 'Review Symposium' on the book, by Atkinson, Singh and Ladwig).

These events not only reposition the theory itself and explicate its dimensions and capacities, but also, and more importantly, demonstrate its strong relations to and with research and discuss its influences on sociology of education as well as on the analysis of institutions and practices of symbolic control, as objects of sociological enquiry, other than those of pedagogy and education *stricto senso*.

This growth of interest in Bernstein's work is, to my belief, related not strictly to a change in the intellectual arena but more specifically to a new globalised need for an explanatory framework and for tools to understand and analyse contemporary changes occurring in work, in education and other regulatory institutions/practices and their consequences for identity construction, particularly in the context of: a) education reforms taking place not only in the U.K. but gradually in many other countries, especially in Europe and America, since the mid-1980s; and b) changes in technology, economy, the labour market and culture, all drastically affecting ways of being, of becoming, of feeling, thinking and relating. These issues may well challenge the generality of the theory and lead to its further development.

One of the many acts of international recognition of Basil Bernstein's work and, as I suggested above, one of the expressions of a trans-national search for a comprehensive explanatory framework of the 'new conditions', has been his nomination as Honorary Doctor of the University of Athens in November 1996, where, in his inaugurative lecture, he treated the subject 'Official Knowledge and Pedagogic Identities'. This is when and where this interview was born, although, technically, it was completed several months later through electronic mail.

In this interview Professor Bernstein responds extensively to questions concerning the concept of pedagogy, its role in the theory and its capacities to deal with different realities of regulation and construction within different contexts and not only formal education; the concept of identities and its relations to 'codes' and 'discourse'; 'boundaries' as a conceptual 'key' of the theory; the transformations of the theory from a 'code-centered' theory to a 'discourse-centered' one, as well as issues concerning the structure, the production strategy and the development of the theory in time. Thus the reader will recognise here not only basic themes of the theory but also some new steps towards extending the horizons of the theory, as well as more personal and usually hidden aspects of authorship and intellectual production as a process.

J. S.: Professor Bernstein, in your predominantly sociological work on cultural production, reproduction and change you retain a very special place to the concept of pedagogy, pedagogy is usually considered elsewhere as a lower order concept referring simply to an undifferentiated set of practices of upbringing and education, to methods and processes of transmission and acquisition, aiming at developing knowledjes, skills and moral order.

In your theory this concept functions, I believe, at a higher level of abstraction referring to varying sets of rules and principles and to devices generating differing sorts of practices producing different sorts of identities. Could you expand on how you understand this concept, why and how you use it in your theory and what are its capacities for addressing cultural practices and experiences other than education?

B. B.: To start with it is necessary to distinguish between pedagogic consequences and a pedagogic relation. All experiencing carries a pedagogic potential, but all experiences are not pedagogically generated.

When I talk about pedagogy, I am referring to pedagogic relations that shape pedagogic communications and their relevant contexts. Three basic forms of pedagogic relation may be distinguished: explicit, implicit and tacit. Explicit and implicit refer to a progressive in time pedagogic relation where there is a purposeful intention to initiate, modify, develop or change knowledge, conduct or practice by someone or something which already possesses, or has access to, the necessary resources *and* the means of evaluating the acquisition. The acquirer may or may not define the relation as legitimate, or accept as otherwise, what is to be acquired. Explicit or implicit refers to the visibility of the transmitter's intention as to what is to be acquired from the point of view of the acquirer. In the case of explicit pedagogy the intention is highly visible, whereas in the case of implicit pedagogy the intention from the point of view of the acquirer is invisible. The tacit is a pedagogic relation where initiation, modification, development or change of knowledge, conduct or practice occurs, where neither of the members may be aware of it. Here the meanings are non-linguistic, condensed and context dependent; a pure restricted code relay. An example would be modelling, perhaps the primary pedagogic mode; primary in the sense of time and primary in the sense of durability. This primary modelling where both transmitter and acquirer are unaware of a pedagogic relation must be distinguished from secondary modelling which is a deliberate and purposive relation only for the acquirer.

Now, take the instance of a request for information. We can distinguish cases where the information is given without regard to the one to be informed, and cases where information is given where the informer adapts the information according to perceived need. In the latter case there is an element of recontextualising which may have a complex backing. I suggest that such a shaped response occurs in what I call horizontal discourse and is a *segmental pedagogic act* often exhausted at the point of its consumption.

In the case of segmental pedagogic acts, there is always present an intention to initiate, or modify or develop or change knowledge or conduct or practice or all three, although the acquisition of the criteria or information may not always be subject to evaluation on the part of the transmitter, nor may the acquirer make him/herself available for evaluation, e.g. a doctor may give an instruction to a patient but not know whether this has been followed correctly.

We can distinguish the above from media presentations and projections as in magazines, newspapers and television, all of which contain a range of different discourses. All these media forms are segmentally organised, where segments may have a variety of modes of discursive realisation and motivation. However in the case of such media, their production is geared to maintaining, developing or changing an audience niche. From the point of view of media productions, these productions presuppose what I call the pedagogic device, but is the output pedagogic communication?

There is rarely strong direct control, or even indirect control over the context, social relations and motivations of the consumers, and so what is acquired, at what level and for what purpose, is open to serious debate. Here we have a case where the pedagogic device, that is, distributive, recontextualising and evaluative rules, is the condition for the production of the discourse, but the segmental organisation of the discourse creates a variety of modes of communication whose outcomes are complex and multi-layered, both for any one segment *and* also with respect to the medium as a *form* of discourse. I propose to call the *form* of media discourse a quasi-pedagogic discourse generated by the pedagogic device but having an embedded segmental realisation. From the point of view of the acquirer any one segment may elicit primary or secondary modelling (tacit pedagogic relation), be part of a temporal pedagogic projection (explicit/implicit pedagogic relation) or a transfer of specially shaped information (pedagogic act) or, as more likely, embedding of all or some of these forms of pedagogic relation.

To sum up my position, here we have defined pedagogic communication (explicit, implicit or tacit) which normally occurs in formal and informal educational agencies, e.g. family, school, religious. However, it is clear that these definitions do not cover situations where there may be some form of pedagogic regulation irrespective of the nature of the acquisition. There are a number of segments within horizontal (i.e. everyday) discourse where information is requested and given. We have distinguished here *pedagogic acts* where the information is specifically recontextualised by the giver, expressly to meet the needs of the requester. We have used the term 'act' as distinct from 'communication' to indicate the specific and limited nature of the pedagogic relation. We can also distinguish pedagogic acts dominated by the recontextualising of vertical discourse, i.e. discourse of specialised knowledge; e.g. doctor-patient, lawyer-client, etc. Such recontextualising may or may not be shaped by the needs of the receiver.

We have found it necessary to distinguish the above pedagogic acts from the potential and actual pedagogic regulation of various media, e.g., newspapers, magazines, television, radio. Here we have distinguished the form of any medium from any segmental realisation. We regard the form as an explicit output of the pedagogic device but creating a quasi-pedagogic discourse. This discourse is realised segmentally and any segment may or may not be a pedagogic act, an explicit, implicit or tacit pedagogic communication or it may be some embedding of each. From this point of view a mass medium takes the *form* of a quasi-pedagogic discourse and its realisation is an embedded segment.

Now, pedagogy is the focus of my theory to the extent that pedagogic modalities are crucial realisations of symbolic control, and thus of the process of cultural production and reproduction. Symbolic control, through its pedagogic modalities, attempts to shape and distribute forms of consciousness, identity and desire. Here one can distinguish between official pedagogic modalities and local pedagogic modalities. The former are official symbolic controls and give rise to macro/ micro regulation of contexts, practices, evaluations and acquisitions at institutional levels. The latter, local pedagogic modalities, are familial, peer and "community" regulations. What interests me in this regard is that there is potential colonising/complementary/conflicting, privileging/marginalising relations between local and official pedagogic modalities.

Clearly, symbolic control has other cultural relays and whether the theory is applicable is a matter of investigation. My own work has concentrated on a limited field of inquiry, essentially official and local pedagogic modalities. I should add here that official is not limited to formal educational institutions, but includes medical, psychiatric, social service, penal, planning and informational agencies. Similarly, local is not limited to the family but includes other social identity forming contexts, agents, practices and acquisitions.

Symbolic control is materialised through what I call a pedagogic device. The device consists of three rules which give rise to three respective arenas containing agents with positions/practices seeking domination. I should say in passing that although I found, as many others, Bourdieu's concept of field immensely valuable, I have had some difficulties over its boundaries, inter-relations and conditions of its existence for my own work. Further, again from my position, the metaphor of field either from classical mechanics or Lewin's topological social psychology does not carry an adequate imaginative projection. I have now settled for the metaphor "arena" which creates a sense of drama and struggle both inside and outside.

Returning to the three rules making up a pedagogic device: Distributive rules attempt to control access to the arena for the legitimate production of discourse, pedagogic discourses are projected from positions in the recontextualising arenas and evaluative rules shape any given context of acquisition. This gives rise to a macro/micro transition which is not necessarily or even rarely a linear translation. The arenas as resources may have different degrees of autonomy from each other and from the state. The pedagogic device, the condition for the materialising of symbolic control, is the object of a struggle for domination, for the group who appropriates the device has access to a ruler and distributer of consciousness, identity and desire. The question is whose ruler, in whose interests or for what consciousness, desire and identity.

So far then we have symbolic control mediated through the pedagogic device, which is the condition for the construction of pedagogic discourses.

But pedagogic discourse as a language has a vast potential of realisations. Despite the expected stability of the pedagogic device as the condition of *any* pedagogic discourse, the discourse itself is contingent upon the activities within the arenas and the relative autonomies within and between the arenas. It is the *activities* within the arenas which create the pedagogic modalities, that is their *generating codes*. The codes are regulative principles which select and integrate relevant meanings (classifications), forms of their realisations (framings) and their evoking contexts. The values (strong/weak) and functions (classification^{ie}/ framing^{ie}) carry the code potential. How this potential is actualised is a function of the struggle to construct and distribute code modalities which regulate pedagogic relations, communications and context management. Conflict is endemic within and between the arenas in the struggle to dominate modalities *and* in the relation between local pedagogic modalities and official modalities. At the micro level of the pedagogic context, colonising, complementary, privileging and marginalising relations may be played out according to the code modality $(\pm C^{ie}/\pm F^{ie})$.

It is important here to repeat, yet again, that rules are not codes but the *re-*

sources for codes, differently resourced by different groups realising different distributions of power and principles of control. Thus codes transform distributions of power and principles of control into pedagogic communication. Codes attempt to suppress contradictions, cleavages and dilemmas in the external order (classification) and set up psychic defences for intra-individual order through the insulation (boundaries) they produce. *But code acquisition necessarily entails both the acquisition of order and the potential of its disturbance.*

J. S. You say that pedagogic modalities, generated in the recontextualising arena, attempt to shape and distribute forms of consciousness, identity and desire. 'Identities', according to the theory, are constructed, distributed, embedded, disembedded, shifted in relation to the nature of and changes in the pedagogic moadlities dominating the symbolic field. Could you elaborate on how you construct and use the concept of identity in your theory? What are its 'references' to other theorists and other theories? Is the concept of identity similar to the structuralist concept of the subject, as indicated, for example, in Sadovnik (1995)? Relatedly, does 'identity' include or depart from other concepts that have attempted to describe some sort of interiority: consciousness, thought, self, subject, etc.? What is the connection between identity and the concept of code (as regulator of experience)? What is the connection between identity and discourse?

Moreover, particularly in your publication of 1990, you make an explicit and extended reference to the 'whole' of the field of the sociology of education and it seems to me that, when you develop your theoretical model of pedagogic practice (classification and framing/recognition and realisation rules), what you attempt to do is to manage the perennial problem of the macro-micro in the sociology of education, this preoccupation with the macro-micro is also evident in your reference to rules, distributive, recontextualising, evaluative. Can you, from this point of view, make more explicit the link between your theoretical model and your analysis of contemporary identities that recent education reforms attempt to construct? Furthermore, to complete this question on identity, in what position does the concept of identity lie in relation to your concepts of 'relations between' and 'relations within' subjects? In other words, is it a concept referring more to relations between categories rather than to 'relations within' subjects or the contrary?

B. B.: The concept of identity was first introduced in a 1971 paper, the 'Classification and Framing of Educational Knowledge' paper, where the concept referred to the subjective consequences of pedagogic discursive specialisation (e.g. as a biologist, physicist, etc.). The strength of this identity was a function of the classificatory relation to other pedagogic discourses. The social basis of the identity was also explored in the aforementioned paper. Briefly the identity was composed of sacred and profane features. The former referred to the relation to the form of knowledge (to its otherness) and to the social and discursive obligations this relation required. The latter, the profane, referred to the contextual demands and constraints of the economic context. Thus the identity could be threatened by a change in its classificatory relation, or by an unfavourable change in the economic context. This analysis did not focus on identity in terms of the forms of its realisation and practice regulating its acquisition.

This analysis of acquisition was developed in a paper 'Codes, Modalities and the Process of Cultural Reproduction: a model' (1981). Here a distinction was drawn between 'voice' and 'message'. 'Voice' referred to the limits on what could be realised if the identity was to be recognised as legitimate. The classificatory relation established 'voice'. In this way power relations, through the classificatory relation, regulated 'voice'. However, 'voice', although a necessary condition for establishing what could be said and its context, could not determine *what* was said and *the form* of its contextual realisation; that is the 'message'. The 'message' was a function of framing. The stronger the framing, the smaller the space accorded for potential variation in the message (what was said and its contextual realisation). Thus the modality of the acquired identity was a function of the classificatory and framing relations which regulated the discursive and contextual realisations. In this way I could talk about the specific codings of the identity in terms of its classification and framing. It was further proposed that there was a tension between 'voice' and 'message' in that the latter could change the former, that is the framing relations could lead to a change in the classificatory relations. In this way framing relations could challenge the power relations imposing or enabling the classification.

So far I have talked about the construction of identity modalities and their change within the institutional level. Later (1996) I analysed contemporary curricula reform at the state level in terms of a struggle to project official pedagogic identities. The question arises as to the relation between the analysis of identity within institutional levels in terms of classification and framing, and the analysis of projected official identities at the level of state. However I do not think it is possible to state these official projections in terms of classification and framing values as there may well be greater variation in the distribution of curricula and their entailed pedagogic practices and contexts in the case of some official projections than others. Tyler (1998) does not hold this view and links codes to official pedagogic projections.

Underlying this particular approach to identity is the issue of how variations in the distribution of power (classifications) and variations in the principles of control (framings) impose or enable variations in the formation of identities and their change, through differential specialisation of communication and of its social base.

Now in terms of the question about whether the concept of identity refers more to relations between categories rather than to the relations within subjects, an answer can now be given. The form and modality of pedagogic identity are an outcome of the classificatory relations (relations between categories) *and* the form of the realisation of the classificatory relations, that is the strength of the framing (relations within). In other words the code modality is the outcome of 'relations between' and 'relations within'.

I will now deal very briefly with official projected pedagogic identities and local identities.

As you know, there is a wide-ranging literature on identity, subjectivity and self, with which I have no wish to engage here. Much of the literature is theoretical description rather than detailed, empirical representative description. I am concerned essentially with *contemporary resources* under conditions of cultural/economic change for constructing a sense of belonging to and different from, and for the management of internal sense making and external relationships in time, space and context.

I have concentrated particularly on official pedagogic discourse, seen as emerging from an official recontextualising arena containing potentially four positions for designing and distributing pedagogic identities—retrospective, prospective (centring identities), therapeutic and market (de-centring) for the management of contemporary economic/cultural change.

An official identity here is constructed by embedding a career (knowledge, moral, locational) in a society's dominating purposes. The same model is used for describing the emerging of local identities under conditions of re-organising capitalism. Here identities are seen as de-centred (present oriented) centring (past-oriented) and re-centring (becoming/future oriented). Briefly, identity here refers to contemporary resources for constructing belonging, recognition of self and others, and context management (what I am, where, with whom and when). Resources refer to their potential for coping with the disembedding of those identities whose collective, stable unambiguous base has been weakened under contemporary conditions of re-organising capitalism. It is now possible to examine the relations between the official pedagogic identities projected and distributed by contemporary curricula reform and the emergence of local identities.

There is clearly, here, a relation to Foucault's technologies of normalisation, discipline and the construction of the subject, but the theory gives a more dynamic picture of the struggle to appropriate, design and distribute these technologies and the conditions for variation and change. Also, the theory offers a stronger language of description of its empirical concerns at both macro and micro levels. It attempts to show the relations between symbolic structure (discourses) and social structures (where the latter are seen as frozen practices). In the case of Bourdieu the theory may make the concept of habitus more transparent with respect to the manner of its specialisation and thus formation. It also does not abstract function from form but rather seeks to show the interdependencies. 'Relation to' and 'relations within' are integrated in the analysis.

J. S.: The concept of the boundary and more specifically the theoretical device of the variation of the strength of boundaries is evidently a cornerstone of your theory. It is not however always very clear to me what is the relation between this concept and the subject (the subject's autonomy, creativity, action, agency, resistance) or between this concept and change. Does, for example, a weakened boundary imply wider capacity or 'space' for the subject or groups of subjects and therefore wider capacity for change, or is it not always or simply the case? How does the notion of social class enter in this discussion?

B. B.: It is fascinating that the perennial questions put to contemporary social theory are: What about autonomy? What about creativity? What about agency? What about the space for change and challenge? Is this because in our lives the space for this potential is so small, its realisation entails complex issues, ambiguities and dilemmas that we need affirmation from our theory? It is perhaps ironic that we understand so much but control so little that we require our theory to confirm so much. Or is it the banality of our personal realisations of choice which motivate the way we interrogate theory and structure our expectation. Theory here as secular vision.

So what does it mean to ask these questions about creativity, autonomy, etc, in the context of my work, and how do these issues relate to the concept of boundary? First, it is crucial to understand that the spatial concept boundary (classificatory relations) should not be separated from its temporal concept (framing). The framing of the pedagogic relations regulate in *what* way and *if* the boundary (classificatory relations) is acquired. Secondly, the thesis does not directly address issues of creativity, autonomy, agency as such, *but* directly addresses how the realisations of creativity, autonomy, agency vary with pedagogic modalities $(\pm C^{ie}/\pm F^{ie})$.

Thus these issues are never addressed abstracted from modalities of symbolic control, where acquisition, challenge, dilemma and contradiction are intrinsic to the respective modality. It may be of interest here to contrast Durkheim and Foucault's concept of discipline. In Foucault discipline equals the death of the subject through the annihilation of transgression in whose act the subject lives. In Durkheim discipline equals life for without it there is no social, no coordination of time, space and purpose. Transgression through its punishment revivifies the social. Foucault homogenises discipline: there are no modalities each with their own consequences. Durkheim in "Suicide" shows the pathologies which inhere in different discipline regulations and the social basis of this variation. My work follows this approach.

I now return to the notion of boundary. There is always a boundary. It may vary in its explicitness, its visibility, its potential and in the manner of its transmission and acquisition. It may vary in terms of whose interest is promoted or privileged by the boundary. From the point of view of your question, the issue is *how* is the boundary acquired. But what is acquired may well not be what is expected.

Is the boundary a prison of the past (*whatever the nature of that past*) or is it a tension point which condenses the past yet opens the possibility of futures?

Finally, social class relations through distributive regulations, distribute unequally, discursive, material and social resources which in turn create categories of the included and excluded, makes crucial boundaries permeable to some and impermeable to others, and specialises and positions oppositionally identities. The theory has addressed these issues.

J. S.: Code, elaborated and restricted, has been the central concept of your theory right from its outset, and was recognised as its main strong feature. And furthermore, it has had a strong influence on research and theory in many areas of the human and social sciences. In more recent developments of the theory 'discourse' seems to have taken over as a focal concept. What is the relation in your theory between 'codes' and 'discourse'?

B. B.: Elaborated and restricted codes have not disappeared, nor have they been abandoned: they have been subsumed under higher order concepts. Thus from 1971 elaborated codes had to be specified as code modalities regulated by classifications and framings which immediately raises the question of, which and where and why, particular modalities were constructed.

Elaborated code orientation originally referred to a class of meaning constructed in a pedagogic relation (family/school) and *realised* according to the classification and framing values of the context. In the economy, access to code modalities were regarded as class regulated. Thus homogenising, local, context dependent and specific work context and social relations, resulted in a restricted code modality of communication. However, this approach took for granted, and left unexamined, the *form* of the discourse and focussed entirely upon interactional practices, contexts and meanings.

The next step was to see code modalities as realisations of forms of discourse. Two basic discursive forms were distinguished and their social base examined. I called these forms vertical and horizontal discourses.

To elaborate on my analysis of forms of discourse: a vertical discourse takes the form of a coherent, explicit, systematically principled structure, hierarchically organised *or* it takes the form of a series of specialised languages each with its own specialised mode of interrogation and specialised criteria for the production and exchange of texts. The contexts of vertical discourse are specialised knowledge of the natural and social sciences, their technologies and those of the humanities and the arts. Vertical discourses have their origin and development in official institutions of the state and economy. The *realisations* of a vertical discourse depend upon who has power over its classification and framing: *that is the code modality.*

Whereas vertical discourse has its origins, and often its development, in official institutions, horizontal discourse has its origins and development in the everyday or life world. Horizontal discourse is *segmentally* not hierarchically organised and is realised in face to face encounters, where meanings are likely to be both context specific *and* dependent. Because a horizontal discourse is segmentally organised, acquisitions are likely to be segmental and context specific, and therefore pedagogic relations may *vary* from one cultural segment (context) to another. The *code modality* may also vary across segments and *within* segments for different social groups. Thus code modalities may interpenetrate or be specialised to different discourses or different segments, for different social groups.

At this point I should add that the distinction between vertical and horizontal discourses gives rise to a variety of forms with their own specialised social base and conditions of existence. It should also be possible to insert other agencies between 'official' and 'local'.

Integration of forms of discourse with code modalities of realisation extended the descriptive power of the theory, showed more clearly its dynamics and increased its explanatory power.

J. S.: Now I would like to take up a more methodological issue. In reading your theory one gets the impression that the position of interpretation is rather weak. Instead, the need to produce accurate 'descriptions' of practices of educational and cultural production and reproduction and especially of educational practices, is permanently stressed.

What exactly do you mean by description and why is so much emphasis put on it? What implications does this emphasis have for research, yours and others? And a related series of questions: you work very much by creating models of relations, mechanisms and transformations. In your texts, very often, concepts and their meanings are condensed, expressed in the form of an actual diagram. What is the function of these models? How do they link with the empirical research that is supported by the theory?

B. B.: Interpretation cannot be separated from the grounds which make it plausible. One of the problems of contemporary social, especially education sociological research, is that there is a great gap between theory (often used only to legitimate the research) and the data which had been collected. One of the difficulties of much social theory is that these theories have a powerful and persuasive internal conceptual language but reduced powers to provide externally unambiguous descriptions of the phenomena of their concern. Thus researchers have difficulty in using the theory to generate the language which will transform the language of enactment, that is the text they are studying (interviews, visual, graphic representations, etc.) into a language which can be read by the theory. These theories rarely generate a language of description: a language which can transform the language of enactment, into a language which the theory can directly read. It seems to me that when I analyse the relation between theory and research in my own work the following seems to be the case.

1. The theory produces models. These models generate modalities of control on the basis of a set of rules which identify and specialise agencies, agents, practices, communications, their inter-relations, external relations and consequences. The consequences then function as hypotheses about the possible performance to which the model can give rise.

2. When the model is referred to something other than itself, then it should be able to provide the principles which will identify that something as falling within the specification of the model and identify explicitly what does not so fall. Such principles we can call the *recognition rules* for identifying an external relevant something. However, this something will always generate, or have the capacity to generate, greater ranges of information than the model calls for. The *realisation* rules of the model regulate the descriptions of the something. They transform the information the something does, or can put out, the language of enactment, into data *relevant* to the model.

   However, if the realisation rules produce descriptions which are limited to transforming only that information into data *which at that time* appear consonant with the model, then the model can never change and the whole process is circular. Nothing therefore exists outside the model.

3. Thus the interface between the realisation rules of the model and the information the something does or can produce is vital. There then must be a discursive gap between the rules specified by the model *and* the realisation rules for transforming the information produced by the something. This gap enables the something, so to speak, to announce itself, it enables the something to re-describe the descriptions of the model's own realisation rules and so change.

4. Thus the principle of descriptions of the something external to the model must go beyond the realisations rules *internal* to the model.

5. The theory encompasses, in the end, everything from 1 to 4. The question is not that it so encompasses it but *how* does it do so.

Finally it is relevant to point out that we all have models, some are more explicit than others; we all use principles of descriptions, again some are more explicit than others; we all set up criteria to enable us both to produce for ourselves, and to read the descriptions of others, again these criteria may vary in their explicitness. Some of our principles may be quantitative whilst others are qualitative. But the problem is fundamentally the same. In the end whose voice is speaking? My preference is to be as explicit as possible. Then at least my voice may be deconstructed. You can see this figure. . . . [See p. 210.]

The theory takes the form of a series of formal models ranging from macro to micro levels. It is possible to abstract a model from the progression for a particular empirical enquiry and ignore logically higher or lower models. All models

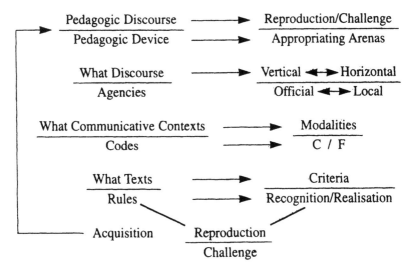

Note 1: It should be noted that the lower term of each pair is the generator.
Note 2: "Text" is anything which attracts evaluation.

are to be found in *Pedagogy, Symbolic Control and Identity: Theory, Research and Critique* (London, Taylor and Francis, 1996).

J. S.: Let me ask you a rather political question, now. I remember you saying in one lecture that the power of the theory is to generate descriptions that are 'interesting and disturbing views' (sic) of the world. Interesting and disturbing for whom, in whose 'hands' and for whose interests? In your mind are descriptions tools for something else? Is there a next step? Do you care to 'model' the next step(s) possible? Or are you satisfied to try to make sure that these 'views' are as clear as possible?

B. B.: For me the political implications, although the initial motivation, are secondary to the long process of understanding and describing the agencies, contexts and practices through which we are both constructed and constructing ourselves and others. This involves understanding how power and control enter into these constructions to include or exclude, or to privilege or marginalise. The theory attempts to show both the limiting power of forms of regulation and their possibilities, so that we are better able to choose the forms we create rather than the forms to be created for us.

Effective choice, effective challenge requires this understanding and failure is often the result of rhetorical solution or ideologically driven aspiration.

J. S.: Your theory and your models have become an object of great appreciation, especially by researchers in many corners of the world, yet they have also given

*rise to, sometimes fierce, criticism and controversy. My last question will not
focus on this criticism and your lengthy reactions to it, but will aim at a rather
delicate task; that is, having you produce your own reflection on your work, some
kind of self-criticism. In short, when you look at the structure and constructs
proper of your theory and at its capacities to do what it has set out to do, i.e., to
describe and bring about a clear understanding of the mechanisms and practices
of cultural reproduction and transformation, which, if any, do you think are its
weaknesses, its vulnerabilities?*

B. B.: In a crucial way the evolution of the theory is a function of the attempt to
develop greater powers of description, greater conceptual clarity and control, increased generality and increased delicacy at the level of detail. This evolution is
directly related to the extensive empirical research which the theory has both
influenced and responded to. One of the problems faced with engaging with the
theory arises out of the manner of its development. Whilst I can see a linear development almost from the first paper published in 1958 until the last, the manner of this development has been obscured by the style of the presentation. Many
of the conceptual formulations of the latter work use a conceptual language which
appeared very much earlier, often in footnotes or asides, but reworked in the latter work. For example the work on pedagogic discourse (1986) was pre-figured
in the conclusion to the Introduction of *Class, Codes & Control*, Vol. III, 1975),
and goes back earlier to a paper published in 1966. Further, although in my mind
I had integrated the sociolinguistic theory with the pedagogic in 1971 (and less
formally much earlier) these two aspects of the work were disconnected by the
intellectual field often for ideological reasons.

However, many of the difficulties stem from my own style of production. Each
paper from the earliest is really part of a future series, which at the time of writing was not known. In a way each paper stands alone incorporating and developing the previous paper and pointing to an unwritten and often unknown text. From
this point of view for me the aim of a paper is productive imperfection. That is it
generates a conceptual tension which provides the potential for development. So
for me the papers are the means of discovering what I shall be thinking, not what
I am thinking. However, whilst this style is beneficial to me it can lead to difficulty for those using the work. It is clearly important to read late papers rather
than earlier ones, and equally as important to understand the progression. But I
recognise that maybe this has been too much to ask.

More specifically, as I see it, the theory is really a part of a more general theory which is beyond me to produce. It is part of a theory of symbolic control and
change, which in turn is part of a theory of culture and its knowledge, which in
turn is part of. . . .

If I now look at vulnerabilities within the theory I think these have been and
will be revealed by empirical research. And as a consequence lead to the development, modifications and replacement of the theory. Thus the theory, for its own

sake, is crucially dependent on research. There is therefore an obligation to construct a conceptual language and provide models which facilitate empirical research. And this I have tried very hard to do.

POSTSCRIPTUM

Much more than simple answers to questions, I think that what we have here is
rather the birth of a new text by Professor Basil Bernstein, as well as an idea of
the rules and resources of the theory. The questions have become vehicles for a
reflexion on a lifetime of theory production but more importantly for what, I believe, are further elaborations of conceptualising, describing, positioning, relating
and analysing pedagogic relations, communications and acts realised in contexts
and practices ranging from informal interactions, formal education and other
(formal/local) agencies to media discourses.

The variety of the contexts actually or potentially addressed by this theory is
something that was pointed at in the past. In Bernstein, 1996, it was noted:

> We have discussed the codes of pedagogic practice in terms of family and
> school, but the conceptual language is not limited to these agencies. It can be ap-
> plied to any pedagogic relation, or more generally to any transmission relation
> of control, e.g. between doctor and patient, social worker and client, psychiatrist
> and patient, prison staff and prisoners, and, of course, to industrial relations
> (Bernstein, 1996, pp. 103–104).

Older references to the psychotherapeutic relationship were recently recalled by
Paul Atkinson (1997, *British Journal of the Sociology of Education*, 18, 1, pp.
115–116); work relations were addressed in Bernstein (1977, 1981). Other researchers have explored the potential of the theoretical framework for the analysis of gender relations and feminist theories of education (c.f. Arnot, 1995;
Delamont, 1995). Furthermore, in Bernstein, (1996), he showed how the theory,
an 'internal language of description', can/must be translated into 'external languages of description', and vice- versa. This illustrates his need to develop strong
relationships between empirical research and theory, particularly within an ethnographic model (pp. 134–144). However, I think that this present text, with its
elaborations on pedagogic acts and communications and vertical and horizontal
discourses clearly sets the basis for new theoretical and empirical work on contemporary powerful agencies and practices of control and regulation. The latter
have arisen out of recent changes of technology, economy and culture which have
marked consequences for identity formation and change. I am referring here to
agencies and practices of the late twentieth century state regulating work/unem-
ployment, health and subsistence, such as in the medical/psychotherapeutic, social and economic services. This creates new or changing curriculum concerns,

linked with new modalities of pedagogy, such as health education information, consumer education information, parental education and, of course, the growing apparatus and practices of 'training', 'professional orientation', etc.

In addition, it is clearly important to focus on the changing nature of regulation and control related to the massive extension and multiplication of agencies and practices of information transmission and communication; not only television and other mass media but also the various electronic networks of information and communication. What are the implications for knowledge/power relations? How do they relate to the establishment of new technologies in education (multimedia, internet, telematics, etc) and their consequences for curriculum and pedagogy? Thus what we have latent in Bernstein's text is a call for the production of a general theory of pedagogy, symbolic control and change, the design of a programme and its research realisation.

J.S.

Joseph Solomon was Vice-President of the Pedagogical Institute, Athens, and is now Associate Professor of Sociology of Education, Department of Education, University of Athens, Greece. He has translated and presented several of Basil Bernstein's basic texts into the Greek language.

Thanks are due to Anna Tsatsaroni, Assistant Professor, University of Patras, for assisting and encouraging the completion and publication of this interview.

Bibliography

Adlam, D.J. with Turner, G.J. and Lineker, L. (1977) *Code in Context*. London: Routledge.

Althusser, L. (1971) 'Ideology and the ideological state apparatus', in *Lenin and philosophy*, trans. Brewster, B. New York: New Left Books.

Apple, M.W. (1993) *Politics and Policy Making*. London & New York: Routledge.

Apple, M.W. (1995) 'Education, culture and class power: Basil Bernstein and the neo-Marxist sociology of education', in Sadovnik, A.R. (Ed.) *Pedagogy and Knowledge: The Sociology of Basil Bernstein*. Norwood, NJ:Ablex.

Arnot, M.M. (1995) 'Bernstein's theory of educational codes and feminist theories of education; a personal view,' in Sadovnik, A.R. (Ed.) *Knowledge & Pedogogy: The Sociology of Basil Bernstein*. Norwood, NJ: Ablex.

Atkinson, P. (1982) 'Bernstein's structuralism', *Educational Analysis*, 31, pp. 85–95.

Atkinson, P. (1985) *Language Structure and Reproduction: An Introduction to Sociology of Basil Bernstein*. London: Methuen.

Atkinson, P., Davies, B. and Delamont, S. (1995) *Discourse and Reproduction: Essays in Honor of Basil Bernstein*. Cresskill, NJ: Hampton Press.

Ball, S.J. (1990) *Politics and Policy Making in Education*. London and New York: Routledge.

Bargh, C. and Scott, P. (1994) 'The new management', *The Times*, 12 December.

Barnes, B. (1982) *T.S. Kuhn & Social Science*. London: MacMillan. Chap. 5.

Barton, L., Barrett, E., Whitty, G., Miles, S. and Furlong, J. (1994) 'Teacher education and teacher professionalism in England: some emerging issues', *British Journal of the Sociology of Education*, 15 (4), pp. 529–543.

Bernstein, B. (1958) 'Some sociological determinants of perception', *British Journal of Sociology*, IX, pp. 159–178 [reproduced in *Class, Codes and Control*, Vol. I, London: Routledge & Kegan Paul, 1971].

Bernstein, B. (1962) 'Linguistic codes, hesitation phenomena and intelligence', *Language and Speech*, 5, pp. 31–42 [reprinted in *Class, Codes and Control*, Vol. I, 1971, p. 91].

Bernstein, B. (1963) 'Family role systems, communication and socialisation', paper presented to International Conference on Cross Cultural Research, University of Chicago.

Bernstein, B. (1965) 'A sociolinguistic approach to social learning', in Gould, J. (Ed.) *Penguin Survey of the Social Sciences*. Harmondsworth: Penguin [reprinted in *Class, Codes and Control*, Vol. I].

Bernstein, B. (1966) 'Sources of consensus and disaffection in education', *Journal of the Association of Assistant Mistresses*, 17, pp. 4–11 [extension in *Class, Codes and Control*, Vol. III, 1975].

Bernstein, B. (1967) 'Open schools, open society', *New Society*, 14 September.

Bernstein, B. (1970) 'Social class differences in communication and control', in Brandis, W. and Henderson, D. *Social Class, Language and Communication*. London: Routledge.

Bernstein, B. (1971a) 'A sociolinguistic approach to socialisation with some references to educability' in Hymes, D. and Gumperz, J. *Directions in Sociolinguistics*. New York: Holt Rinehart & Winston [reprinted in *Class, Codes and Control*, Vol. I, 1971].

Bernstein, B. (1971b) 'On the classification and framing of knowledge', in Young, M.F.D. (Ed.) *Knowledge and Control*. London: Collier-Macmillan [reprinted in *Class, Codes and Control*, Vol. I, 1971].

Bernstein, B. (1971c) *Class, Codes and Control*, Vol. I. London: Routledge & Kegan Paul.

Bernstein, B. (1971d) 'Social class, language and socialisation', in *Class, Codes and Control*, Vol. I.

Bernstein, B. (1973) *Class and Pedagogies: Visible and Invisible*. Paris: OECD, CERI Paris.

Bernstein, B. (1975, 1977, 1991) 'Class and pedagogies: visible and invisible' [reworked in *Class, Codes and Control*, Vol. III, Vol. III revised and Vol. IV as 'Social class and pedagogic practice'].

Bernstein, B. (1975) *Language et Classes Sociales: Codes Sociolinguistiques et Contrôle Social*. Presentation de Jean Claude Chamboredon. Paris: Les Editions de Minuit.

Bernstein, B. (1981) 'Codes, modalities and the process of cultural reproduction: a model', *Language and Society*, 10 pp. 327–363 [reprinted with some expansion in *Class, Codes and Control*, Vol. IV: *The Structuring of Pedagogic Discourse*. London and New York: Routledge].

Bernstein, B. (1986) 'On pedagogic discourse', in Richardson, J.G. (Ed.) *Handbook of Theory and Research for the Sociology of Education*. New York: Greenwood Press.

Bernstein, B. (1987) *Elaborated and Restricted Codes: An Overview, 1958–1986*. Occasional Paper No. 2. Amsterdam: Amsterdam University, Centre for Race & Ethnic Studies [expanded version in *Class, Codes and Control*, Vol. IV, London: Routledge, 1990].

Bernstein, B. (1990) *Class, Codes and Control*, Vol. IV: *The Structuring of Pedagogic Discourse*. London: Routledge.

Bernstein, B. (1995a) 'Response' in Sadovnik, A.R. (Ed.) *Pedagogy and Knowledge: The Sociology of Basil Bernstein*. Norwood, NJ:Ablex.

Bernstein, B. (1995b) *Pedagogy, Symbolic Control and Identity: Theory, Research and Critique*. London: Taylor & Francis.

Bernstein, B. and Cook-Gumperz, J. (1973) *The Coding Grid in Socialisation and Social Control: A Study of Class Differences in the Language of Maternal Control*. London: Routledge & Kegan Paul.

Bernstein, B. and Diaz, M. (1984) 'Towards a theory of pedagogic discourse', Collected Original Resources in Education, *C.O.R.E.*, 8 (3).

Bernstein, B., Peters, R. and Elvin, L. (1966) 'Ritual in education', *Philosophical Transactions of the Royal Society of London*, Series B. 251 (72) [reprinted in *Class, Codes and Control*, Vol. III, 1973].

Blackledge, D. and Hunt, B. (1985) *Sociological Interpretations of Education*. London: Croom Helm.

Bliss, J., Monk, M., Ogborn, J. (1988) *Qualitative Data Analysis and Educational Research: A Guide to Uses of Systemic Networks*. London: Croom Helm.

Bourdieu, P. (1977) 'Sur le pouvoire symbolique' *Annales*, 3 (May–June) [English trans. 'Symbolic power' in Gleeson, D. (Ed.) *Identity and Structure*. Driffield: Nufferlin Books].

Bourdieu, P. (1984) *Homo Academicus*. Oxford: Polity Press.

Bourdieu, P. (1991) *Language and Symbolic Power*, translated by Raymond, G. and Adamson, M. Oxford: Polity Press, p. 260.

Bourdieu, P. (1993) *The Field of Cultural Production*. Oxford: Polity Press.

Bourdieu, P. and Passeron, J.-C. (1977) *Reproduction in Education and Culture*, trans. Nice, R., Beverly Hills, CA: Sage.

Bourdieu, P., Passeron, J.-C. and de Saint Martin, M. (1994) *Academic Discourse*. Oxford: Polity Press.

Brandis, W. and Bernstein, B. (1974) *Selection and Control: Teachers' Ratings of Infant School Children*. London: Routledge & Kegan Paul.

Cazden, C. (1988) *Classroom Discourse: The Language of Teaching and Learning*. Portsmouth, NH: Heinemann.

Christie, F. (1999) *Pedagogy and the Shaping of Consciousness: Linguistic and Social Processes*. London and New York: Cassell.

Collins, J. (2000) 'Bernstein, Bourdieu & the new literacy studies', *Linguistics & Education* (forthcoming).

Cooper, B. and Dunne, M. (1988) 'Anyone for tennis? Social class differences in children's response to national curriculum testing'. *Sociological Review* 46 (1), pp. 117–148.

Cox Donoso, C. (1986) 'Continuity conflict and change in state education in Chile: a study of the pedagogic projects of the Christian democrat and popular unity governments', *C.O.R.E.*, 10 (2) [also PhD, University of London, 1984].

Dale, R. (1994) 'Marketing the educational market and the polarisation of schools', in Kallós, D. and Lindblad, S. (Eds.) *New Policy Contexts for Education. Sweden and the United Kingdom*. Pedagogiska institutionen. Umea: Uméa University, Pedagogiska rapporter No. 42/1994, pp. 35–66.

Daniels, H.R.J. (1988) 'An enquiry into different forms of special school organisation; pedagogic practice and pupil discrimination', *C.O.R.E.*, 12 (2).

Daniels, H.R.J. (1989) 'Visual displays as tacit relays of the structure of pedagogic practice', *British Journal of the Sociology of Education*, 10 (2), pp. 123–140.

Daniels, H.R.J. (1994) *Charting the Agenda: Educational Activity after Vygotsky*. London and New York: Routledge.

Daniels, H.R.J. (1995) 'Pedagogic practice, tacit knowledge and discursive discrimination: Bernstein and Post-Vygotskian research', *British Journal of the Sociology of Education*, 16 (4), pp. 517–532.

Demaine, J. (1981) *Contemporary Theories in the Sociology of Education*. London: Macmillan.

Diaz, M. (1984) 'A model of pedagogic discourse with special application to Columbian primary level', PhD, University of London.

Diaz, M. (Ed.) (1985) *Revista Colombain de Educacion*, 15 (with introduction).

Diaz, M. (Ed.) (1990) *La Construccion Social del Discurso pedagogica*, also Introduction, pp. 1–36, Bogota: Prodic—El Griot.

Dittmar, N. (1976) *Sociolinguistics: A Critical Survey of Theory and Application*, trans. Sand, P., Seuran, A.M. and Whiteley, K. London: Edward Arnold.

Douglas, M. (1966) *Purity and Danger.* London: Routledge & Kegan Paul.

Dowling, P. (1993) 'A language for the sociological description of pedagogic texts with particular reference to the secondary school mathematics scheme SMP, 11–16', PhD, University of London.

Dowling, P. (1994) 'The sociological analysis of pedagogic texts and English for development', unpublished. [Available from Dept. of Maths. Stats. and Computing, Institute of Education, University of London].

Dowling, P. (1995) 'Spectres of Schooling and Utopia', Arena New Series, 4, pp. 191–200.

Dowling, P. (1997) *The Sociology of Mathematics Education: Mathematical Myths/ Pedagogic Texts.* London: The Falmer Press.

Durkheim, E. (1893) *De la Division du Travail Social: Étude sur l'Organisation des Sociétés Superior,* Paris, trans. Simpson, G. as *The Division of Labour in Society.* New York: Macmillan, 1993.

Durkheim, E. (1915) *The Elementary Forms of the Religious Life,* trans. Swan, J.S. London: Allen and Unwin.

Durkheim, E. (1938) *L'Evolution Pedagogique en France,* Paris: Alcan, trans. Collins, P. as *The Evolution of Educational Thought: Lectures on the Formation and Development of Secondary Education in France.* London: Routledge.

Durkheim, E. (1950) *The Rules of Sociological Method,* trans. Solovay, S.A. and Mueller, J.H., Catlin, C.E.G. (Eds.). London: Collier-Macmillan.

Durkheim, E. (1952) *Suicide: A Study of Sociology,* trans. Spaulding, J.A. and Simpson, G. (Eds.) London: Routledge & Kegan Paul.

Eraut, M. (1994) *Developing Professional Knowledge and Competence.* London: Falmer Press.

Faria, I.H. (1984) 'Para a Analise de Voriacao Socio—sementica', PhD, Faculdade da Letras Universidad de Lisboa.

Foucault, M. (1976) *The Birth of the Clinic: An Archaeology of Medical Perception,* trans. Sheridan, L. London: Tavistock Press.

Gee, J.P. (1990) *Sociolinguistics and Literacies: Ideology in Discourses.* London: Falmer Press.

Gibson, R. (1977) 'Bernstein's classification & framing: a critique', *Higher Educational Review,* 9, pp. 23–45.

Gibson, R. (1984) *Structuralism and Education.* London: Methuen.

Giddens, A. (1986) *The Class Structure of Advanced Societies,* 2nd edn. London: Hutchinson.

Giddens, A. (1990) *The Consequences of Modernity.* Oxford: Polity Press.

Giddens, A. (1991) *Modernity & Self-Identity.* Oxford: Polity Press.

Grace, G.R. (1995) *School Leadership: Beyond Education Management. An Essay in Policy & Scholarship.* London: Falmer.

Halliday, M.A.K. (1977) 'Text as semantic choice in social context', in Le, T. and McCausland, M. (Eds.) *Grammar and Descriptions.* Berlin: De Gruyter.

Halliday, M.A.K. (1978) *Language as a Social Semiotic: The Social Interpretation of Language and Meaning*. London: Edward Arnold.

Halliday, M.A.K. (1985) *An Introduction to Functional Grammar*. London: Edward Arnold.

Halliday, M.A.K. (1993) *Language in a Changing World*, Applied Linguistics Association of Australia, Occasional Paper No. 13.

Handlemann, S.A. (1982) *The Slayers of Moses: The Emergence of Rabbinic Interpretation in Modern Literacy Theory*. Albany: State University of New York Press.

Harker, R. and May, S.A. (1993) 'Code and habitus: comparing accounts of Bernstein and Bourdieu', *British Journal of the Sociology of Education*, 14 (2), pp. 160–178.

Harvey, D. (1989) *The Condition of Post Modernity: An Inquiry into the Origins of Cultural Change*. Oxford and New York: Blackwell.

Hasan, R. (1991) 'Questions as a mode of learning in everyday talk', in McCausland, M. (Ed.) *Language Education: Interaction and Development*, Proceedings of the International Conference held in Ho Chi Minh City, Vietnam. Launceston: University of Tasmania.

Hasan, R. (1992) 'Meaning in sociolinguistic theory', in Bolton, K. and Kwok, H. (Eds.) *Sociolinguistics Today: International Perspectives*. London and New York: Routledge.

Hasan, R. (1993) 'Contexts for Meaning', in Alatis, J.E. (Ed.) *Language, Communication and Social Meaning*. Washington, DC: Georgetown University Press.

Hay, C., O'Brian, M. and Penna, S. (1993/4) 'Giddens, modernity and self-identity, the "hollowing out" of social theory', *Arena* 2, pp. 45–75.

Heath, S.B. (1984) *Way with Words*. Cambridge: Cambridge University Press.

Hickox, M. & Moore, R. (1995) 'Liberal-humanist education: the vocationalist challenge', *Curriculum Studies*, 3 (1), pp. 45–59.

Holland, J. (1981) 'Social class and changes in the orientations to meanings', *Sociology*, 15 (1), pp. 1–18.

Holland, J. (1986) 'Social class differences in adolescents' conception of the domestic and industrial division of labour', *C.O.R.E.*, 10 (1).

Hyland, T. (1994) *Competence Education and NVQs: Dissenting Perspectives*. London: Cassell.

Hymes, D. (Ed.) (1964) *Language in Culture & Society: Reader in Linguistics & Anthropology*. New York, Evanston and London: Harper & Rowe.

Hymes, D. (1977) *Foundations of Sociolinguistics: An Ethnographic Approach*. London: Tavistock Press.

Hymes, D. and Gumperz, J.J. (Eds.) (1964) *Ethnography of Communication, American Anthropologist*, Special Issue, 66 (6), part II.

Jenkins, C. (1990) 'The professional middle class and the origins of progressivism: a case study of the new education fellowship 1920–1950', *C.O.R.E.*, 14 (1).

Jones, L. and Moore, R. (1995) 'Approaching competence: the competency movement, the New Right and the "culture change" project', *British Journal of Education of Work*, 2, pp. 78–92.

King, R. (1974) *Values and Involvements in a Grammar School*. London: Routledge & Kegan Paul.

King, R. (1976) 'Bernstein's sociology of the school: some propositions tested', *British Journal of Sociology*, 27, pp. 430–443.

King, R. (1981) 'Bernstein's sociology of the school', *British Journal of Sociology,* 32, pp. 259–265.

Labov, W. (1972) 'The logic of non-standard English', in Giglioni, P.P. (Ed.) *Language and Social Context,* Penguin Modern Sociology Readings. Harmondsworth: Penguin.

Lancaster Regionalism Group (1985) *Localities, Class and Gender.* London: Pion Press.

Latour, B. (1979) *Laboratory Life: The Social Construction of Scientific Facts.* Beverly Hills and London: Sage Publication.

Latour, B. (1987) *Science in Action: How to Follow Scientists & Engineers Through Society.* Milton Keynes: Open University Press.

Lave, J. (1988) *Cognition in Practice: Mind Mathematics and Culture in Everyday Life.* Cambridge: Cambridge University Press.

Lave, J., Murtaugh, M. and de la Roche, O. (1984) 'The dialectic of arithmatic in grocery shopping', in Rogoff, B. and Lave, J. (Eds.) *Everyday Cognition: Its Development in Social Context.* Cambridge MA: Harvard University Press.

Lemke, J.L. (1995) *Textual Politics: Discourse and Social Dynamics.* London: Taylor & Francis.

Li Puma, E. (1993) 'Culture and the concept of culture, a theory of practice', in Calhoun, C., Li Puma, E. and Postone, M. (Eds.) *Bourdieu: Critical Perspectives.* Oxford: Polity Press.

Lynch, K. and O'Neil, C. (1994) 'The colonisation of social class in education', *British Journal of the Sociology of Education,* 15 (3), pp. 307–324.

Lyons, L. (1973) 'Structuralism and linguistics', in Robey, D. (Ed.) *Structuralism: An Introduction.* Oxford: Clarendon Press.

Mace, J. (1995) 'Funding matters: a case study of the response of two universities to recent funding changes', *Journal of Policy Studies,* 10 (1), pp. 57–74.

Manpower Services Commission (1977) *Analytic Techniques for Skill Comparison.* Sheffield: MSC.

Manpower Services Commission (1981) *Young People Starting Work.* Sheffield: MSC.

Maton, K. (2000) 'Recovering pedagogic discourse. Basil Bernstein and the rise of taught academic subjects in higher education', *Education & Linguistics,* Vol II. (forthcoming).

Mauss, M. (1935) 'Les techniques du corps', *Journal de Psychologie,* 32, pp. 271–293.

Moore, R. and Hickox, M. (1995) 'Vocationalism and educational change', *Curriculum Studies,* I, pp. 45–60.

Moore, R. and Muller, J. (1998) 'Sociology of education and the discourse of voice: a critique', available from Homerton College, University of Cambridge.

Morais, A.M., Fontinhas, F. and Neve, I.P. (1993) 'Recognition and realisation rules in acquiring school science: the contribution of pedagogy and social background of pupils', *British Journal of the Sociology of Education,* 13 (2), pp. 247–70.

Morais, A., Neve, I.P., Maderios, A., Peneda, D., Foninhas, F. and Antunes, H. (1995) *Socializacão Primeria E Prática Pedagógica,* Vol. II: *Análise de Aprendiza Gens Na Família E Na Escola.* Lisboa: Fundacão Calouste Gulbenkian.

Moss, G. (1991) 'Media texts, English texts and how to read differently in English', Australia No. 95.

Moss, G. (1993) 'Girls tell teenage romance: four readings histories', in Buckingham, D. *Reading Audiences: Young People & the Media.* Manchester: Manchester University Press.

Moss. G. (1996) 'Negotiated literacies: how children enact what counts as reading in different social settings', PhD, Open University.

Moss, G. (2000) 'Informal literacies and pedagogic discourse', *Linguistics & Education*, Vol. II (forthcoming).

Muller, I. and Taylor, N. (1994) 'Schooling and everyday life: knowledge sacred & profane', unpublished [available from Dept. of Education, University of Cape Town, South Africa].

Nader, H. (Ed.) (1996) *Naked Science: Anthropological Inquiry into Boundaries, Power & Knowledge*. New York: Routledge.

O'Neil, J. (1995) *The Poverty of Post Modernism*. London: Routledge.

Pedro, E.R. (1981) *Social Stratification and Classroom Discourse*. Lund: Liber, Laromedal.

Plowden Report (1969) *Children: Their Primary Schools*. London, HMSO.

Pring, R. (1975) 'Bernstein's classification and framing of knowledge', *Scottish Educational Studies*, 7, pp. 67–74.

Robinson, W.P. (1973) 'Where do children's answers come from?' in Bernstein, B. (Ed.) *Class, Codes and Control*, Vol. II: *Applied Studies Towards a Sociology of Language*. London: Routledge & Kegan Paul.

Sadovnik, A.R. (1991) 'Basil Bernstein's theory of pedagogic practice: a structuralist approach', *Sociology of Education*, 64, (1), pp. 48–63.

Sadovnik, A.R. (Ed.) (1999) *Pedagogy and Knowledge: The Sociology of Basil Bernstein*. Norwood NJ: Ablex.

Scribner, S. and Cole, M. (1981) *The Psychology of Literacy*. Cambridge MA: Harvard University Press.

Serres, M. (1995) 'Conversations on science culture & time', Serres, M. with Latour, B. trans. Lapidus, R. Anne Arbor: University of Michigan Press.

Shilling, C. (1992) 'Re-conceptualising structure and agency in the sociology of education: structuralism and schooling', *British Journal of the Sociology of Education*, 13 (1), pp. 69–87.

Singh, P. (1993) 'Institutional discourse: a case study of the social construction of technical competence in the primary classroom', *British Journal of the Sociology of Education*, 14 (1), pp. 39–58.

Singh, P. (1995) 'Discourses of computing competence evaluation and gender: the case of computer use in primary schools classrooms', *Discourse Studies in the Cultural Politics of Education*, 16 (1), pp. 81–110.

Solstad, K.J. (1997) *Equity & Risk, Planned Educational Change in Norway: Pitfalls & Progress*. Oslo: Scandinavian University Press.

Swope, J. (1992) *The Production, Recontextualising and Popular Transmission of Religious Discourse in Eight Basic Christian Communities in Santiago Chile, C.O.R.E.* 16 (3).

Taylor, W. (1969) *Society and the Education of Teachers*. London: Faber & Faber.

Training Agency (1989) *Developing Standards by Reference to Functions, Development of Assessible Standards for National Certification*, Guidance Note 2. Sheffield: Training Agency.

Tyler, W. (1984) 'Organisational structure, factors and codes: a methodological inquiry into Bernstein's theory of educational transmission', PhD, University of Kent.

Tyler, W. (1988) *School Organisation: A Sociological Perspective*. London and Sydney: Croom Helm.

Tyler, W. (1995) 'De-coding school reform: Bernstein's market oriented pedagogy and postmodern power' in Sadovnik, A.R. (Ed.) *Knowledge and Pedagogy: The Sociology of Basil Bernstein.* Norwood, NJ: Ablex, also Bernstein's response, pp. 407–412.

Walford, G. (1994) 'Classification and framing in English public boarding schools', in Atkinson, P., Davies, B., and Delamount, S. (Eds.) *Discourse and Reproduction.* New Jersey, Hampton Press.

Wells, C.G. (1985) *Language Development in the Pre-School Years.* Cambridge: Cambridge University Press.

Wells, C.G. (1987) *The Meaning Makers: Children Learning Language and Using Language to Learn.* London: Hodder & Stoughton.

Wertsch, J.V. (1985a) *Vygotsky and the Social Formation of Mind.* Cambridge, MA: Harvard University Press.

Wertsch, J.V. (1985b) 'The semiotic mediation of mental life: L.S. Vygotsky & M.M. Bakhtin', in Mertz, E. and Paramentier, R. (Eds.) *Semiotic mediation: sociocultural and psychological perspective.* New York: Academic Press.

Wexler, P. (1995) 'Bernstein: a Jewish misreading' in Sadovnik, A.R. (Ed.) *Knowledge and Pedagogy: The Sociology of Basil Bernstein,* Norwood, NJ: Ablex, also Bernstein's response, pp. 396–399.

Wexler, P. (1996) *Holy Sparks: Social Theory, Education and Religion.* New York: Saint Martin's Press.

Wexler, P. (1996) *Critical Social Psychology,* 2nd edn. New York: Peter Lang.

Whitty, G. (1991) 'The new right and the national curriculum', in Moore, R. and Ozga, J. (Eds.) *Curriculum Policy.* Oxford: Pergamon/Open University.

Whitty, G., Rowe, G. and Aggleton, P. (1994a). 'Discourse in cross-curricular contexts: limits to empowerment', *International Studies in the Sociology of Education,* 4 (1), pp. 25–41.

Whitty, G., Rowe, G., and Aggleton, P. (1994b) 'Subjects and themes in the secondary school', *Research Papers in Education Policy and Practice,* 9 (2), pp. 159–179.

Williams, G. (1995) 'Joint book-reading and literacy pedagogy: a sociosemantic examination', PhD, Macquarie University.

Wolpert, L.L. (1992) *The Unnatural Nature of Science,* London: Faber & Faber.

Index

acquisition: code acquisition, 103–6, 203; democracy of, 43; of Hierarchical vs. Horizontal Knowledge Structures, 163–65; and Horizontal and Vertical discourse, 158–60, 160f; and identity, 204; of the language device, 26; and the pedagogic device, 36–37, 36f, 37f; and the school, xxii–xxiii; and segmental pedagogy, 158–59; translator's language acquisition, 139; and visible vs. invisible pedagogic practice, 110
actor (defined), 62n1
Adlam, D. J., 104, 186
agents, location of in fields/sectors, 110, 111f
Aggleton, P., 20–22, 23n4, 52, 71, 174n11
Antunes, H., 101–2, 121, 184
appeal subsystem, 137t
Apple, M. W., xxvin2
art, 106–7
ascribed identities, 72
Atkinson, P., 124, 177, 197–98
author (defined), 62n1
autonomous mode, 55, 56f
autonomy, 45f, 48–49, 56, 58, 68–69, 206
avoidance subsystem, 137t

baby feeding, 180–81
Bakhtin, 62n2
Ball, S. J., 38, 79n
Bargh, C., 62–63n3
Bernstein, Basil, interview of, 197–213
bias, xiii–xix, 39, 65, 90

'The Birth of the Clinic' (Foucault), 172n8
Blackledge, D., 127n3
Blair, Tony, 68
Bliss, J., 139
Bloomfield, Leonard, 172n7
boundaries, xiii, xx, 5, 54–55, 96, 206–7. See also classification; framing
Bourdieu, P., xivn1, xxii, 104, 122, 155, 166, 171n1, 172n7, 175–77, 179, 187–89, 205
Brandis, W., 94
Bruner, Jerome, 62n2

career, student's, 66
carrier and the carried, 27
Cassirer, Ernst, 89, 145
categories, 6–7, 96, 98f, 99. See also types of discourse
Cazden, Courtney, 149
centreing resources, 66
Chamboredom, 177
change, 15, 77, 79n, 124, 206
Children: Their Primary Schools (Plowden Report), 44, 56
Chile, 116–19
Chomsky, Noam, 42–44, 147–48, 172n7
Christian Democratic Party (Chile), 116–17
Christianity, 8–9, 81, 83–86, 118–19
Christie, Frances, 90
Cie (defined/explained), xvii, 14–15. See also classification
Class, Codes and Control series (Bernstein), 89, 103–4, 113, 127n3, 188, 211

class, social/economic, xxv, 18–20, 72, 90, 94, 104–5, 110–13, 206. *See also* middle class; social groups

classification, xvi–xvii, 99–102; classificatory principles, 7–11, 14; in competence vs. performance models, 45, 45f; and context, 17, 20–22; development of, 99, 101–3; external and internal values of, 23n2, 99; between family and school, 104–5; and the language device, 27; in the medieval university (*see* Quadrivium; Trivium); and recognition rules, 16–20; and the relations between categories, 6, 100; in schools, 9–11, 10f, 22–23n1; social space constructed by, 12; strong vs. weak, 7–11, 10f, 14–15; studies, 18–20, 106–8; voice established by, 12, 204. *See also* pedagogic codes; recognition rules

Closed Type schools, 97, 98f

'Code Modalities and the Process of Cultural Reproduction: A Model' (Bernstein), 93, 106, 113

codes, 109, 186, 202–3; and change, 15; code acquisition, 103–6, 203; code meanings, 178; code modalities, 38–39, 185–88; code theory/thesis, 148, 191–93; collection code, 10–11, 10f; concept of code, 92, 186–88; and discourse, 207–8; elaborated codes, 14–15, 178, 207; formulations, 14–15, 187; location of, 176; misrecognition and clarification of, 175–90. *See also* classification; framing; pedagogic codes

communication, 99; 'discussion' vs. 'talk', 23n4; and framing, 12–13, 99 (*see also* framing); pedagogic acts differentiated from pedagogic communication, 200–201; and the pedagogic device, 26–28, 26f; pedagogic practice as, 179; and recognition rules, 16–17

competence: competence models of pedagogic practice, 44–50; competence modes, 50–51, 54–57, 56f (*see also* liberal/progressive mode; populist mode; radical mode); competence theories, 42–43; concept of, 147–48; and generic modes, 53; segmental

competences, 159–60; social logic of, 42–44

comprehensivisation, 57

computers, 119–20

concessional subsystem, 95, 137t

Contemporary Theories in the Sociology of Education (Demaine), 127–28n3

content, 35–36, 35f

content analysis, 133

context: classification and, 104–5; and the classificatory principle, 17; contextual rules and the language/pedagogic device, 26–28, 26f; evoking contexts, 109, 109f; and the identities produced by regions, 55; and languages of description, 134; and meanings, 30; and pedagogic discourse, 35–36, 35f; and recognition and realisation rules, 16–17, 16f, 20–22, 105; translated as interactional practices, 186. *See also* pedagogic context

control: in competence vs. performance models, 45f, 47; defined, 55; distinguished from power, 5; family studies in positional/personal control, 94, 112, 121, 135–36, 140–41; models of, 95f, 135–38, 150; subsystems of, 94–95, 137–38. *See also* framing; symbolic control

Cook-Gumperz, Jenny, 94, 95, 121, 129–30, 140–41

Cooper, B., 173–74n11

Cox (Donoso), Christian, 116–18, 189

creativity, 43, 206

cultural reproduction, xivn1, 4, 15

curricula and curricula reform, 20–22, 60–61, 65–66, 70–72, 98f, 204

Dale, R., 79n

Daniels, H. R. J., 62n2, 106–8, 121

Davies, B., 197–98

de la Roche, O., 174n11

de Saint Martin, M., 122, 188

de-centred (pedagogic) identities, 67f, 68–74, 74f, 205; De-centred Market (D.C.M.) identity, 67f, 68–72; De-centred Therapeutic (D.C.T.) identity, 67f, 70

Delamont, S., 197–98

Demaine, J., 127–28n3

democracy, xix–xxv

social order, 13, 66. *See also* regulative
 discourse
social sciences, 41–42, 85, 161–64,
 166–67
socialisation, theories of, 89
Socialist Party (Chile), 117
'society as organism' myth, xxiii–xxv
sociolinguistics, 112–13, 121, 128–30,
 145–53
Sociological Interpretations of Education
 (Blackledge and Hunt), 127n3
Sociological Research Unit, 89–90
sociology/sociological theory, xii–xiii, xvi,
 3–4, 9, 42, 161–63, 166, 171
Solomon, Joseph, 68, 197–213
spaces, 14, 35, 35f, 45f, 46
specialist performance mode, 55, 56f
stability, 39–40
staff/teachers, 10–11, 10f, 22–23n1,
 45–50, 56, 58, 98f
state, 56–58, 60–61, 63n4, 70–71, 114,
 204
strategy system of control, 95
stratified schools, 96–97
structuralism, 124, 187–88, 190n1
'Suicide' (Durkheim), 124, 206
Swope, J., 118–19, 121
symbolic control, xxvi, 54, 110; mediated
 through the pedagogic device, 202 (*see
 also* pedagogic device); place in
 Bernstein's theory, 123, 201–2;
 research, 110–13

text, xvi, 18, 35, 35f, 40n3, 45f, 47–48,
 105f
textbooks, xvi, 127n3, 168, 173–74n11
Thatcherism, 67–68
theory of pedagogic discourse: criteria for,
 90–93, 120; criticisms and responses,
 127–28n3, 175–90, 211–12;
 development of, 89–106, 108–10,
 113–15, 120–23, 126–27n2, 155,
 188–89; external assessment of, 90, 92,
 184–85; limitations of, 97;
 methodology, 123–26; models of, 103f,
 210f; political implications, 210;
 research, 89–90, 93–94, 96–97,
 100–101, 106–8, 110–13, 115–20,
 120–22

'Therapeutic Control' (Bernstein), 96
therapeutic identities, 73–74, 74f, 205
thinkable knowledge, 29
time, 35, 35f, 43, 45f, 46, 72
Torah, 84–85
trainability (defined), 59
transmission: and acquisition, 16–18, 16f;
 changeability of, 189; costs of, in
 competence vs. performance models,
 49–50; and de-centred pedagogic
 identities, 69, 70; explicit vs. tacit,
 168f, 169, 199–200; instrumental vs.
 expressive order, 102 (*see also*
 expressive order; instrumental order);
 and the pedagogic device, 36–37, 36f,
 37f; and recognition and realisation
 rules, 106; of skills vs. values, 32;
 transmission systems, models of,
 95–99. *See also* pedagogic discourse
Trivium, 8–9, 82–83, 85
Turner, G. J., 104, 186
Tyler, W., 79n, 97, 122, 125, 204

United Kingdom, 56–58, 60, 62–63n3,
 63n4, 70–71, 110–11
unthinkable knowledge, 29–30

*Values and Involvements in a Grammar
 School* (King), 96
Vertical discourse, xviii–xix, 157, 159–60,
 160f, 168f, 169–70, 173–74n11, 207–8
voice, 12, 204
Vygotsky, Lev Semenovich, 62n2, 145,
 171n1, 177–78

Walford, G., xv
Weber, Max, 36, 78
Wells, C. G., 112
Wertsch, J. V., 62n2
Whitty, G., 20–22, 23n4, 52, 71, 174n11
Whorf, Benjamin Lee, 177
Williams, G., 128
Willis, 147
Wittgenstein, Ludwig, 42

Youth Training Scheme (YTS), 53

About the Author

Basil Bernstein is Emeritus Professor of the Sociology of Education, University of London. Prior to 1990, he was the Karl Mannheim Professor of the Sociology of Education.

Printed In Poland
by Amazon Fulfillment
Poland Sp. z o.o., Wrocław